Additional Praise for *Savings and Trust*

"In lucid prose, Justene Hill Edwards tells the tragic history of the rise and fall of the Freedman's Bank in a devastating, page-turning saga of predation, plunder, and trust betrayed."
—**W. Caleb McDaniel, Pulitzer Prize–winning author of** *Sweet Taste of Liberty: A True Story of Slavery and Restitution in America*

"Following a rogue's gallery of bankers and politicians, Justene Hill Edwards deftly investigates a monumental financial crime. *Savings and Trust* is a significant contribution to the long and shameful history of America's racial wealth gap."
—**Claudio Saunt, author of** *Unworthy Republic: The Dispossession of Native Americans and the Road to Indian Territory*

"Justene Hill Edwards give us the first modern and comprehensive history of the Freedman's Bank, beautifully capturing the hopes of its African American depositors after emancipation and their betrayal by speculators, feckless allies, and racist opponents. A brilliant, riveting, and timely book."
—**Manisha Sinha, author of** *The Rise and Fall of the Second American Republic: Reconstruction, 1860–1920*

"*Savings and Trust* offers a fresh look at the remarkable ascent and tragic downfall of the Freedman's Savings and Trust Company. In this well-researched, brilliantly analyzed, and compellingly told account, Justene Hill Edwards brings to life the dramatic expansion of America's racial wealth gap with a focus on Black resourcefulness and trust and white betrayal and plunder during Reconstruction."
—**Kidada E. Williams, author of** *I Saw Death Coming: A History of Terror and Survival in the War against Reconstruction*

"A gripping read. Justene Hill Edwards's *Savings and Trust* tells the heartbreaking story of what began as an unqualified good and would become an origin story for subsequent iterations of anti-Black race discrimination perpetrated by the banking industry."

—**Dorothy A. Brown, author of** *The Whiteness of Wealth: How the Tax System Impoverishes Black Americans—and How We Can Fix It*

"*Savings and Trust* is a crucial piece of the story of the racial wealth gap and the financial violence that produced it with such devastating consequences into the present."

—**Stephanie McCurry, author of** *Women's War: Fighting and Surviving the American Civil War*

"*Savings and Trust* is a work of restorative justice, boldly holding accountable those who tragically privileged self-interest over the possibility of a just and equitable interracial democracy after the Civil War."

—**Martha S. Jones, author of** *Vanguard: How Black Women Broke Barriers, Won the Vote, and Insisted on Equality for All*

"In Justene Hill Edwards's hands, the Freedman's Bank's story is about much more than economics. With elegant prose and the flair of a master storyteller, she captures the promises of Reconstruction and their betrayal, which dashed the lives of Black Americans who dared to trust in the prospect of change and left the United States with a toxic legacy that persists today."

—**Laura F. Edwards, author of** *Only the Clothes on Her Back: Clothing and the Hidden History of Power in the Nineteenth-Century United States*

SAVINGS AND TRUST

ALSO BY JUSTENE HILL EDWARDS

*Unfree Markets: The Slaves' Economy and
the Rise of Capitalism in South Carolina*

SAVINGS
AND
TRUST

The Rise and Betrayal of
the Freedman's Bank

JUSTENE HILL
EDWARDS

W. W. NORTON & COMPANY
Independent Publishers Since 1923

Manufacturing by Lake Book Manufacturing
Book design by Beth Steidle
Production manager: Lauren Abbate

ISBN 978-1-324-07385-7

W. W. Norton & Company, Inc.
500 Fifth Avenue, New York, NY 10110
www.wwnorton.com

W. W. Norton & Company Ltd.
15 Carlisle Street, London W1D 3BS

1 2 3 4 5 6 7 8 9 0

To my mother, Deborah Bryan, for her
unconditional love, support, and affection

CONTENTS

CHRONICLE OF EVENTS

NOVEMBER 6, 1860: Republican Abraham Lincoln elected as the sixteenth president of the United States

DECEMBER 20, 1860: South Carolina declares secession from the federal Union

FEBRUARY 4, 1861: Delegates from Alabama, Florida, Georgia, Louisiana, Mississippi, and South Carolina meet to form the Confederate States of America

APRIL 12, 1861: Confederate forces fire on Fort Sumter, South Carolina, igniting the Civil War

FEBRUARY 25, 1862: Congress passes the Legal Tender Act, creating a national currency, and issues $500 million in bonds to fund the Civil War

JULY 17, 1862: Congress ratifies the Second Confiscation Act and Militia Act of 1862

JANUARY 1, 1863: Emancipation Proclamation goes into effect

1864: Military savings banks are created for Black soldiers in Beaufort, South Carolina; New Orleans, Louisiana; Norfolk, Virginia

FALL 1864: Union general William T. Sherman begins March to the Sea, from Atlanta to Savannah, with the Union army

JANUARY 16, 1865: General Sherman issues Special Field Order No. 15

JANUARY 27, 1865: John Alvord organizes a meeting of bankers, philanthropists, abolitionists in New York City to establish Freedman's Savings and Trust Company

MARCH 3, 1865: President Lincoln signs the Freedman's Bank Act

APRIL 4, 1865: Freedman's Bank central office opens in New York City

APRIL 9, 1865: Lee surrenders to Grant at Appomattox Courthouse, Virginia

APRIL 14, 1865: Lincoln assassinated

JANUARY 10, 1867: Henry D. Cooke nominated to the bank's board of trustees

MARCH 1867: Bank's central office moves to Washington, DC

APRIL 16, 1867: First Black trustees added to the bank's board of trustees

APRIL 19, 1867: The bank makes the first illegal loan, to D. L. Eaton

MAY 2, 1867: D. L. Eaton appointed as bank actuary

FEBRUARY 24, 1868: The House of Representatives impeaches President Andrew Johnson

MARCH 12, 1868: Alvord elected to be the president of the Freedman's Savings and Trust Company

MAY 26, 1868: The Senate acquits President Andrew Johnson

MARCH 4, 1869: Presidency of Ulysses S. Grant begins

MAY 6, 1870: Congress approves of amending the Freedman's Bank charter to allow the board of trustees to issue loans

DECEMBER 7, 1871: Freedman's Bank new central office opens at 1507 Pennsylvania Avenue in Washington, DC

JUNE 1872: Congress closes the Freedmen's Bureau

FEBRUARY 1873: Examiner Charles Meigs conducts first examination on behalf of the comptroller of the currency

SEPTEMBER 18, 1873: Jay Cooke & Company declares bankruptcy

PANIC OF 1873: A transatlantic financial crash that began in Europe spreads in the United States by the failure of Jay Cooke & Company

MARCH 10, 1874: Examiner Charles Meigs conducts second examination on behalf of the comptroller of the currency

MARCH 14, 1874: Alvord retires from the presidency and remains on the board of trustees; Frederick Douglass becomes the fourth president of the Freedman's Savings and Trust Company

JUNE 20, 1874: Congress approves an amendment to the bank's charter, to alter the bank's operating guidelines

JUNE 29, 1874: Freedman's Bank trustees vote to cease operations and close the bank

JULY 1, 1874: Alvord proposes that the trustees reconsider the vote to close the bank; the trustees conduct a second vote and Alvord is outvoted, with nine trustees voting to close the bank and four voting to keep the bank open

JULY 2, 1874: Trustees alert the secretary of the Treasury and Congress of the bank's closure

JULY 1874–DECEMBER 1874: Freedman's Bank commissioners investigate and take an accounting of the bank and its thirty-four branches

DECEMBER 11, 1874: Freedman's Bank commissioners report findings to Congress

1876: Congressman Beverley Browne Douglas of Virginia begins congressional hearings into Freedman's Bank collapse

1879–80: Senator Blanche K. Bruce, the second Black senator elected to a full term, conducts an investigation and subsequent hearings into the bank's failure

APRIL 13, 1911: Republican Congressman Ernest W. Roberts of Massachusetts introduces the final bill in Congress to reimburse Freedman's Bank depositors

DRAMATIS PERSONAE

JOHN W. ALVORD: Congregationalist minister and founder of the Freedman's Bank; third president of the Freedman's Bank

HENRY D. COOKE: Freedman's Bank trustee; finance committee chairman; president of the First National Bank of Washington, DC (DC branch of Jay Cooke & Company); first territorial governor of the District of Columbia (1871–73)

FREDERICK DOUGLASS: Fourth and last president of the Freedman's Bank (March 1874–June 1874); abolitionist, writer, orator, intellectual

D. L. EATON: Freedman's Bank actuary (1867–72)

MARY SUSAN HARRIS: Depositor at the Richmond, Virginia, branch

MAHLON HEWITT: First vice president of the Freedman's Bank

GENERAL OLIVER O. HOWARD: Union general; commissioner of the Freedmen's Bureau; founder of Howard University

WILLIAM HUNTINGTON: Member of the board of trustees and the finance committee; resigned from the board of trustees in February 1872

ANDREW JOHNSON: Vice president of the United States (March 4, 1865–April 15, 1865); seventeenth president of the United States (April 15, 1865–March 4, 1869); impeached in 1867

EDGAR KETCHUM: Freedman's Bank trustee, elected in 1867, member of the finance committee

JOHN MERCER LANGSTON: First African American congressman from Virginia; Freedman's Bank trustee (1872–74); member of the bank's finance committee; first Howard University Law School dean

ABRAHAM LINCOLN: Sixteenth U.S. president

ELLEN BAPTISTE LUBIN: Depositor at the Freedman's Bank branch in New Orleans

CHARLES A. MEIGS: Bank examiner with the Office of the Comptroller of the Currency and the Department of the Treasury

DR. CHARLES B. PURVIS: Freedman's Bank trustee elected in 1867; one of the founders of Howard University Medical School

C. S. SAUVINET: Cashier of the New Orleans Freedman's Bank branch

GENERAL WILLIAM T. SHERMAN: Union general, issues Special Field Order No. 15

ROBERT SMALLS: Formerly enslaved member of the South Carolina General Assembly; bank depositor

ANSON M. SPERRY: Army paymaster; Freedman's Bank paymaster

GEORGE W. STICKNEY: Freedman's Bank actuary (1872–74); nephew of D. L. Eaton

ENON AND EPHER WRIGHT: Depositors at the Mobile, Alabama, branch

PREFACE

IF YOU'VE EVER VISITED THE NATIONAL MALL IN WASH-
ington, DC, and stood in front of the White House at Sixteenth Street
and Pennsylvania Avenue, you've probably strolled past the site where
the Freedman's Savings and Trust Company's central office once stood.
Positioned adjacent to the White House and the Department of the
Treasury on 1509 Pennsylvania Avenue, in the southeast corner of Lafayette Square, the bank's main office from 1871 to 1874 stood mere steps
from the seats of executive and financial power during Reconstruction.

Today, on the corner of Madison Place and Pennsylvania Avenue
NW, in the heart of the nation's capital, stands a plaque that commem-
orates the Freedman's Savings and Trust Company, also known as the
Freedman's Bank. The inscription on the plaque reads:

> On this site stood the principal office of the Freedman's Savings
> and Trust Company founded on March 3, 1865 to receive deposits
> from former slaves. Frederick Douglass served as its last president.
> The bank was closed on June 29, 1874. The building was sold in
> 1882, and razed a few years later.

These four short lines are all that remain to honor one of the most pro-
found, and tragic, stories in American history.[1]

Hopefully, the plaque piques your interest. Unfortunately, it doesn't
fully capture the bank's story. While it's true that the bank was established on March 3, 1865, to "receive deposits from former slaves," the
bank did much more. Its administrators also made loans, allowing white
people with connections to the bank's trustees to borrow Black depositors' money. Black depositors, however, were barred from borrowing

money from the very institution into which they were funneling millions of dollars.

And there's more. Though Frederick Douglass did serve as the bank's last president, the trustees, most of whom were white, appointed Douglass knowing that it was on the verge of complete collapse, which occurred three months after he accepted the position.

Furthermore, the bank did not simply close. After the trustees voted on June 29 and again on July 1, 1874, to cease operations, the bank officially suspended payments to depositors on July 2, 1874. Bank administrators had loaned out so much of Black depositors' money to white borrowers that African Americans who wanted to make withdrawals could not access their hard-earned funds. The administrators operated the bank with such malfeasance, lending money without collateral and at times stealing deposits, that members of Congress called for the bank's closure to fully account for the wrongdoing.

At its height, freed people had opened over one hundred thousand accounts and deposited over $50 million ($1.4 billion today).* When the bank closed, it left the remaining 61,144 depositors without access to

---

* All monetary figures in modern terms come from MeasuringWorth.com.

the almost $3 million still left in bank accounts. After it ceased oper-
ations, depositors and their descendants spent decades, into the 1930s
and 1940s, pleading with members of Congress, attorneys general, and
even U.S. presidents to help them recoup their money—to no avail.

Given the bank's heartrending history, it is surprising that a plaque
is all that remains to commemorate the Freedman's Savings and Trust
Company. After reading the plaque, one might ask: What happened to
the depositors after the bank failed? *Savings and Trust* seeks to answer
this question—and many more. It tells the history of the bank's rise and
of the Black Americans who helped make the bank a success. It also
tells a story of betrayal and theft. This book shows how a group of white
Americans gambled with, plundered, and stole from Black people as
they climbed out of slavery into a new era of freedom. It establishes how
people at the highest levels of finance and government pillaged a bank
filled with African Americans' money and destroyed the economic
foundations on which recently freed people were building their lives.
Ultimately, *Savings and Trust* shows that one of the origins of America's racial wealth gap can be found in the failure of the Freedman's
Bank in 1874.

SAVINGS AND TRUST

INTRODUCTION

Save the Small Sums

ON JULY 20, 1868, BLACK FARMER ENON T. WRIGHT made the almost nine-mile journey from Dog River, Alabama, to Mobile, Alabama. Born enslaved in 1821, in Greene County, Alabama, Wright was likely familiar with the region's waterways, as he spent the first thirty-six years of his life living and working within the alluvial landscape that characterized Alabama's Gulf Coast. He made the voyage by boat or on foot or maybe a combination of both. He surely traveled past cotton plantations and a factory or two as he made his way into Mobile. The city was a major port and a hub of industrial and economic enterprise during the period of slavery. His relationship to enslavement, however, differed from the over 430,000 enslaved people who lived in Alabama in 1860, before the outbreak of the Civil War.[1]

Enon Wright was extraordinary by many standards. And maybe the decisions that brought him to this moment, the exceptionality of his life as a formerly enslaved Black man, permeated his thoughts. Using a mixture of skill, ingenuity, and a dash of luck, Wright did what most other enslaved people could not have done: he purchased his own freedom. For $900 ($31,100 today), he negotiated with his enslaver to buy his way out of slavery in 1857. With his freedom papers in hand, he worked to earn and save as much money as he could, through the danger of being a free man in a slave state, and through the Civil War, where the potential for universal freedom hung in the balance. After the war, he labored as a farmer in Dog River, surviving the unpredictability of Reconstruction, setting aside money as he went along.

Then, on that day in July 1868, the forty-seven-year-old Wright traveled from his home in Dog River to Mobile. His intended destination was 41 Saint Michael Street, mere blocks away from the Mobile River, which separated Alabama and the Florida panhandle. By entering the building on Saint Michael Street, Wright decided to take a chance on—and to put his *trust* in—a financial institution that he hoped would support his life as a freed person. He strolled into the Mobile branch of the Freedman's Bank, established in January 1866, to open an account.

Wright spoke with the branch's cashier, a twenty-nine-year-old white New Yorker named C. A. Woodward.[2] At this time, Woodward was preparing for publication a short treatise on the history of savings banks, in which he included his thoughts on the "National Savings Bank for Colored People." In it, Woodward celebrated the Freedman's Bank and its goal of bringing banking to the recently emancipated. He even lauded depositors such as Wright for their investments in the institution and for embracing the bank's messages that connected citizenship to the morality of saving and thrift. In fact, he wrote, "It seems almost incredible, when we reflect that this money has been accumulated from the meager earnings of a people but recently emerged from slavery, who were necessarily in a condition of extreme destitution, and who since their liberation have been subject to a continuous system of fraud and pillage by their former masters."[3] Woodward's arguments for savings banking exemplified the experiences of African Americans who decided to open Freedman's Bank accounts. He probably did not fully appreciate the clairvoyance with which he deployed the language of "fraud and pillage." His insight, though, was prescient. Nevertheless, it was people such as Enon Wright who helped Woodward cultivate a deeper understanding of the bank's mission and of why the branches were so valuable to African Americans throughout the South.

In his conversation with Woodward about opening an account, Wright provided a variety of information. He gave his race as "Black," he was "single," which meant that he was unmarried, and he was a member of a large family that included eight siblings. He did not list the name of his employer or the plantation on which he lived because he worked for himself as a farmer, and he was a free man at the end of the Civil War in 1865.[4] Importantly, Wright came prepared to make a substantial first deposit. By the end of 1868, the average deposit across the twenty-three branches was $69.[5] Enon Wright deposited far more than that. His opening deposit was an impressive $1,000 ($21,200 today).[6] He had accepted the bank's charge to "Save the Small Sums" and "Put the Money You Save into the Freedman's Savings Bank." He joined the chorus of Black Americans eager to build their wealth through investing in the bank.

Enon Wright was not alone when he ventured into 41 Saint Michael Street. In fact, he was not the only member of his family to do so. His older brother, Epher, experienced a similar trajectory. By purchasing his freedom in 1847, a decade earlier than his brother, for $1,000 ($36,700 today), the sixty-year-old Epher Wright entered the Civil War as a free man as well, and entered the bank branch in Mobile ready to open an account with a starting balance of $600 ($12,700 in today's dollars).[7] Together, Epher and Enon Wright were two of the five people on July 20, 1868, who decided to take calculated gambles with their savings by opening accounts at the Mobile branch of the Freedman's Bank.[8]

Together, the Wright brothers embraced the messages that the bank espoused: Black people's political and economic freedom through saving money and banking. The bank represented the promise of capitalism in the age of emancipation. And while that message encouraged depositors, it also spurred the bank's demise.

⚜

THERE ARE VARIOUS WAYS to tell the history of the Freedman's Bank. One is from the perspective of people such as Enon and Epher Wright, African Americans who toiled and saved to buy themselves out of slavery. In many ways, the Wright brothers epitomized the dream of the almost four million enslaved men, women, and children who embarked on the harrowing trek to claim their freedom at the end of the Civil War. By patronizing their local Freedman's Bank branch, the

Wright brothers and tens of thousands of African Americans like them invested in their own economic futures.

Another perspective comes from the bank's white administrators. Some of the abolitionists, bankers, and philanthropists, such as Mobile cashier C. A. Woodward, used the bank to demonstrate their support of freed people and their support of the newest banking infrastructure, which emerged during the Civil War. The new regulatory architecture, with a standardized currency, capital requirements for national banks, and a regulator, the Office of the Comptroller of the Currency, was supposed to stabilize the national economy. White philanthropists in Northern cities such as Philadelphia and New York believed in savings banking as a vehicle to help the poor and working classes become self-sufficient. For these philanthropists, the Freedman's Bank was a grand economic experiment in savings banking for former slaves just emerging out of the tribulations of bondage.

Yet another perspective comes from a figure who was the most visible Black man in America during the nineteenth century: Frederick Douglass. Douglass's involvement with the bank temporarily marred his reputation as a Black man dedicated to African American political and economic advancement, especially for the formerly enslaved. His entanglement with the bank at the time of its demise was one of his greatest regrets. He would spend the rest of his life restoring his good name.

Savings and Trust explores these intertwined stories, telling the history of the Freedman's Bank from the perspective of the freed people who invested in the bank as depositors, as well as through the experiences of the bank's administrators. Fundamentally, the history of the Freedman's Bank is the story of a web that connected the almost four million African Americans who strode proudly into the era of freedom in 1865 to white men at the highest levels of American finance and politics. Whether they opened accounts or not, African Americans used the bank to test whether the federal government would make good on the promise to protect freed people and to extend them citizenship and voting rights. The bank became a proxy for the federal government's commitment to the ideals of the Civil War. At a fragile moment in

Frederick Douglass, ca. 1879

the history of the American republic—the reconstitution of a nation obliterated by the violence of civil war—the Freedman's Bank represented the economic potential of the nation's formerly enslaved people. It was animated by the benevolent work of white bankers and philanthropists, supported by congressional Republicans and the federal government more broadly. The bank was supposed to symbolize the twin engines of capitalism and democracy made manifest.

Instead, Black people's generational distrust of financial institutions can be traced to the founding and failure of the Freedman's Bank. African American depositors could not escape the rapaciousness that defined Gilded Age capitalism. White bankers pillaged the bank, mishandling and stealing Black depositors' savings in the process. African Americans' economic livelihoods were at stake, and the bank's demise bankrupted Black communities across the nation. In the end, they were the victims of white capitalists' greed. Their experiences with the bank, and the federal government's unwillingness to hold the perpetrators accountable, represented an underexplored aspect of the white racial violence that characterized Black people's lives in Reconstruction and during the Gilded Age.

Historians familiar with the Civil War and Reconstruction eras are aware of the Freedman's Bank and its history. But the story of the bank has often been an addendum, or sometimes a literal footnote, in larger accounts of a nation emerging out of the vagaries of war. *Savings and Trust* places the Freedman's Bank at the center of a larger narrative about Reconstruction and the economic aspirations of millions of African Americans. It also illuminates the extent to which America's banking industry has preyed on the nation's most vulnerable populations. During Reconstruction, it was the millions of African Americans recently emancipated from slavery who were the victims of the financial industry's predation.[9]

꒒꒦

ESTABLISHED ON MARCH 3, 1865, and signed into existence by President Lincoln in the month before his assassination, the Freedman's Bank grew steadily in its first five years, with depositors from New York to New Orleans opening accounts and depositing their hard-earned savings into the bank's coffers. Between 1865 and 1870, African Americans deposited a total of $12.6 million ($303 million today) into accounts at branches in states as far north as New York, as far south as Florida, and as far west as Texas. By 1870, depositors had earned over $1.6 million ($38.5 million today) from the bank in interest payments on their deposits.

Black depositors received clear messages from administrators about the advantages of saving money. These trustees and branch cashiers were Republicans who not only actively supported the Union's war efforts but also supported a free labor ideology that infiltrated the bank's advertisements within Black communities with bank branches. "Save the Small Sums—Cut Off Your Vices—Don't Smoke—Don't Drink—Don't Buy Lottery Tickets—Put the Money You Save into the Freedman's Savings Bank," were splashed in Black newspapers and disseminated in Black communities across the nation, primarily in the former Confederate South.[10] Designed to persuade depositors that morality and saving went hand in hand, the bank's predominantly white administrators worked to convince Black people to patronize local branches and deposit as much money as possible into bank accounts. The messages—and the propaganda—communicated to freed people that banking would help them climb the ladder to full freedom.

By 1874, depositors had collectively placed over $57 million ($1.51 billion today) into over one hundred thousand bank accounts in thirty-four branches.[11] By anyone's estimation, freed people made the Freedman's Bank one of the most successful financial institutions of the nineteenth century. For a short time, African Americans used the bank to build a stable economic foundation for themselves and their families after the Thirteenth Amendment abolished legal slavery in 1865.[12] During this time, the Freedman's Bank epitomized the economic power of African Americans unleashed from the bonds of enslavement.

In their public-facing messaging, the founders and trustees of the Freedman's Bank wanted to democratize finance, to make banking accessible to working-class and poor people. Bank officials believed that they needed to teach freed people about banking and finance to help them understand the responsibility and burden of freedom. This message formed the core of the bank's mission. The trustees and administrators circulated public messages to freed people about the federal government *not* helping them economically in their climb out of slavery. They urged Black people not to rely economically on the federal government and instead to cultivate a sense of self-sufficiency. By working for the bank and guiding its mission, administrators were agreeing to help freed people navigate the economic minefield that defined Reconstruction.

Bank administrators, however, did not fulfill the terms of their promise to depositors. Instead of offering simple banking services to freed people, the trustees decided to take a gamble. First, it was an illegal loan to a trustee in April 1867. Then, in May 1870, the bank's predominantly white trustees, led by famed (and infamous) banker Henry D. Cooke, lobbied Congress, which allowed them to alter the bank's fundamental mission.

By mid-1870, the bank ceased operating as a savings bank or, as the bank's name suggested, a *savings and trust company*. The trustees, with

Henry D. Cooke, ca. 1865

congressional approval, began to operate the Freedman's Bank as a commercial bank. Instead of merely accepting freed people's deposits, the trustees began making loans, using the millions of dollars of Black Americans' money to invest in speculative ventures. Most of the loans went to white businessmen, members of Congress, and investors in and around the bank's central office in Washington, DC. Some of the trustees even stole depositors' money to fund their own business ventures. Initially, when the bank operated as a savings bank, the trustees' and administrators' intentions may have benefited the depositors. But as African Americans' money flowed into their accounts, the bank administrators' intentions changed. Corruption seeped in. This corruption jeopardized the bank's fundamental mission, to serve African Americans.

The bank could sustain only so much instability. So when a financial panic in the fall of 1873 toppled some of the nation's most prominent financial institutions, this event proved to be too much risk for the Freedman's Bank to withstand. The trustees, therefore, made one final decision to salvage the bank's reputation among Black depositors. In March 1874, the trustees convinced Frederick Douglass to help steer the bank toward prosperity. But not even Douglass could rescue the institution, or the depositors' money. After nine years of operation, the bank's exponential growth came to an abrupt stop. On July 2, 1874, the bank officially closed its doors. The remaining depositors, all 61,144 of them, lost access to a collective $2,939,925.22 ($77.9 million today). Though depositors recovered $1,731,845.01 ($45.9 million today), 59 percent of the total deposits at the bank's closing, by 1909 depositors still had $1,208,071 ($40.1 million today) outstanding that they had not received. The damage was done.[13] Freed people received clear messages about their value in the financial services marketplace. Though slavery was no longer legal, white capitalists could exploit them and their hard work, and they would have little recourse.

❧

SAVINGS AND TRUST CHARTS the rise, expansion, and untimely collapse of the Freedman's Bank. It also illuminates the multifaceted violence of Reconstruction. Though white racial terrorism against African Americans, especially in regions of the former slave South, is well documented, physical violence was not the only form of terrorism that white Americans waged on freed people.[14] The bank's plunder by white bankers, financiers, and capitalists was brutal. While not the interpersonal atrocities that white vigilantes pursued against freed people, the strategic pillage of the Freedman's Bank by white capitalists represented another type of violence against African Americans. It encompassed the ruthlessness of capitalism left unchecked. It was the financial violence of theft.

Through interrogating the bank's inner workings, including the machinations of the bank's trustees and administrators, *Savings and Trust* shows how a small well-connected group of men—some wealthy and some naïve—built the bank up and tore it down, with over sixty thousand freed people in July 1874 losing their economic safety net in the process. African Americans such as Enon and Epher Wright put their faith—even their *trust*—in the Freedman's Bank, and in the institution's trustees, administrators, and cashiers. And after the Panic of

1873 and the bank's closing, the white men of finance and economic means came out of the financial collapse on firm ground. They reestablished their reputations. They found new ways to build their empires.

African Americans did not have the same fortune. Depositors hoped that by putting money into Freedman's Bank accounts, they could save money, buy land, provide for their families, and, importantly, bequeath the money in their accounts to their families and loved ones in the event of their death. But with the bank's collapse in 1874, African Americans faced financial losses that shattered their dreams of real economic uplift. They were subsequently forced to the fringes and ignored by the banking industry.

The data reveals that depositors confronted a distressing financial reality. Researchers have estimated that after the bank failed, depositors could recoup only 20 percent of their deposits on average, meaning that they lost a staggering 80 percent of the money that remained in their accounts as of July 1874.[15] The losses faced by the bank's Black depositors amounted to 10 percent of the total wealth of Black communities that surrounded the branch locations.[16] Some lost all the wealth that they had accumulated.

The depositors bore the financial burden of bank administrators' corruption. According to economists Claire Célérier and Purnoor Tak, African Americans made up 90 percent of the bank's depositors, yet they received less than 5 percent of the total amount of money loaned out by the bank. Moreover, the administrators of the Washington, DC, branch issued 90 percent of the loan volume, but collected approximately 11 percent of the bank's total deposits.[17] They leveraged Black people's money and in turn made loans to white borrowers in Washington, people with direct connections to members of the bank's board of trustees. The administrators turned into a cabal composed of businessmen and politicians who unabashedly gambled with depositors' money. Freed people put millions of dollars into bank accounts only to have their money given at favorable rates to white people who used the money to fund their own risky investments. In the end, it was Black people who took all the risk, and lost everything in the process.

❧

IN THE LATE NINETEENTH and early twentieth centuries, African Americans, still shaken by the bank's failure, began to construct their own economic and business infrastructure. Because of the banking industry's practice of exclusion, African Americans were forced to create their own sources of capital and credit. If the financial services industry and the federal government were going to exploit and ignore them, then they would construct their own avenues to achieve economic stability. African Americans, though, did not forget the harm that the Freedman's Bank failure wrought on freed people. Black organizations of the early twentieth century such as the National Negro Bankers Association encouraged Congress to give serious consideration to a more robust program of depositor compensation. Advocates such as W. E. B. DuBois argued that the federal government had failed to protect African Americans during Reconstruction. He asserted that such negligence, by bank administrators and federal authorities, would bankrupt African Americans for generations to come. He did not have confidence in the political will of white politicians to advocate for Black Americans. When asked in 1927 about the possibility of further compensation for depositors for the bank's failure, DuBois wrote a sobering assessment. He concluded, "I assure you that there isn't the slightest chance in the world of your receiving any further funds from this deposit."[18]

White Americans used the bank's failure to fuel stereotypes about Black people's laziness and their lack of fitness for the responsibility of political and economic inclusion. White Democrats and Republicans alike dared to argue that Black people were ill-prepared for the privileges of freedom. This was why, they contended, the bank failed. As one of the bank's commissioners told a depositor after the bank's collapse, it was Black people's fault for entrusting bankers with their money. These types of criticisms continued to infiltrate public discussions of African Americans, especially in the postwar South. Even Frederick Douglass sought to rebut the claim of Black financial ignorance and misguidedness. "The failure of that institution," he clarified, "was not due to the ignorance and incompetency of colored men, but to the shrewdness and rascality of white men."[19] Despite the bank's temporary success, white Americans blamed African Americans for the bank's tragic demise.

In the longer term, African Americans were pushed out of the financial marketplace. In the late nineteenth and early twentieth centuries, without large banks to serve their needs, African Americans created financial institutions of their own. Left behind by traditional banks, Black communities around the nation, from Richmond, Virginia, to Durham, North Carolina, and Tulsa, Oklahoma, invested in their own communities through establishing a variety of types of institutions to suit their specific economic needs.[20] They created joint stock companies, their own banks, and Black economic enclaves. The Capital Savings Bank in Washington, DC, incorporated in October 1888, and the True Reformers Bank founded in Richmond, Virginia, which began operations in April 1889, serve as examples.[21] Despite the continued threat of racial and economic violence, African Americans were compelled to create avenues through which to combat the ever-increasing reality of economic exclusion.

As a result, African Americans lost what little confidence they had in the increasingly speculative nature of traditional finance. They came to believe that bankers were voracious and immoral, willing to dupe anyone foolhardy enough to entrust them with their money. As one historian has noted, capitalism was a confidence game, and banking required that economic actors be willing to gamble. African Americans were not interested in playing the game. In many ways, they could least afford to.[22]

The history of the Freedman's Bank shows that America's racial wealth gap started with slavery and continued during Reconstruction, the era that was supposed to inaugurate freedom for African Americans. America's banks have historically both ignored and exploited Black communities. Only when financial institutions, supported by the federal government, believed that they could profit from African Americans' desire to build wealth did they extend financial services to them. But if redlining, predatory inclusion, and the subprime mortgage crisis of the early 2000s have proved anything, it's that America's banking industry has preyed on populations of people least likely to have the economic or political power to fight back.[23]

The Freedman's Bank was created to symbolize the highest ideals of American capitalism and the democratic promise of freedom during the second founding.[24] For freed people, however, the bank came to represent a new form of exploitation. The connections among the bank's rise, collapse, and continued influence on Black communities have been buried. *Savings and Trust* recovers this history.

PART ONE

Savings

CHAPTER ONE

The Bank's Founding, 1864–65

Do nothing to foster and encourage speculation. . . . Pursue a
straightforward, upright, legitimate banking business. Never
be tempted by the prospect of large returns to do anything but
what may be properly done under the National Currency Act.

—HUGH McCOLLOUGH, FIRST COMPTROLLER
OF THE CURRENCY, DECEMBER 1863[1]

And be it further enacted, That the general business and object of
the corporation hereby created shall be to receive on deposit such
sums of money as may from time to time be offered therefor, by,
or on behalf of persons heretofore held in slavery in the United
States, or their descendants, and investing the same in the stocks,
bonds, treasury notes, or other securities of the United States.

—"AN ACT TO INCORPORATE THE FREEDMAN'S
SAVINGS AND TRUST COMPANY," SECTION 5

BY THE SUMMER OF 1864, THE BLACK SOLDIERS WHO served under Union general Rufus Saxton struggled with a logistical problem. In June, Congress approved equal pay for members of the U.S. Colored Troops (USCT). This was a watershed moment, one in which Black soldiers could rejoice. Their efforts to have the Union army and the federal government recognize their sacrifices had come to fruition. Yet their celebrations were mixed with frustration. Though they won an increase in pay, Black soldiers struggled with how to save their hard-earned money. Their problem did not revolve around their spending habits. They faced the opposite dilemma. Black soldiers wanted to save their money, many in hopes of sending much-needed financial resources to their families, specifically their wives and children.

Saxton decided to implement a temporary solution. As a brigadier general in the Union army and military governor of the Department of the South, Saxton carried out the army's policies in South Carolina, one of the major hubs of the war effort. In addition to bringing his military prowess to administering crucial tactical strategies, especially regarding the region's freed people, Saxton also brought a distinct perspective on financial literacy. He was known to encourage soldiers under his command, both Black and white, to save as much of their wages as possible.[2] But Saxton was concerned about Black soldiers, especially since they had just received an increase in pay. Therefore, he made a special effort on their behalf. He decided to follow in the footsteps of his colleague General N. P. Banks, who was serving in Louisiana. He created a military savings bank so that Black soldiers would have a safe place to keep their money.

On August 29, 1864, Saxton made a pronouncement, issued "to the Freedmen in the Dept. of the South," from his headquarters in Beaufort, South Carolina. In Circular No. 5, he established the South Carolina Freedman's Savings Bank. Saxton announced to the region's freed people, "You will thus have a secure place of deposit for your money, where it will yield you a fair rate of interest, and will, at the same time, indirectly aid in sustaining the government which is doing so much for you." Saxton also offered freed people several assurances. He promised, "All the colored people who deposite [*sic*] their money in it will take a receipt from the Treasurer for the amount, and can feel assured that it will be returned to them again with interest when called for."[3]

Saxton intended that the South Carolina Freedman's Savings Bank, located in Beaufort, would have a simple mission. He appointed the bank's administrative team—which included Captain J. P. Low as the bank's president, Lieutenant A. P. Ketchum as treasurer, and S. L. Harris as the cashier—and made these men responsible for ensuring that the soldiers' deposits were "invested in safe and valuable United States Government Securities."[4] Harris, as the cashier, would accept deposits as small as five cents, and after depositors accumulated twenty-five dollars in their accounts, they would earn 5 percent interest. And when the bank earned profits on their investments, the profits would be divided among the depositors with over twenty-five dollars in their accounts.[5]

To encourage the depositors to keep their money in the bank for as long as possible, Saxton instructed the bank's administrators to place limitations on how easily depositors could make withdrawals. These limitations reflected the behavior that Saxton wanted depositors to adopt. Depositors, for example, could withdraw their money on demand if they wanted less than twenty-five dollars. If they wanted to withdraw over twenty-five dollars, then it was up to Harris's discretion. Harris could require that depositors wanting over twenty-five dollars give thirty days' notice. These types of strategies reflected Saxton's priority of encouraging prudence among the Black soldiers under his command.

The idea of creating a mission-based, nonprofit financial institution such as the military savings banks emerged not in the Civil War era but in the early nineteenth century. In the period after the American Revolution, bankers in the Northeast embarked on a movement to create financial institutions to encourage working-class populations to develop the habit of saving. Clustered in cities such as New York, Boston, and Philadelphia as early as the 1810s, savings banks were founded by bankers and philanthropists as nonprofit institutions. Bankers established savings banks to help members of the laboring classes rise out of poverty through saving. In contrast to commercial banks, which were institutions created to generate profits for shareholders, savings banks had a benevolent, as opposed to a moneymaking, mission.[6]

Savings banks played an integral role in introducing predominantly white working-class Americans to engaging with financial institutions. This population of people had few resources to help them save. Savings banks were chartered—given permission to operate—by state governments, which had begun to regulate the financial institutions that emerged during this period. Though banks were helping spur economic growth and expansion, state legislators realized that they needed to create a regulatory framework for ensuring that depositors' investments were secure. Regulation became even more important because a variety of financial institutions appeared in the landscape of banking in the first half of the nineteenth century, including savings banks and commercial banks.[7]

Commercial banks, joint stock companies, and savings banks dominated financial services in the years between the 1810s and 1850s. Commercial banks, in particular, represented the rewards and risks of American-style financial capitalism. They existed to make money. Commercial banks made loans with the intention of profiting from lending to entrepreneurs and businesses. Savings banks were different. Combining civic and economic uplift, savings banks grew in northern cities, as business-minded philanthropists sought ways to improve the conditions of the working class and poor. In essence, the task of these early financial institutions was to help the poor escape poverty through encouraging them to both work *and* save. And through the simple process of receiving depositors' money, storing it for safekeeping, and offering a modest return on deposits, the early crop of savings banks attempted to fulfill the founders' goal of curbing indigence among working-class people in cities such as Philadelphia, Baltimore, and New York.[8] Ultimately, savings banks served both bank founders and future depositors. The depositors had access to a vehicle of economic growth, while bank founders had an outlet to fulfill their civic responsibilities. The military savings banks would operate within this banking landscape.

The South Carolina Freedman's Savings Bank opened in October 1864 and operated under the Department of War, which meant that the bank, and the deposits, would not be under the aegis of the Department of the Treasury. The bank functioned as an extension of the war effort. This fact, however, did not elicit much scrutiny. Instead, Saxton framed the bank's establishment as part of the effort to ensure that Black soldiers, and freed people more generally, began to live self-sufficient lives. He proclaimed, "[I]t is your duty to provide against a future time of need in such a way as to sustain the administration which, under Providence, has brought you all these blessings, and to prevent your families or yourselves from ever becoming a tax upon its bounty." Saxton wanted to ensure that Black soldiers, especially those who were formerly enslaved, did not rely economically on the federal government. He did not want Black people to depend on the government's largesse, despite the reality that it was freed people who had toiled to bring wealth to Confederate enslavers who rebelled against and seceded from the Union.[9]

Saxton, though, did make a concession. He decided *not* to exclude white soldiers. "The bank will not be exclusive for the freedmen," he declared, "although established primarily for their benefit." Perhaps he was communicating his message about saving and independence to white soldiers as well—an extension of his belief that "[i]n a time of plenty and prosperity, a wise man lays up in store out of his abundance something for a time of need in the future."[10]

It is difficult to discern the percentage of deposits that the bank received from white versus Black soldiers, but by the end of 1864, soldiers had deposited over $65,000 into the South Carolina Freedman's Savings Bank ($1.15 million today). By any estimation, the bank proved to be a success. A year later, Saxton would celebrate the bank, writing, "Of the other means by which the negroes are preparing themselves, or being prepared, for their new condition, and the new career opened to them, I will mention . . . the Savings Bank in Beaufort, in which are deposits amounting to nearly $100,000, invested in United-States bonds."[11]

White businessmen and capitalists from the North observed with interest. A savings bank for freed people, as a financial experiment, demonstrated to them that the formerly enslaved were prepared for the economic challenges of freedom. Indeed, northern capitalists realized that freed people were an untapped market for banking services.

As freed people began to see lives for themselves without the bonds of enslavement, their economic priorities began to shift into focus. And they had one economic goal above all else: to buy land.

❧

ON THE EVENING OF January 12, 1865, a group of twenty Black men arrived at the home of Charles Green, an Englishman, cotton merchant, and former Confederate sympathizer. Located in Madison Square, in the heart of Savannah, Georgia, Green's home reflected a Gothic Revival architectural aesthetic, complete with red sandstone and iron railings, designed to reflect Green's status and wealth. As the men glanced at the two-story mansion, perhaps they noticed candles illuminating the medieval bay windows, and once they stepped into the home, they were ushered past marble mantels and chandeliers. Maybe, as they entered one of the most expensive homes in Savannah, they wondered why this meeting was taking place in a site of such opulence, made possible through the toil of the region's formerly enslaved people.[12]

The men selected Garrison Frazier to speak for the group. Frazier was sixty-seven years old, from Granville, North Carolina. He had bought himself and his wife out of slavery in 1857, paying "$1,000 in gold and silver," an achievement that he pronounced with great pride. Even as an enslaved person, Frazier had dedicated his free time to the ministry. A preacher for thirty-five years, Frazier was in declining health, which forced him to retreat from his pastoral duties. Despite his lack of physical vitality, Frazier accepted the group's proposal that he speak on their behalf.[13]

The men were summoned by Union general William T. Sherman, who at the time called Green's mansion his home and his operational headquarters. Sherman invited the men to his Savannah headquarters at the behest of Secretary of War Edwin Stanton. Stanton had made a surprise visit to Georgia and requested to speak with a small group of Black men in the city. His trip, and his conversation with the freedmen, belied a larger concern that he and other members of the Lincoln administration had about the recent southern military campaign. Stanton's goal was to take a full accounting of the aftermath of the Union army's recent victories—and to evaluate rumors he'd heard about Union general William T. Sherman's treatment of freed people.

A decorated officer, Sherman had been racking up military conquests as he led Union troops against the Confederacy in Tennessee and Georgia. During the late summer and fall of 1864, he delivered the Union with a decisive series of military triumphs, which culminated in his capture of Atlanta on September 2, 1864. His success proved to be so pivotal that it would provide Lincoln with the political ammunition he needed to win reelection that fall. As Sherman moved eastward, setting Atlanta ablaze in the process, he initiated what was known as the "March to the Sea," a six-week campaign from Atlanta to Savannah that concluded with his army capturing Savannah on December 21. By late December 1864, news of his military dominance reverberated across the nation. It would be the most destructive, and one of the most effective, campaigns of the war.[14] Despite Sherman's achievements, which galvanized the Union's optimism, freed people witnessed and were the victims of his and his troops' violence.

Reports had been leaked about Sherman's treatment of freed people and his thoughts on emancipation. He received a letter dated December 30, 1864, from Henry Halleck, a senior officer in the Union army, from the army's headquarters in Washington, DC. In this letter, Halleck wrote that even though Sherman was universally praised for his victories over the past months, Lincoln had been hearing about his enmity toward freed people. Halleck wrote, "They say that you have manifested an almost criminal dislike to the negro."[15] Freed people were receiving the message that those who followed Sherman's army, in search of freedom and protection by Union forces, were not fully a part of the Union army's efforts to win the war, despite Lincoln's proclamation of freedom for enslaved people in rebel states.[16] Union military forces would use, ignore, sacrifice, or discard freed people at will. *This* was what Stanton traveled to Georgia to understand.

When Stanton arrived in Savannah on January 11, he notified Sherman that he wanted to speak to a group of freed people. He wanted to ask them what they understood about the Emancipation Proclamation and their thoughts on living with and near white people. Ultimately, Stanton was seeking a better understanding of their plight and how they were navigating the practicalities of freedom. He wanted to hear their experiences for himself, in their own words.

The group of Black men, handpicked by Sherman because he considered them "the most intelligent of the negroes," sat with Sherman and Stanton "to have a conference upon matters relating to the freedmen of the State of Georgia."[17] These men were exceptional in many ways. Of the twenty, eleven were free before the beginning of the Civil War. All were ministers or leaders in their church communities. Each had a vested interest in using this meeting to convey their perspectives on slavery, the war, and freedom to the audience before them. William J. Campbell, for example, stated that he was born enslaved in Georgia. But in 1849, at thirty-five years old, he gained his freedom "by will of his mistress." In 1855, he worked as pastor of the First Baptist Church of Savannah, and he counted 1,800 members in his congregation. Perhaps Campbell's proudest statement was that his congregants owned the property on which the church was built. It was worth $18,000 ($346,000 today).[18]

After the men formally introduced themselves to Stanton, providing a bit about their personal histories, making sure to highlight their greatest accomplishments, Frazier then proceeded to answer Stanton's queries. As Stanton asked his questions, twelve in total, ranging from what they would do if members of the Confederacy armed them to how they felt about General Sherman, the Black men's eyes drifted to Frazier as he gave measured, thoughtful, and tempered responses.

Stanton's third line of inquiry was perhaps his most poignant. He requested that Frazier "[s]tate in what manner you think you can take care of yourselves, and how can you best assist the Government in maintaining your freedom." Frazier's response was revealing. He asserted: "The way we can best take care of ourselves is to have land, and turn it and till it by our own labor—that is, by the labor of the women and children and old men; and we can soon maintain ourselves and have something to spare."[19] Land, according to Frazier and the men, was what freed people wanted most of all. He finished answering the question by stating, "We want to be placed on land until we are able to buy it and make it our own."[20] Frazier's declaration perfectly captured freed people's financial goals. They wanted land, but they were also willing to work and save money to buy it. They were not looking for governmental largesse. Instead, freed people wanted to earn the profits of their labor to purchase property. This was how freed people defined freedom. Freedom meant the ability to buy and own land and to reap the financial benefits of landownership.

Freed people's understanding of their economic objectives clashed with what white Union officials such as Stanton and Sherman believed. Freed people positioned their financial goals around property. For African Americans, full freedom required land because land equaled true political and economic independence. Union army officials' ideas about what Black people needed to survive in freedom were different. They believed that freedom required waged labor. The land and labor question reflected the misalignment between freed people's financial goals and those of white northern Republicans and leaders in the Union army. The Republican Party's platform in 1860, for example, included messages that connected freedom to labor. The motto "Free Soil, Free Labor, Free Men" infiltrated Lincoln's political campaign and underscored the economic goals of capitalists from the North. These differences played out in important ways during the war. In a December 1863 order on the recruitment and treatment of Black soldiers, Union general Benjamin Butler argued, "Political freedom rightly defined is liberty to work and to be protected in the full enjoyment of the fruits of labor."[21] By connecting freedom to being paid for one's labor, Butler communicated to freed people that their freedom hinged on their willingness to work. He continued, "[N]o one with ability to work should enjoy the fruits of another's labor," and for this reason, Butler made it known that the federal government would not support "any Negro or his family . . . who is able to work and does not work."[22] Freed people had different economic priorities. They did not frame freedom in terms of waged labor or work. Instead, as Frazier articulated, freed people wanted the *opportunity* to work and save money. But for the millions of formerly enslaved African Americans, freedom meant the right to purchase land for themselves and their families—and to have that right protected by the federal government.[23]

During Stanton's five-day stay in Savannah, he and Sherman continued to discuss a path forward for freed people. They decided on a radical course of action. Their solution revolved around what freed people wanted most: land. Therefore, Sherman drafted, and Stanton approved, what would be known as Special Field Order No. 15, on January 16, 1865.

Special Field Order No. 15 designated four hundred thousand acres of prime coastal land between South Carolina and Florida for freed people. Stated as the "islands from Charleston, south, the abandoned rice fields along the rivers for thirty miles back from the sea, and the country bordering the St. Johns river, Florida," the order made land immediately available to the region's formerly enslaved population. Sherman designed the military initiative to accomplish two goals.[24] First, the order to confiscate land held by prominent white planters in South Carolina and Georgia who joined the Confederacy was meant to be a final blow to secessionists. By divesting them of land, Sherman sent white planters in South Carolina and Georgia the message that their violent recalcitrance would be rewarded by dispossessing them of capital.

Sherman's second, and equally important, goal in issuing the order involved dealing with what he believed was the problem of freed people themselves. During his rampage across the South in 1864, he witnessed tens of thousands of freed people celebrating the Union army's arrival. They would often leave their homes and communities to eagerly join Sherman's march. For freed people, his arrival represented the opportunity to claim their freedom under the protection of Union military forces. Sherman and his troops, however, came to see the freed people who followed them as a nuisance and a burden. He had complained earlier in 1864 to Lieutenant General Ulysses S. Grant of the "refugees and negroes that encumber us."[25] The order, therefore, solved Sherman's immediate problem of relocating freed people.

The crux of Sherman's initiative entailed parceling out land to Black families in forty-acre plots. The order offered coastal plots of the Georgia and South Carolina Sea Islands to freed people "[w]henever three respectable negroes, heads of families, shall desire to settle on land."[26] In addition to the mandate that no white people were allowed to live in the cordoned-off land, the order outlined that "blacks may remain in their chosen or accustomed vocations" and that "the sole and exclusive management of affairs will be left to the freed people themselves, subject only to the United States military authority, and the acts of Congress."[27] This meant that freed people could live on their own, organize their own families and communities, and be free to work as they chose. Theoretically, freed people could live and thrive without white supervision.[28]

Formerly enslaved people were enthusiastic about acquiring homesteads like the parcels of land offered by the federal government to white Americans under the Homestead Act of 1862. The Homestead Act offered 160-acre plots of land to American citizens, in particular American citizens who had "never borne arms against the United States Government or given aid and comfort to its enemies." Those who could pay a small fee to the federal government would be allowed to take advantage of this program, which was a federally subsidized initiative that redistributed over 240 million acres of land to American citizens, most of whom were white.[29] Freed people considered Special Field Order No. 15 a step in that direction.

When Sherman enacted Special Field Order No. 15, he temporarily transformed the lives of the approximately forty thousand freed people who settled on the land.[30] But Sherman did not issue the order as an agent of racial harmony and equality. Though he enacted a policy that had the potential to provide freed people with tangible economic assets as they entered the era of freedom, his goals were not altruistic. Instead, he believed that military dominance superseded freed people's claims of freedom and property. If *temporarily* releasing four hundred thousand acres of land to the formerly enslaved would give him the decisive military victory that he desired, then that is what he would do.[31] Furthermore, if segregating freed people on their own land prevented them from following him and his troops, then it was a worthy short-term measure.

The order was not, however, merely about segregating freed people. Special Field Order No. 15 was also a colonizing effort.[32] Mirrored after ideas that emerged in the early nineteenth century that free Blacks threatened the goal of political harmony in the new nation, the order was an extension of the colonizationist beliefs expressed by politicians such as Thomas Jefferson and James Madison. They argued that free Blacks undermined the stability of a nation where slavery continued to be legal—and politically contentious. For white Americans, free Blacks represented an existential threat because enslaved people would always see them and aspire toward freedom. Enslavers believed that this aspiration would undermine the foundations of the United States as a slave-holding republic. Therefore, the colonization movement, which began on a formal scale with the founding of the American Colonization Society in 1817, sought to relocate free Blacks to regions of West Africa (Liberia) or the West Indies (Haiti).[33]

The colonization movement lost traction during the antebellum era due to free Black people's rejection of forced removal from a nation that they helped build. It reemerged during Lincoln's presidency. During his first two presidential years, Lincoln entertained colonization as a panacea to the political upheavals around the war and slavery's (and enslaved people's) role in it. In August 1862, he suggested to a group of Black men who visited the White House that Liberia was a location to which freed Blacks could relocate.[34] They unilaterally rejected his suggestion, with Frederick Douglass as one of the plan's most vehement critics.

In September 1862, Douglass published an article in which he excoriated Lincoln and his colonization plans. Douglass wrote, "The argument of Mr. Lincoln is that the difference between the white and black races renders it impossible for them to live together in the same country without detriment to both." He further argued, "Colonization, therefore, he holds to be the duty and the interest of the colored people." He was furious at Lincoln for supporting the idea that people of African descent did not have the right to make political claims to American citizenship. Considering that Black people were willing to fight and die for the Union, Douglass asserted that colonization was a derogation of Black people's continued sacrifice for the nation. He understood Lincoln's argument for colonization as recognition that white Americans would never accept the presence of Black people in the United States.

"[I]t is not the presence of the Negro that causes this foul and unnatural war," Douglass highlighted, "but the cruel and brutal cupidity of those who wish to possess horses, money and Negroes by means of theft, robbery, and rebellion."[35] In some ways, Special Field Order No. 15 allayed freed people's concerns about the federal government's foreign colonization plans—and extinguished, albeit temporarily, their anger about Union army officials disregarding their sacrifices.

Despite the underlying motives of Sherman, Stanton, and Lincoln, the order was a short-term success. Freed people understood Sherman's decree to be a move toward reconciliation. It represented a promise, that their Union and Republican allies would support their desire for compensation and for land.[36] Freed people considered land to be the federal government's first step in repaying them for generations of enslaved service. For freed people, the land symbolized a form of reparations.

⚜

SPECIAL FIELD ORDER NO. 15 was not the Union army's first efforts during the war to confer tangible economic benefits on Black people, in particular Black men. In July 1862, Congress passed the Second Confiscation Act, which allowed the Union army to officially recruit Black soldiers into its ranks.[37] This was a pivotal move for Lincoln, for the Union army, and for African American men. Congress went a step further the same day by ratifying the Militia Act of 1862, which allowed Black men to enlist.[38] The numbers of Black men who joined the Union army rose considerably. By 1865, over 180,000 Black men served in the military fight for slavery's end.[39]

Lincoln's and Congress's approval of recruiting Black men in the fight for freedom was a watershed moment. In addition to serving in the army and taking up arms against their enslavers, Black men who served in the Union army would receive, for the first time, payment for their military service. Therefore, when the Union army accepted Black men as soldiers, the federal government recognized Black men not as property but as people who were willing and ready to fight for the Union— and importantly, for themselves. And they would also be compensated for their sacrifice.

Despite this development, Black soldiers who did enlist quickly recognized that their contributions on the battlefield, to the Union's quest for victory over the Confederacy, did not translate into equality in pay. On September 28, 1863, Corporal James Henry Gooding wrote to Lincoln from Morris Island, South Carolina. Gooding had enlisted on February 14, 1863, and served in the Fifty-Fourth Massachusetts Volunteer Infantry Regiment, one of the war's first all-Black companies.[40] In his letter, he made his case for Black soldiers receiving pay equal to their white counterparts. "We have done a Soldiers Duty," Gooding stated. "Why cant we have a Soldiers pay?" He argued that Black men had been doing their duty, serving in every military capacity their superiors asked. What's more, they had wives and families, and "three dollars per month, for a year" was not enough to provide their "needy wives, and little ones, with fuel."[41] Gooding's letter to Lincoln illuminated Black men's wartime economic struggles. Their fight for freedom could not supersede the more immediate economic needs of their families.

On June 15, 1864, Congress heeded Black soldiers' calls for equal pay. The U.S. Colored Troops received retroactive equal pay and "the same uniform, clothing, arms, equipments, camp equipage, rations, medical and hospital attendance, pay and emoluments, other than bounty, as other soldiers of the regular or volunteer forces of the United States."[42] Though Black men rejoiced that Lincoln and members of Congress finally recognized their contributions to the Union's fight, the increase in pay presented Black soldiers with a logistical quandary. Practically, what would they do with their earnings?

Three Union generals came up with a plan. They decided to open savings banks. The first of three military banks was the Free Labor Bank in New Orleans, established by Union general N. P. Banks in February 1864. He founded the bank so that Black soldiers under his command would have access to a financial institution in which to deposit their earnings from serving in the war. Union generals Benjamin Butler and Rufus Saxton followed suit. Butler established a military savings bank in Norfolk, Virginia, and Saxton founded one in Beaufort, South Carolina.[43] Though these three banks served a need among soldiers in New Orleans, Norfolk, and Beaufort, the banks lacked federal oversight.

Established under the Department of War, the banks were not under the Department of the Treasury's direct supervision. Even though General Banks stated in his initial February 1864 announcement that "authority will be asked to connect the Bank with the Treasury of the United States," this proposal did not come to fruition.[44] Despite insufficient regulation from federal authorities, African American interest in these savings banks grew. For example, by December 1864, Black soldiers in Norfolk deposited about $65,000 ($1.2 million today) and in New Orleans, they deposited over $24,000 ($461,000 today).[45]

The experiment in military banking combined with Special Field Order No. 15 proved that African Americans greatly desired financial services. Savings banking had the potential to be a vehicle to help freed people save money, buy land, and build wealth. But just because freed people steadily earned money, engaged in banking, and purchased land in the final months of the war for freedom did not mean that their achievements would be safeguarded. They needed the increased support of the federal government to protect their investments.

As judiciously as Sherman issued Special Field Order No. 15, and as speedily as the three Union generals established the military savings banks, freed people understood that the federal government was not legally bound to protect their investments in property and in financial institutions. After all, though Lincoln had issued the Emancipation Proclamation and Sherman had carried out his orders, slavery continued to be a legal institution in the United States. Freed people were not citizens, and therefore did not enjoy citizenship rights. For this reason, African Americans recognized the need to secure their economic investments at all costs. As the military savings banks ushered a new generation of Black men and women into the world of finance, so too did a new national financial institution. It would be created less than two weeks after the field order went into effect. It would be known as the Freedman's Savings and Trust Company.

🙠

CONGREGATIONALIST MINISTER John Alvord had not expected to remain in South Carolina and Georgia in early January 1865. He had planned to travel back to New York at the beginning of the year. But he was serving as an attaché with Sherman's army, and he was hesitant to return home, despite missing his wife and children. Instead, he decided to continue following Sherman's army. In doing so, he would witness Sherman's campaign from Atlanta to Savannah. It proved to be a thrilling experience. "Things here are so full of interest," he raved, "that, now I am out, it is thought I should not hurry back."[46] Alvord's enthusiasm was not about Sherman's campaign. Instead, he delighted in interacting with freed people. As a white man who lived with his family in the North, he wanted to take advantage of the opportunity to talk with them and learn about their needs as they made the transition into freedom. The freed people that Alvord encountered kept him occupied. "Had a number of large meetings with the [colored] people—now free—helped in organizing schools & so," he relayed.[47] This experience helped him understand the hope that freed people felt amid the war's brutality.

Alvord's conversations with freed people would have an indelible influence on him. He began to wonder how Black people would manage their financial lives in freedom. One highlight of his trek with Sherman's army was his front-row seat to observe how the military savings bank in Beaufort functioned. He encountered a white officer in Hilton Head, South Carolina, who showed him a truck filled with $75,000 in Black soldiers' pay. They had no secure place to keep their earnings and they believed the best solution was to give their money to someone they hoped would keep their money safe. These observations inspired Alvord's next steps. "I came North full of the idea," he wrote, "and called together gentlemen in New York who agreed to take hold of the enterprise."[48]

With this new goal, Alvord realized that he had two main hurdles to confront. First, did the Black soldiers understand how the military banks functioned? Second, were they interested, beyond their USCT service, in banking? Alvord decided that the only way to answer these questions would be to put his plan in motion. His next step, one that he spent the remainder of his time in the South entertaining, would be to quietly gather support from powerful and wealthy allies in New York for a mission-driven, benevolent financial institution that could serve the economic needs of the formerly enslaved. With the proposition of a bank on his mind, he realized that his trip to witness Sherman and his campaign had proved to be more fruitful than anticipated. Engaging with freed people captured Alvord's attention—and shaped his new mission, to start a savings bank for the nation's former slaves.[49]

At fifty-seven years old, John Alvord led his adult life guided by a commitment to the tenants of Congregationalism and abolitionism. Born in Connecticut and armed with a degree from Yale College, he had decided to work on behalf of the abolitionist movement during the antebellum era. At the start of the Civil War, he aligned himself with the Union's effort to not only defeat the Confederacy but end slavery. He believed that white evangelicals from the North who supported abolitionism had a duty to serve the Union by helping enslaved people. He disseminated religious information to troops and enslaved refugees. He was also passionate about teaching freed people how to read. He demonstrated his abilities to teach and proselytize, honed by years of religious and political service. And while his training as a member of the clergy made him a skilled teacher, Alvord did not have the same knowledge of finance. A banker he was not.[50]

Whether it was hubris, eagerness, or a mix of both, Alvord did not let his ignorance of the intricacies of banking and finance hinder the pursuit of his newfound, and perhaps what he even believed was his divine, calling. He assumed that the work of establishing a bank for freed people would help them attain what they needed for self-making in the era of freedom—money and what one historian called "landed independence."[51] Alvord finally arrived in New York City in late January 1865, fortified with a resolve to found a bank. His conversations with the freed people of Savannah and Charleston helped him to better understand their needs and to determine how he could use his time, connections, and political influence to support them. He believed that God had called him to do this work, to aid freed people as they made the unprecedented journey out of slavery, through war, and into freedom. Through his conversations, he learned about freed people's desire for education and for land. On the cusp of Special Field Order No. 15, he witnessed as they began to plan for their economic futures. Alvord believed that a bank of their own would serve them well. He would not let his lack of knowledge about banking stop him.

Upon his arrival in New York, he tapped into his network, drawing interest in the formation of a savings bank for freed people from the world of banking and philanthropy. On January 27, 1865, a group of twenty-two men, "gentlemen together (of the very highest standing in this city)," met at 3 p.m. in the American Exchange Bank in New York City. The esteemed assemblage of people included Hiram Barney, a prominent lawyer and abolitionist, and Rev. George Whipple, an abolitionist who worked with the American Missionary Association.[52] Financiers and antislavery activists were invited to consider "the wants of the Freedman for some safe depositing for their bounty money."[53]

As the men began to consider his grand plan for bringing savings banks to freed people, Alvord hoped that the men could sense his enthusiasm for the idea.[54] They were discussing an unprecedented proposal to arm the formerly enslaved with the financial literacy necessary to support their ascendance out of slavery. He recounted for the group the details of his recent trip to Savannah and Charleston as he followed Sherman's troops. He reported that freed people were having a hard time keeping their money safe. He told the meeting's attendees about his conversation with General Littlefield, who reported to Union general Rufus Saxton. Littlefield revealed to Alvord that "the Freedmen generally insisted upon leaving in his Hands and then other recruiting officers, their bounty money as well as considerable portion of their pay."[55] Furthermore, these were "large sums, which promised to increase," and the freed people asked for Littlefield's help. They implored him to encourage his "friends to establish some institution to receive this trust."[56]

When the freed people communicated to Littlefield and Alvord their needs, they conveyed that they required access to a trustworthy financial intermediary. Simply put, they needed a safe place to store their money. Most of the Black men who served in the Union army, for example, could not securely save their earnings. Since only three Union generals established savings banks, in disparate parts of the nation, most Black soldiers, even most white men who enlisted, did not have access to a savings bank. Alvord foresaw military savings banks as test cases for the grand experiment of introducing savings banks in newly freed Black communities across the nation. He did not fully understand that enslaved and free Black people had been experimenting with their own form of economic uplift, which was why he and the other men were surprised by the success of the military savings banks. Nevertheless, he endeavored to build on the military savings banks' prosperity by creating for freed people a bank of their own.

Alvord was eager—too eager. His enthusiasm about opening a savings bank to serve the communities of Black people he met on his tour of the South prevented him from fully understanding what freed people desired—and to reckon with his ability to fulfill their demands. Yes, they wanted land. And yes, they wanted economic stability. But what Alvord overlooked, which surely seeped into the message that he conveyed to the men he lobbied to support his audacious proposal, was that Black people, even those who had been enslaved, were not ignorant. It is true that freed people did not have the same level of knowledge about finance and banking as some of the men in the room at the American Exchange Bank. One such man was A. S. Hatch. He was the cofounder of Fisk & Hatch, a New York investment firm, who by 1865 had been one of the agents responsible for selling Union bonds to domestic and foreign investors in support of the Union's war efforts. But the freed people that Alvord met *did* have a measure of financial literacy. The difference, however, was that freed people's knowledge of finance was forged through the violence and exploitation of slavery—not through the exciting world of investments and bond sales. Neither Alvord nor his New York partners fully appreciated this detail.

In fact, enslaved people had been finding ways to work for themselves and earn money from the earliest moments of slavery in colonial America. The traditions of producing and selling homemade goods, for example, were omnipresent in American slave societies. Enslaved people's economic pursuits were embedded in the fabric of colonial slavery and woven into the structures of slavery as the institution evolved in the nineteenth century. So omnipresent were enslaved women selling their wares in marketplaces and enslaved men selling their labor to willing payers that enslavers often accepted these activities. They recognized that turning a blind eye toward such endeavors was a price that they were willing to pay to prevent enslaved people from running away or, worse, inciting insurrection. This was why freed people understood ideas of saving, lending, and borrowing.[57]

Freed people's experience of being bought, valued, and sold on the auction block shaped their education in the language of finance. For example, they learned about mortgaging, as one self-emancipated man, William Craft, wrote, through witnessing family members being "mortgaged" to free up capital for their enslaver to make other potentially lucrative investments. Craft revealed in 1860 that his enslaver had "sold my brother, then mortgaged my sister . . . and myself, then about sixteen, to one of the banks, to get money to speculate in cotton."[58] Unfortunately for Craft, his enslaver defaulted on his debt obligation, which resulted in his being put up for auction along with his sister. These experiences taught freed people very specific lessons about finance. Freed people brought this education with them as they made the transition from slavery to freedom.

As Alvord chronicled his interactions with freed people, he convinced the group of men to support his plan. The men who attended the first meeting on January 27 agreed that a "National Freedman's Trust Company" was "not only practical, but very important" to helping freed people save their earnings. The future bank trustees believed that by "devoting all the profits to the education and elevation of their race" and "paying interest theron to the depositors or their heirs," they would help freed people be better equipped to take advantage of the privileges of freedom. But there was a caveat. The profits made by the bank would be invested "through such channels as might be deemed best by the Trustees." That is, the trustees wanted to maintain control of how the bank's profits were to be spent.[59]

It was telling, however, that everyone in attendance was white. The political momentum for the bank's creation emanated from a group of white men who never had the experience of living under the violent regime that defined the lives of enslaved people in America. As they put together a course of action, it is possible that at least one person in the room expressed a practical concern. If the bank was going to succeed, they needed the public support of not only politicians but prominent Black people who might draw potential depositors to the institution. But that was an idea for another day.

They agreed to meet soon to detail a plan. After the January 27 meeting, Alvord continued to spread the gospel of the Freedman's Savings and Trust Company. In February 1865, his goal was to gather as much support from as wide a cross section of power brokers as possible. He made it his goal that some of the most prominent and well-respected white Americans, from titans of industry to heads of financial firms, would fill the bank's board of trustees. For example, Alvord appealed to Major General O. O. Howard. An officer in the Union army, Howard had his own plans for helping the millions of freed people in the South. He witnessed lawmakers drafting new legislation to create what would be called the Bureau of Refugees, Freedmen, and Abandoned Lands, also known as the Freedmen's Bureau.[60] He and Alvord were working toward similar goals, to help freed people during a period of transition and unpredictability. Alvord conveyed to Howard that General Saxton wanted him to "get formed in New York a Trust Fund Co for the bounty money of the negroes."[61] Alvord believed that the freed people with whom he spoke were eager to open bank accounts, not only for their own individual benefit but to help other Black people climb out of slavery.[62] He hoped that they could work with each other to establish both the Freedmen's Bureau and the Freedman's Bank.

During the second and third trustee meetings, on February 1 and 5, the men who signed on to be trustees etched out the bank's bylaws and acts of incorporation. They also agreed that representatives for the proposed bank needed to garner more political support for the institution.[63] The trustees believed that lobbying members of Congress and officials in the Lincoln administration would bring positive attention to the bank. They needed future depositors to have faith that their money would be well protected. The trustees therefore approved sending representatives to the nation's capital to secure the support of men such as the chief justice of the Supreme Court (and former Treasury secretary), Salmon P. Chase, and General Littlefield.[64] They selected Alvord to travel to Washington on their behalf.

The conversations in the trustees' meetings convinced Alvord that he needed to move with urgency. Before leaving New York, he reached out to his new friend and confidant General O. O. Howard on February 5. He expressed his enthusiasm for an "ordinary Savings Bank . . . for this now degraded people" and asked him to put in a good word with General Saxton. At this point, Saxton oversaw administering Special Field Order No. 15 and ensuring that the military savings bank in Beaufort ran smoothly. Alvord believed that Saxton held a lot of influence among the freed people *and* among politicians in Washington. "I wish you would therefore drop him a line," Alvord pleaded, "& especially say that I am an honest man—a long time friend of the negro, with some knowledge of men & of business affairs."[65] He hoped that Howard, and therefore Saxton, would see him as an honest man who would protect freed people's economic interests despite his lack of business acumen. He also hoped that Saxton and Howard would advocate on his and the bank's behalf.

Alvord prepared for his trip to Washington with a sense of excitement. Before he left New York, he convinced his colleague in the American Missionary Association and fellow trustee Rev. George Whipple to make the trek with him. Classmates who had graduated from Oberlin Theological Seminary in Ohio in 1836, Alvord and Whipple shared a dedication to missionary work, which made their partnership in this venture one that they had been cultivating for decades.[66] Within days of the February 5 meeting, they made the voyage from New York to Washington to lobby key figures in the Lincoln administration and members of Congress.[67] They visited senators and congressmen and members of the Department of the Treasury, singing the praises of their savings bank proposal. They worked to convince major political players in Washington to support a forthcoming bill to incorporate the bank.

During their visit, several members of Congress insisted to Alvord and Whipple that the bank be "a National, rather than state institution."[68] This was an important distinction. By obtaining a charter from Congress instead of the New York state legislature, for example, the bank would be able to operate branches across the nation, not just in the state of incorporation. Alvord and Whipple understood that there were incentives to following the new regulations. According to the banking rules imposed during the Civil War, the bank would be under higher levels of regulatory scrutiny with a national charter; theoretically, charters were designed to protect the stability of the banks—and therefore protect depositors' interests.

The newest laws transformed the landscape of banking in the 1860s. The Legal Tender Act of 1862 and the National Banking Acts of 1863 and 1864, established under President Lincoln and implemented by then secretary of the Treasury Salmon P. Chase, sought to stabilize the national economy. Prior to 1863, individual states were responsible for regulating banks. There were not only hundreds of banks but also thousands of bank notes and forms of legal tender. No standard currency existed.[69] These banking acts therefore created a uniform national currency. The Legal Tender Act permitted the federal government to issue paper money and made paper currency legal tender secured by the federal government. The Banking Act of 1863 established the Office of the Comptroller of the Currency (OCC), which chartered and regulated national banks. Banks had to maintain standard capital requirements and submit to quarterly reporting, and could issue only banknotes backed by government bonds.[70] The Freedman's Bank would operate under this new regulatory architecture. But since the bank was proposed as a savings bank, not a commercial bank, it would not endure the same scrutiny.

Furnished with the backing of cabinet members and prominent congressional Republicans, Whipple journeyed back to New York while Alvord stayed in Washington. Whipple entered the fourth trustee meeting on February 15 with a report of his and Alvord's activities. He revealed to the ten other attendees that even though the members of Congress expressed enthusiasm for the bank and its mission, some members proposed amendments to the charter. Whipple detailed, "[T]he fear was expressed that the effort to introduce any material changes might prevent its passage by this Congress."[71] This piece of information prompted the trustees to request Whipple's speedy return to Washington. He would help Alvord ensure that the bill for the bank's incorporation would receive congressional approval.

Meanwhile, Alvord believed that he needed to remain in Washington because "some one must stay to <u>keep it</u> going."[72] Though he and Whipple had garnered support from some of the most influential Republicans in Washington, he felt anxious about receiving enough support for the bank's creation. He felt confident, however, that he could use his skills as a minister to advocate on the bank's behalf.

Their lobbying efforts were paying off. Senator Henry Wilson of Massachusetts, a staunch opponent of slavery, introduced the bill to incorporate the bank on February 13.[73] The bill was then referred to the Committee on Slavery and Freedom for consideration. Massachusetts senator Charles Sumner, chair of the committee, invited Alvord to a special meeting on February 16 to speak about the bank to committee members. Once the committee met and agreed to move forward with a full vote of the Senate, the real work of moving the bill through Congress began.

The legislative tug-of-war started on March 2, two days before the end of the legislative calendar for the Thirty-Eighth Congress and two days before Lincoln's second inauguration. In the political flurry, Sumner, the bank's designated advocate, moved for the Senate to consider Senate Bill 443, the incorporation of the Freedman's Savings and Trust Company. Sumner began the discussion by assuring his fellow senators that the whole bill did not need to be read aloud. Instead, they needed only to review the amendments made by the members of his special committee. But he was not so easily appeased. Missouri Senator Benjamin G. Brown, elected as an Unconditional Unionist, demanded, "I move to dispense with the reading. Let the Senator state whether it is an ordinary savings bank charter." Sumner assuaged Brown and his fellow senators, arguing, "It is an ordinary savings bank," and that it would enjoy no "extraordinary privileges" because "its object is a simple charity."[74] Senator Charles Buckalew, a Democrat from Pennsylvania, then posed an important question: Would the bank be allowed to operate outside of Washington, DC? Sumner responded that the question had been addressed in committee and that the bank could conduct business across the nation, not just in Washington—a detail that, Sumner reminded Buckalew, he had agreed to during the committee meeting.

The Senate's presiding officer declared that he would forgo reading the bill with a unanimous yes vote from the Senate. He then asked, "Is there objection?" Senator James McDougall, a Democrat from California, uttered a simple, "I object."[75] His objection must have startled Michigan senator Jacob M. Howard because he responded, for the record, "I hope my friend from California will withdraw his objection."[76] Senator McDougall's unanticipated protestation might not have been too surprising for his fellow senators. He was known for his profligate consumption of alcohol, often showing up on the Senate floor in an "apparent stupor."[77] This might have been one of those moments.

Even after Howard's gentle reprimand, McDougall did not back down. He continued by announcing, "I object to the whole thing."[78] The Senate secretary John Forney then proceeded to read the bill, surely to placate McDougall and to prevent another outburst. The reading, however, did not stop McDougall. He intervened again before Forney could fully read the bill's contents. This time, McDougall declared, "I withdraw the call," and Forney ceased reading, presumably to Sumner's relief.

But McDougall's interjection was not the only one, nor was it the last. Senator Lazarus Powell, a Democrat from Kentucky, chimed in. He expressed serious concerns about the bank's potential geographic reach. He called the proposal "a roving kind of commission for these persons to establish a savings bank in any part of the United States." For this reason, he pronounced, "I think the bill is wholly unconstitutional."[79] He argued that he did not believe that the bank had the legal standing to operate outside of the District of Columbia. Powell had cultivated a reputation in Congress as having very strong ideas about banking and regulation. He believed that banks' primary responsibility was to serve the communities in which they resided. To operate a national bank, therefore, would undermine this mission.[80] So his opposition to the bank was consistent with his perspective on national banking. Sumner agreed with Powell and offered a compromise. He stated, "Very well, let it be limited to the District."[81]

In the bill that the Senate sent to the House for approval, Sumner kept the amendment that the bank's corporate charter would be confined to Washington.[82] When the House of Representatives opened debate about the bill on the evening of March 3, there was one line of questioning that temporarily halted the vote. Congressman John Ganson, a Democrat from New York, asserted that someone from Washington should be among the people listed as bank trustees. Massachusetts Republican Thomas Eliot suggested Supreme Court justice Salmon P. Chase. No member of the House objected to Chase's addition. And when members of the House of Representatives hurriedly voted to pass the bill on March 3, it was the last piece of legislation approved before the end of the congressional session.

President Lincoln signed "An Act to Incorporate the Freedman's Savings and Trust Company" on the night of March 3. Congressional Republicans rushed to get the approved bill on Lincoln's desk so that it would become one of his final political acts on the final day of his first term as president. As Lincoln showed his support for the Freedman's Bank late that evening, he also signed "An Act to Establish a Bureau for the Relief of Freedmen and Refugees," which established the Freedmen's Bureau. That the Freedmen's Bureau was created on the same day as the Freedman's Bank meant that the two institutions—the bank, which was independent of the federal government, and the bureau, which was wholly connected to it—would be attached. The bank complemented the bureau's mission, which was "the supervision and management of all abandoned lands, and the control of all subjects relating to refugees and freedmen from rebel states."[83] The white philanthropists and bankers who served as the first group of bank trustees, and those who worked for the Freedmen's Bureau, agreed that the bank could serve as a vehicle for helping freed people adapt to the realities of freedom. The following day, on March 4, Lincoln was sworn in at his second presidential inauguration. As the Confederacy was preparing to make its last military stand against the Union forces, Lincoln had been reelected to end the war and bring the nation into a new era.[84] The Freedman's Savings and Trust Company was a part of that vision.

Speed would have its consequences. The swiftness with which Congress moved to get an approved bank-charter bill ready for Lincoln's signature meant that they overlooked key inconsistencies. The version approved by the House was not the version signed by Lincoln. Instead, it was the Senate's version. This meant that the bank was officially incorporated in Washington, DC, not New York, and Chief Justice Chase's name was not included in the charter, not that he approved of being a bank trustee. What is perhaps most important, the bank would not be under the regulatory supervision of the newly established OCC. Instead, the charter stated that Congress had the authority, and the responsibility, to appoint someone to inspect the "books of the corporation."[85] These errors did not change how the bank could go about its business, initially. Yet these mistakes suggest that Alvord, the trustees, and members of Congress were too hasty in their creation of a bank to support freed people's economic progress.

THE FEDERAL CHARTER that Congress awarded Alvord and the trustees to operate the Freedman's Bank continued the nineteenth-century savings bank revolution. The bank's mission was clear: to receive deposits. And its mandate was to keep the deposits of "persons heretofore held in slavery in the United States, or their descendants."[86] The bank's core principles came from the benevolent message of self-help as a means of helping freed people gain greater access to citizenship rights and helping them elevate their economic status. And the bank's fifty-member board of trustees was made responsible for ensuring that the bank operated in a way that manifested its mission.

By design, savings banks were supposed to operate with less risk. These institutions did not make loans or seek to aggressively make a profit. But there was an ever-present allure of shifting bank business to more lucrative yet risky investments, especially with the growth of American finance in the decades before the Civil War. In an environment where the potential for profit making shaped American economic growth, savings banks did not offer the financial benefits to bankers who wanted to grow their capital. Savings banks, though, continued to be a popular idea, especially for northern antislavery reformers. These northerners, such as Alvord and the bank trustees, involved in the effort to aid freed people, were some of the most outspoken champions of the Freedman's Bank.

The Freedman's Bank symbolized the nineteenth-century savings bank project, while comporting with the new banking rules. The bank, and its founders, were necessarily bound by the newest regulatory infrastructure created to stabilize the currency, the banking system, and ultimately the American economy. The management of risk was the highest priority for the Department of the Treasury and the OCC. The Freedman's Bank mandate aligned with avoiding the unpredictability associated with operating a commercial bank.[87]

The bank's congressionally approved charter outlined how it would function. Its fifty-member board of trustees was responsible for ensuring that the bank operated in a way that protected depositors' money. According to the charter, the trustees were expected to serve on committees that would make important decisions about staffing, where to open branches, and how to cover the costs of running the bank. The trustees, however, were not required to have financial ties to the institution. There were no financial or legal incentives to ensure that board members would act in the depositors' best interests. Because the bank was established as a nonprofit institution, the trustees had no legal responsibility to work on behalf of depositors.[88] The trustees earned the social capital of their affiliation with the bank. But they did not have to be accountable for ensuring that the depositors' money was handled in a fiscally responsible way.

Despite the bank's modest purpose, its mission was revolutionary. With a central branch in one city and given permission to open branches throughout the nation, the Freedman's Bank was in the vanguard of branch banking in the nineteenth century. In the new regulatory landscape, the Freedman's Bank would operate with a central office in New York, and administrators would slowly establish satellite branches throughout the country, especially in regions with a high concentration of freed people, mostly in the South.[89]

The bank was allowed to invest *only* in "stocks, bonds, treasury notes, and securities of the United States."[90] By investing in government debt, the bank was loaning money to the federal government. This was considered—and is still considered—to be a safe, low-risk, and stable investment. In buying financial instruments issued by the federal government, depositors were indirectly supporting the economic stability of the United States as it emerged out of a fractious war. Additionally, according to the bank's charter, no more than one third of the bank's deposits were to be invested in government securities. Another third would be kept on hand to pay for the bank's operating expenses, for when depositors wanted to withdraw funds, and to cover the president's and vice president's salaries. The charter, however, did not clearly articulate how the remaining third would be used. It was to be kept in an "available fund." This fund was to be used "at the discretion of the Trustees."[91]

The Freedman's Bank was extraordinary by the standards of the American banking industry in the nineteenth century. It brought together disparate groups of people: bankers in New York, philanthropists in Boston, Union generals, members of the Lincoln administration, free Blacks, and recently emancipated African Americans. And the bank's first depositors were the soldiers who opened accounts and made deposits in the three military savings banks.

The administrators, though, would have to resolve depositors' wants and needs with their own priorities. How would freed people actually act as bank customers? Would they trust the intentions of a group of white, northern, Republican capitalists? Even though *trust* was built into the bank's name, the administrators, namely Alvord, had to contend with the reality that freed people needed to have faith in the bank's directors. Though it was not the first savings bank to embrace the word *trust*, the founders of the Freedman's Savings and Trust Company surely had a greater responsibility to its depositors. The bank was furnished with a name meant to suggest ownership by freed people and inspire trust in the bankers who were made responsible for their money. With this important mission in mind, Alvord led the charge to begin planning for the bank's opening and future expansion.

CHAPTER TWO

Growing Pains, 1865–66

FREEDMAN'S SAVINGS BANK
Come One! Come all!
And deposit your money in one among the best
institutions in the United States,
and thereby save your money and get the interest.

—*THE COLORED TENNESSEAN*, MAY 24, 1866[1]

Deposits from Military Savings Banks in Norfolk
and Beaufort into Freedman's Bank, July 1865:
$180,000 ($3.34 million today)[2]

THREE WEEKS AFTER LINCOLN SIGNED THE FREED-
man's Bank Act in early March 1865, an article appeared in the *Christian Recorder*, a Black newspaper published by the African Methodist
Episcopal Church. Simply titled "Brooklyn Correspondence," the Black
writer, who went by the name "Junius," began by stating, "Our whole
relationship is changed in this country." With a nod to the millions
of former slaves gaining freedom during the last throes of war, Junius
offered a pragmatic assessment of Black people's changed status in the
nation. Instead of immediately celebrating emancipation, he urged African Americans to be judicious. Just because the end of slavery seemed
to be near did not mean that they would enjoy rights equal to whites,
he argued. "PREJUDICE has robbed the colored citizen of every sem-
blance of equal justice," he contended. One only needed to look, Junius
prompted, at the plight of free Black people in Northern states over the
previous six decades. They were disenfranchised. During the last decade,
they had lived in fear because of draconian fugitive slave laws. Junius
even underscored that "the jury-box, the palladium of American liberty,
has been denied us."[3] In sum, the persistence of slavery threatened every
Black person in the nation. But the end of slavery did not mean that
Black people would be welcomed instantly into the body politic. For
this reason, African Americans needed to support, defend, and protect
themselves, especially in a moment of unprecedented transformation.

Maybe the recent creation of the Freedmen's Bureau and Freedman's Bank spurred his message. Though Lincoln supported these two
entities to help usher freed people into freedom, Junius encouraged
Black people to embrace freedom on their own terms. But their methods had to change, to evolve. Though their forefathers and foremoth-
ers "held conventions, and passed resolutions, our eloquent orators have
held, spell-bound, the most enlightened audiences, and have convinced
many of our opponents of the intellectual ability of the race," these

strategies were no longer viable. This era of liberty required a different approach. The new objective was not the end of slavery, or even equality. For Junius, it was "the thousands of poor people who are living in poverty and disgrace in our large cities." Black people's new hurdle was economic prosperity as much as it was attaining political rights. He argued, "We want a moneyed interest awakened among the masses."[4] He was encouraging the free and freed people of the nation to consolidate their power, to save money, buy land, and become economically independent.

The writer of the essay was teacher and journalist Junius C. Morel. He was so frequent and respected a commentator that he simply went by his first name when publishing his incisive critiques.[5] His perspective on racial uplift was shaped by his childhood as the son of a white planter and an enslaved woman in North Carolina. After escaping North Carolina as a teenager, he lived and worked in Philadelphia, then made his home in New York. But he became disillusioned with what he considered apathy among the elite communities of African Americans in the North during the antebellum era. No longer would oration and moral suasion protect Black people. With slavery on its last legs, Morel believed in more radical solutions. Economic empowerment was the key to Black people's political advancement.[6]

With the establishment of the Freedman's Bank, Morel's vision of Black economic self-determination took center stage. But in his essay, he made a pronouncement about what he believed Black people required to attain real, true, and lasting independence. "No people," he declared, "can become great by the efforts of another."[7] The Freedman's Bank would test this theory. Could African Americans achieve economic freedom through putting their money and their trust in an institution created by whites? The experiment was about to begin.

APRIL 4, 1865, WAS an auspicious day for the Freedman's Savings and Trust Company. At 3:30 p.m., the Director's Room of the American Exchange Bank in Manhattan was reserved for the trustees of the newly created savings bank for freed people. Fourteen men entered the American Exchange Bank's office at 50 Wall Street, each having accepted

Alvord's invitation to serve on the bank's esteemed board of trustees. Most of the men had personal connections to Alvord. The trustees would be responsible for shepherding the bank—and its depositors— into a new economic and political future.[8]

The day's agenda included a robust set of priorities. The trustees needed to determine who would be the bank's president and decide on the structure of the various committees. They also had to address the problem of not having a full fifty-person board. The fact that only four-teen of the fifty appointed trustees attended the first board meeting did not bode well for the trustees' anticipated involvement. The board was also missing seven trustees, who had resigned or not officially accepted Alvord's invitation to join. In the month between Lincoln's signing the bill that established the bank on March 3 and the meeting, the official list of trustees had dropped from fifty to forty-three.

The loss of seven trustees, such as wealthy abolitionist and polit-ical firebrand Gerrit Smith, was an early crack in the bank's founda-tion. Little is known about why the trustees resigned. Perhaps once they understood the commitment of time and resources that Alvord had requested—that they attend regular committee meetings and open accounts of their own—they decided to step away from the bank before becoming more intertwined with the business. It is possible that their names were added in the bank's charter to give it a veneer of credibility with members of Congress.[9] The charter's speedy approval implies that the ploy may have worked. But this strategy would present a problem when the bank became a functioning financial institution—and when the trustees and administrators started serving freed people.

Despite the relatively small number of trustees present on the after-noon of April 4, the bankers and philanthropists, accustomed to frat-ernizing and receiving economic information from banking houses on Wall Street, entered the Director's Room with a specific goal. They intended to lend their knowledge and political capital to the success of a financial institution born out of the nineteenth-century idea of *thrift*. Some perhaps believed that their contributions of money and time to the bank fulfilled a moral obligation to help the most downtrodden members of American society. Men such as Alvord expressed this position. Other trustees perhaps believed that an affiliation with the bank would bolster their social and political standing, to curry favor with members of Lincoln's administration. Whatever their personal reasons for accepting the appointment, the trustees proceeded with the meeting's agenda, to determine the bank's administrative structure.

The first agenda item was the selection of the bank's president. William A. Booth, a Connecticut-born New York merchant, businessman, and philanthropist, won the nomination. Clothing merchant and missionary Mahlon Hewitt was elected the first vice president. Hewitt was likely one of the more principled members of the bank's executive committee. He had been working with the American Union Mission during the Civil War and, in the month before he accepted a position with the bank, he had expressed concern about the freed people of Charleston, specifically wanting to figure out a way to alleviate their "suffering and want occasioned by the rebellion."[10] And Walter S. Griffith, president of the Home Life Insurance Company, was chosen as the second vice president.

Though Booth assumed the role of bank president, he had little authority. According to the bank's bylaws, the president was "subject at all times to the control and direction of the Board, or of the Finance Committee." The first vice president had more influence—and more responsibilities. As the first vice president, Mahlon Hewitt was required to "attend at the office of the Company during the hours of business, and to exercise, under the direction of the President, a general supervision and control."[11] The responsibilities of the second vice president amounted to stepping into the first vice president's or the president's role if either of them could not fulfill it.

The one position that they did not fill on that day was that of the bank's secretary. The person in the secretary's position would "transact the business of the Company," meaning the secretary would do the work of running the bank and maintaining its branches.[12] Though the bylaws articulated the duties of the person in each position, the trustees did need to agree on how to delegate the most basic of operational tasks, that is, how the bank would function on a day-to-day basis. By creating committees, the board, guided by Alvord, agreed that the first vice president and the secretary would manage the bank's essential functions. More directly, the first vice president and the secretary would run the bank.[13]

The trustees had one final mission that day. One of the seemingly more mundane, but no less important, goals of the April 4 meeting was to discuss a proposal from March to add a Black person to the board. The trustee who made the proposal was Philadelphia merchant Thomas Webster, a staunch opponent of slavery with a public hatred of enslavers.[14] Webster may have introduced the idea of adding a Black board member as a demonstration of the bank's support of Black economic uplift. It may have also been a strategy to convince freed people to open and deposit money into accounts. Booth announced that the members of the subcommittee responsible for nominating trustees and officers "were not yet prepared to nominate any persons heretofore held in slavery in the United States or their descendants to fill any vacancy now existing in the Board."[15] Perhaps certain trustees did not want an African American man to shift the bank's main focus: encouraging freed people's investments in capitalism not through charity but through thrift, prudence, and hard work. So, despite Webster's urging, the bank's board remained all white as of April 1865.

The all-white and male board of trustees promptly ended the meeting once they decided that they would discuss the executive committees' salaries a few days later. The president and vice presidents did not take the positions merely for financial gain. Booth, Hewitt, and Griffith had outside careers and obligations. For example, Booth's role as bank president was not his only responsibility. By the 1860s, he was known in New York society as much for his business acumen as for his philanthropy. While he was a banker and merchant, in addition to assuming the role as the bank's president, he also served as the president of the American Tract Society *and* of the Children's Aid Society.[16] No one publicly questioned Booth's array of professional obligations. Though the trustees initially understood their affiliation with the bank as a form of philanthropy, time would tell whether their varied commitments would stand in the way of their engagement with the bank. After all, even though the bank was a philanthropic venture for the trustees, the trustees were still responsible for ensuring that the day-to-day business of the institution was handled. There was a member of the executive committee, however, who took his role more seriously than the others.

One of the trustees with the least amount of knowledge about the intricacies of finance was the most eager. On April 7, the board elected Alvord as the bank's corresponding secretary. This position on the bank's executive committee required the most dedication of time and energy. Alvord was enthusiastic. His plan was finally coming to fruition. But with his official appointment to the bank's executive committee, he held two positions: bank secretary *and* inspector and superintendent of schools for the Freedmen's Bureau. These posts made Alvord a busy man. He had to balance his administrative responsibilities for the bank with his role at the Freedmen's Bureau. He believed that both positions were important to helping the millions of freed people in the South. He hoped that through economic security and education, African Americans could carve new identities, establish a strong economic foundation, and become esteemed new citizens of the nation.

Despite these lofty aspirations, Alvord felt overwhelmed by the mandates of his positions. He reflected on his dual responsibilities, writing to his wife, "I cannot tell what work awaits me. I am now endeavoring to labor faithfully for both institutions—the field of both being the same mainly, at the moment there is <u>much to be done</u> here & everywhere."[17] He was overwhelmed not only by his responsibilities with the Freedmen's Bureau and the bank but also by his family's economic circumstances. He and his wife corresponded frequently in the spring and early summer of 1865, expressing to each other concerns about collecting and paying rents and taxes.[18] Despite his uneasiness, Alvord forged ahead. He took seriously, but underestimated, what would be required of him to fulfill his roles in the Freedmen's Bureau and the Freedman's Bank.

Alvord's work, and the work of the bank, would only heighten in the coming weeks. The early-April meetings occurred as Lincoln and his generals were moving decidedly toward the war's end. That the fighting in Northern Virginia and the fall of Richmond to Union forces would result in the surrender of Confederate general Robert E. Lee to Union lieutenant general Ulysses S. Grant at Appomattox Court House on April 9 was an auspicious backdrop. The atmosphere in Virginia during the beginning of April was one of anticipation and celebration. The men in the Director's Room at the American Exchange Bank felt the same, a sense of excitement mixed with relief that the military fight that characterized the bloody civil war, and slavery, were coming to an end.[19]

On April 4, as the trustees began to establish the foundation on which the bank would grow, the bank's central office also opened. Located on 87 Cedar Street in New York City, it was two blocks away from the New York Stock Exchange and Wall Street in lower Manhattan, in the heart of New York's burgeoning financial district. The location of the bank's central office was not selected haphazardly but reflected what the bank symbolized. It was filled with bankers and philanthropists who were connected to American finance. And while members of the board supported the Union's war efforts, they also strove to show their patriotism through economic success.

It was telling that the bank's central office was not in a Black New York neighborhood.[20] Instead, it was near Wall Street, the heartbeat of the American economy. The central office's location also augured a potentially unfavorable outcome for freed people. After all, white bankers on Wall Street were often indifferent to and sometimes openly hostile toward Black people, especially runaway slaves during the era of enslavement.[21] Despite this reality, by establishing the bank's small foothold near other financial institutions, the board was communicating their grander intention of making the bank a prosperous institution. But for whom—the freed people or board members themselves—would become a larger concern.

❧

SEVEN DAYS AFTER the bank's central office opened in New York, Washington was thrown into chaos. On the evening of April 14, Abraham and Mary Todd Lincoln traveled by carriage from the White House to Ford's Theater for a night of entertainment. The evening's performance of the comedy *Our American Cousin* drew the Lincolns, accompanied by Union major Henry Rathbone and his fiancée, Clara Harris, to a special box in the theater. The celebratory ambience turned to pandemonium when actor John Wilkes Booth pointed his .44-caliber Derringer pistol at the back of Lincoln's head, firing at point-blank range. Lincoln never recovered. He died at 7:22 a.m. the following day.

The assassination of President Lincoln and the ensuing political fallout from Andrew Johnson's ascension to the presidency marked the beginning of the Reconstruction period. But the challenges ahead, in the aftermath of war and a dramatic reorganization that marked the shift away from slavery, required Freedman's Bank administrators to deploy new strategies if the institution was to thrive.

The bank got off to a slow start in the summer of 1865. Its opening had not garnered the popular celebration for which Alvord or perhaps even William Booth had hoped. Several factors contributed to the bank's slow initial pace. Bank administrators had not laid the groundwork for establishing branches outside of New York City. The political repercussions that emanated from Lincoln's assassination, President Johnson's dramatic shifts in Reconstruction policies, and African Americans' uncertainty about the slow end of slavery stymied the quick spread of the gospel of the savings bank for the formerly enslaved.

Because of the inertia that the bank's opening garnered in the press, members of the board began to fear that freed people might hesitate to open accounts. The biggest hurdle for African Americans involved trust. Would they give unknown white men access to their hard-earned wages? Could they have confidence that the bank would protect their financial interests? These were perhaps questions that the trustees asked at a May 17 subcommittee meeting at the bank's central office in New York. The agency committee agreed that it would make sense for Vice President Hewitt and Alvord to travel to Washington, Richmond, Norfolk, and "to other points South if they think proper" to establish bank branches in "such points as the interest of the Freedmen may require."[22]

The trustees decided that Hewitt and Alvord would do a traveling tour of the South, taking time away from the bank's headquarters. Their mission would be to encourage African Americans to put their faith in the bank's white administrators, cashiers, and staff. They needed to persuade potential depositors that the bank would function with their best financial interests in mind. By meeting as many African Americans as possible, and deploying their politicking skills, Hewitt and Alvord would work to ensure that the freed people would embrace the bank's message of prosperity through depositing money in accounts.

The board resolved that Hewitt and Alvord would visit cities that had some of the highest formerly enslaved populations. They had to be creative if they were going to motivate freed people who had not previously interacted directly with the financial services industry to open accounts and deposit their wages. Therefore, they developed a strategy. To calm African Americans' fears about banking and about white men protecting their money, they made a strategic choice. Hewitt, with Alvord in tow, would address Black people's concerns by appealing to African Americans in the heart of their communities: Black churches.[23] So, at the beginning of May, the two went south.

Their first stop was Washington, DC. Though the board initially wanted Alvord and Hewitt to encourage Black Washingtonians to patronize the bank, this first visit had a broader goal. The rapid shift in Washington's political climate after Lincoln's assassination warranted bank representatives making the rounds in the nation's capital. With Alvord taking the lead, the men met with members of the Johnson administration, including the new president himself, who wrote a letter for Alvord stating his support of the bank and its mission. Though Johnson was a Democrat, Alvord believed that his endorsement would go a long way toward helping him sway members of Congress. With Johnson's blessing, Alvord then met with Treasury Secretary Hugh McCulloch and Assistant Secretary of War Charles Anderson Dana. Alvord wanted to guarantee that the bank had the backing of influential political officials as he and Hewitt continued their journey to the southern states. In addition to appealing to prominent Black businessmen in the city, they lobbied politicians in Washington to convince members of the new administration that a national savings bank for African Americans was a prudent idea.[24]

After spending the last week of May 1865 traveling around Washington, lobbying Black and white Washingtonians, Alvord and Hewitt made the voyage to Norfolk, Virginia. Norfolk was the bank's first branch, and, in many ways, it was one of the easiest for bank administrators to establish. Since one of the military savings banks established in 1864 was in Norfolk, the bank's executive committee agreed that it would not be difficult to roll the deposits into the branch. Alvord established a branch in the city and collected $8,000 from "the Negroes on deposit for my Bank, & established a permanent branch there."²⁵ He and Hewitt hoped that the momentum of the Norfolk branch would expand to other cities.

During the bank's first three months, Alvord grappled privately with fears about the future of freed people in the nation. He divulged these inner frustrations to his wife. In a May 30, 1865, letter, he pondered, "Will there be any place for the negroes? Will the lands hitherto abandoned be repossessed by their former owners?"²⁶ As optimistic as Alvord was about freed people's status and their potential to enjoy the benefits of emancipation, he was also unsure about white people's willingness to respect the new political and social order. He hoped that the bureau would support freed people's claims to land as a key to securing their economic and political stability in this fractious, but promising, postwar period. "Is there to be any confiscation as penalty for traitors," he wondered, "so the colored population have some space wherein to develope their industry, secure education, & thrive in the enterprizes [sic] of life?"²⁷ Alvord felt that freed people needed not only education and political rights but also economic power to move successfully from slavery to freedom—and from enslaved person to American citizen. But he was naïve about the road ahead. Though he truly believed that the bank could be a stepping stone for the formerly enslaved, he also underestimated how whites—both from the South and from the North—could stand in their way.

In early June 1865, after their stops in Norfolk and Washington, Hewitt and Alvord, joined by three other representatives from the Freedmen's Bureau, made the trip to Richmond to round up support for the city's bank branch. They selected Ebenezer Baptist Church as one of the venues for their task. This church—filled with a congregation of freed people—was a strategic choice. Alvord deployed his religious beliefs in his messages to bank trustees, politicians, and advocates about the bank's glorious mission. For him, the religious and the financial were intertwined. It was no accident that several of the bank's trustees were also affiliated with evangelical organizations such as the American Missionary Association and the American Tract Society. The bank's mission was informed as much by Christian evangelical beliefs as by the moral messages that infiltrated the financial language of saving.

So, Ebenezer Baptist Church was the perfect setting for their goals. Established in 1857 by enslaved people and free people of color in Richmond, the church was a beacon of Black political activism during the Civil War. The church's early years, however, were marred by the state's legal regulations that forbade groups of Black people, enslaved and free, from congregating without the presence of a white person. White fear of slave insurrection shaped Virginia's slave laws and therefore the early structure of Ebenezer Baptist Church. Yet on June 6, 1865, the church's governing body, which consisted of approximately one hundred Black male congregants, was "earnestly engaged in reorganizing their church." They had gotten "rid of the old rebel preacher" and installed an African American pastor who would "give them the true gospel as preached in the North, as they had tried the Southern religion long enough."[28]

At some point over the previous two weeks, Hewitt and Alvord decided that Hewitt would take the lead at this meeting. As they made their way into the church, located in the center of the city, Hewitt was reminded that he needed to connect the bank's work of economic uplift to the church's role in helping formerly enslaved people survive and thrive in the era of freedom. The men entered the church and witnessed a common occurrence in Black religious congregations in the former Confederate South. Approximately one hundred Black men were engaged in an intense discussion about a new church constitution. What would be the church's governing principles? How would they guide their newly freed congregation through the promise and unpredictability of freedom? Without white oversight, African Americans could openly design the religious communities that best reflected their congregants' needs.

Hewitt, Alvord, and the Freedmen's Bureau agents waited as the congregants carried on their debate. Perhaps they expected a vigorous greeting. Only after the congregants adopted the new church constitution did they turn to welcome Hewitt and the other men into their sacred space. Hewitt stood before them, with approximately one hundred pairs of eyes interrogating his posture, his clothing, and his disposition, and unveiled his plan for the Richmond branch of the bank.

In his remarks, Hewitt attempted to convince the congregants to embrace the benefits of capitalism through banking. By positioning a branch in Richmond, the heart of the former slave South, Hewitt informed the men, bank depositors would have access to an institution created to bolster their economic success. As he spoke, the congregants listened with "earnest attention," perhaps weighing the pros and cons of his appeals for them to open accounts.[29]

Once Hewitt completed his comments, several "older gentlemen" responded to his plea for the church members to become depositors. One man spoke up saying that he was in dire need of a financial institution in which to securely store his money. Over the years, he had lost about $5,000 because "he had no place to keep it." His only options were to give money to white men for safekeeping or to bury it in the ground. In the latter case, he could never remember where he buried his cash. The man seemed enthusiastic about the bank, arguing that he "was glad that now he could have some place to put his money where it would be safe."[30] Another man in the congregation announced that he had accumulated $700 in gold during the war. He was forced to bury it as well, and when he returned to retrieve the money, someone had stolen it. As the men told stories about the challenges they faced with saving money, it became clear that their problems had little to do with earning wages. Their biggest concern was that there were no financial institutions available to African Americans, especially recently emancipated people. The men shared a common desire to have "a bank of their own."[31]

Hewitt surely saw an opportunity in the stories that the men told, sensing that the bank would fulfill a need in African American communities across the South. He was even more enthusiastic and surprised by their knowledge of money, saying that the men conveyed a "surprising degree of business shrewdness and intelligence."[32] His shock at their economic acumen shows the extent to which he believed that African Americans needed the bank's help to understand the benefits of saving and banking. In communicating to him the hardships that they faced with saving money, the men revealed that what they needed was *not* hand-holding by white benefactors. Instead, they needed access to financial services to help them protect their financial interests. This reality was evident in the final exchange.

One "old" man raised his voice to ask how the deposits would be secured. Hewitt was perhaps not prepared for such a direct question about the fundamentals of banking. It is even possible that he had not anticipated that he would be questioned about the bank's soundness. He told the man, and the other congregants, that the bank "was composed of a large number of the best and wealthiest men in the United States." But he also disclosed that the "best and wealthiest men" at the bank's helm were not "personally responsible" for securing the bank's deposits, a fact that would prove to undermine the bank's stability in the future. Hewitt concluded his answer by saying that the congregants needed to trust the men's "honor and integrity of character."[33]

The man continued to interrogate Hewitt, not satisfied with his answer. "Were there any old Rebels and slaveholders among them?" he inquired. His question got to the heart of Black depositors' concerns about the bank's ideological foundations. Was the Freedman's Savings and Trust Company a front for scheming Confederates or avaricious former enslavers? "No," Hewitt replied, "they are all Northern men, and your friends."[34]

Hewitt might not have fully appreciated the men's concerns. He was communicating that there were no former members of the Confederacy or slaveholders as bank managers or trustees. He was trying to convey that they could trust that bank administrators would be responsible and honorable economic actors. But in the aftermath of Lincoln's assassination and President Johnson's political move to reinstall ex-Confederates in positions of power, the men's concerns were well founded. While other church members replied with a hearty sense of acceptance, a few murmuring "Den, dat's alright," the inquiring man was still not fulfilled by Hewitt's responses. The "old" man continued his scrutiny. "But . . . what's done wid de money?" he insisted. Hewitt proudly stated that the deposits were invested in U.S. stocks, a safe and low-risk investment. What he didn't mention was that according to the bank's act of incorporation, the bank would invest in not only stocks but also treasury notes, bonds, and "other securities of the United States."[35]

Hewitt's explanation must have placated the man because he stood and paused, as if meditating on Hewitt's final words. The man then concluded, "Well, den, the bank can't break widout de United States breaks, and dar's no danger of that, though de Rebels tried mighty hard to break it."[36] The man's final comment elicited a round of laughs that echoed throughout the church. His remark lifted the fog of uncertainty that had hung around the church as he questioned Hewitt. But the man's comment and his economic reasoning presented a problem. He connected the bank's success to the nation's economic stability. If the country could climb its way out of wartime economic insecurity and emerge stronger than before, then the bank would be safe from the tumultuousness of economic risk that characterized banking in nineteenth-century America.

The man's logic was not entirely accurate. And, interestingly, Hewitt did not attempt to correct him. What he should have said was that the Freedman's Savings and Trust Company was established as a savings bank. The institution's success, and its failure, depended on the trustees' and administrators' prudent financial decision-making. The bank's stability relied on judicious accounting practices, with the cautious oversight of bank managers and branch cashiers. And according to the bank's original charter, the institution could accept only deposits. Bank administrators could not extend lines of credit or originate loans to borrowers. The bank's stability relied on minimizing risk, not entirely on the nation's economic stability. The man did understand, however, that the bank was tethered to the success of the federal government through the Treasury. Because the bank invested approximately a third of deposits in governmental securities, its stability also relied on the federal government's ability to pay back loans. The bank invested in Treasury bonds, meaning that one-third of bank deposits were loaned to the federal government at a relatively low interest rate. Governmental securities were a stable investment. The man's understanding of the bank's structure—and Hewitt's failure to set the record straight—reflected the unevenness of the relationship that would evolve between white bank administrators and African American depositors.[37]

Hewitt, his team, and the congregants expressed a shared enthusiasm about the bank, which led them to make an agreement. When the Richmond branch opened, Ebenezer Baptist Church would open an account. The congregants celebrated the newly established "friendship" between themselves and their "white friends." They hoped that the rapport with Hewitt, Alvord, and representatives from the Freedmen's Bureau would result in the building of a stable financial institution in their city to usher them more securely into freedom.

As excited as the congregants were about the prospect of a bank of their own in Richmond, they were also impatient. They urged Hewitt and Alvord to expedite the process of breaking ground. Not only did the congregants agree to open accounts when the bank branch was established, they offered Hewitt and Alvord additional help. They elected a group of fifteen men to "canvass the City and surroundings" to spread the bank's gospel. They also agreed to "appoint a permanent Advisory Committee to carry it into effect."[38]

Both Hewitt and Alvord rushed to report back to the committee a week after the meeting. They wrote of the rousing crowd, the welcoming residents, and the enthusiasm with which freed people in Richmond received news of the bank. Alvord asked for "instructions in regard to establishing an Agency at Richmond."[39] They were eager to increase the bank's visibility within the Black population in the former capital of the Confederacy.

Alvord and Hewitt also relayed information about the desire of the Black men in Richmond to act as agents of the bank, that is, to work as administrators, taking deposits when the bank opened. They hoped that by allowing Black men to advocate in an official capacity on the bank's behalf, they could recruit more depositors. Moreover, by partnering with Black "agents" in Richmond, the bank would be showing its embrace of African Americans as collaborators to bring Alvord's vision of uplift through economic prosperity to the masses.

The trustees, however, were less willing to accept the freed people's requests. The subcommittee responsible for placing agents in bank branches shot down the proposal. They argued, "Colored agents going among the negros to get deposits, while they would not in fact be our agents nor make us legally responsible for the funds until they were passed on our books, still if a loss should occur the depositors might assume that they were acting as our agents and make us much trouble." And in a direct rebuff, the committee responded, "[T]hat mode of obtaining deposits is looked upon as dangerous."[40] Despite Alvord's support, members of the committee on agents did not embrace Black men as full partners in the grand experiment of banking for African Americans. They were willing to accept Black people's money, but not the idea of Black people being responsible for handling the bank's deposits.

This series of interactions between the Black people in Richmond and the bank's representatives became an example of the stark differences between what the freed people wanted and the behavior that administrators expected from depositors. In biblical terms, they were "unequally yoked." Freed people expected that the bank would act on behalf of the Freedmen's Bureau and the federal government. Their questions about the relationship between the bank and the federal government suggested that they hoped the bank's mission would make real the goals of Reconstruction: reconciliation and repair. Freed people yearned for federal authorities to protect their interests in the name of reunion. They also wanted to exercise some influence over how the bank was run and who would represent them in their local branches. For freed people, the bank represented the promise of Reconstruction.

Bank administrators had different expectations. They assumed that freed people would defer to the wisdom and guidance of the bank's white founders on financial matters. The agency committee's response to the requests of the Ebenezer Baptist Church congregation demonstrated this belief. They were less than enthusiastic about Black men working at the bank. Neither the bank's philanthropic mission nor the founding members' antislavery and abolitionist affiliations convinced bank administrators that Black people should be involved beyond their role as depositors. This policy would evolve quickly as African Americans began to advocate for more representation among the bank's personnel.

Their lobbying paid off in Washington, DC. The first exception was the bank's second branch, established in Washington in August 1865. William J. Wilson was a Black teacher in Washington who had garnered Alvord's support to work as the bank's cashier.[41] Yet the clashes between Black depositors' desires and bank administrators' beliefs would persist as more branches opened across the South.

The ideological misalignment between the bank's prospective depositors and the administrators, however, did not stymie the bank's opening in the city. Though there would be no Black agents in Richmond as of 1865, Hewitt and Alvord's goals were partially fulfilled. The Richmond, Virginia, branch of the Freedman's Bank opened in October 1865. Located at the corner of Tenth and Broad Streets, in the heart of the city, it was the fourth bank location opened, after branches were founded in Washington, Lynchburg, and Norfolk.

The Richmond branch sat in an auspicious location. Not only did Richmond house one of the biggest slave-auction sites in the nation between 1820 and 1860, but mere months before the branch opened, the city was the capital of the Confederate States of America.[42] The bank was situated only four blocks away from the White House of the Confederacy, the executive residence of Jefferson Davis, president of the Confederacy. The branch represented a new vision for economic freedom in America. And as the capital of the former Confederacy, Richmond encapsulated the tragedy of slavery for the almost four million people of African descent in the nation.

In 1865, African Americans exercised their newly endowed freedoms as they embraced the new era of emancipation. Against this backdrop, the interaction between the Ebenezer Baptist Church congregants and Hewitt offered a new symbol of what the economic and political relationship could be between African Americans in the former Confederate South and white Americans. The exchange represented how the bank and the African American community hoped to work together to topple the vestiges of slavery in Richmond—and in the nation as a whole.

AS HEWITT AND ALVORD made their way through regions of the South to bolster support and attract depositors for the bank, the reordering of Washington's political foundation continued. The vacuum left in the wake of Lincoln's assassination and filled by the ascendance of President Johnson meant a shift in Reconstruction policies. This shift affected freed people the most. During Johnson's first months as president, he enjoyed broad support from Republicans in Congress. They wanted him to carry on Lincoln's legacy of supporting freed people and their gaining of political rights. Johnson even garnered support from prominent African Americans, such as Virginian John Mercer Langston. Langston, like many other African Americans, held on strongly to the belief that Johnson would carry out Lincoln's political vision. They hoped even more that Johnson would make Black people's goal of inclusion in the creation of a biracial democracy a reality.[43]

In early May 1865, Johnson made a choice to openly express his enthusiasm about the bank. His pronouncement was timely—and strategic. On April 10, four days before Lincoln's assassination, the bank's president, vice presidents, and secretary, as well as ten trustees, sent a letter to Lincoln asking him to communicate his support of the bank to "colored people . . . the Secretaries of War and the Treasury." They wanted Lincoln's help to spread news of the bank's good work "for the safe keeping and transmission of funds."[44]

Lincoln never read the letter. Instead, Johnson responded a month later, on May 6. "I cordially approve of the laudable and benevolent object of the Freedman's Savings and Trust Company," he wrote. "I commend it to the Secretaries of War, Navy, and Treasury," he promised, "for such facilities in reaching the freedmen, and for the safe keeping and transmission of funds, as the Company may need, and as will be consistent with the public service."[45]

Johnson's support of the bank, however, did not translate into his making a broader push for African Americans' economic or political rights, especially for freed people in the former Confederate South. Voicing support for the bank was one thing. Enacting real legislative change in favor of the bank's potential customers was something else completely.

On May 29, six weeks into his presidential term, Johnson made a bold step in demonstrating his eagerness to overturn Lincoln's wartime policies. On that day, Johnson issued his Amnesty Proclamation, a comprehensive plan for his administration's approach to Reconstruction. In it, he extended an official pardon to former Confederates, welcoming them back into the body politic. To ensure that "the authority of the Government of the United States may be restored, and that peace, order and freedom may be established," Johnson pardoned "all persons who have directly or indirectly participated in the existing rebellion."[46] But amnesty was not automatic.

Johnson's proclamation required ex-Confederates to swear allegiance to the United States and to agree to defend the Constitution. It also required high-ranking officials in the Confederate army and influential members of the Confederate political elite to appeal to him directly for amnesty. Though the proclamation made it seem as though the bar for amnesty was high, in reality, thousands of ex-Confederates readily appealed to Johnson and regained their rights as citizens. And the president's administration graciously offered them concessions. Johnson made a strategic move *not* to require them to reject the grounds on which the Confederacy stood: secession. And though the Thirteenth Amendment, which abolished slavery, had been passed by Congress in January 1865, it had not yet been made into law by the time Johnson issued the proclamation. That would occur in December 1865. During the period between his proclamation in May and the ratification of the Thirteenth Amendment in December, Johnson's plans for Reconstruction and reunion scaled back the amendment's political potential.[47] The proclamation of amnesty was only the beginning.

For the tens of thousands of freed people in coastal regions of South Carolina, Georgia, and northern Florida, Johnson's proclamation nullified their land claims. Freed families quickly asserted property claims to Confederate land after Sherman's Special Field Order No. 15 in January 1865. When Johnson reversed that order in September 1865 by issuing Circular No. 15, freed people lost property rights that they had fought to preserve. On September 12, 1865, the federal government would support the policy of redistributing land to former Confederates. According to Johnson's policy, "Abandoned Lands held by this Bureau may be restored to owners pardoned by the President." The ex-Confederates who received a pardon needed only to take an oath of allegiance.[48] Johnson made a calculated gamble with the livelihoods of freed people. He traded Black economic survival for ex-Confederate loyalty.

This decision, perhaps even more than Johnson's offer of political amnesty to rebels, undermined freed people's economic momentum. In October 1865, mere weeks after Circular No. 15 went into effect, Union general O. O. Howard traveled to South Carolina. He set up two meetings. The first was in Charleston with former Confederates to relay Johnson's new policy of the divestment of land from freed people and the restoration of property rights to them. He was surely met with enthusiasm by former Confederates who could reestablish themselves as both citizens and property owners.

The second meeting was on Edisto Island on October 19. Howard proceeded carefully as he spoke with his audience of "several hundred of the colored people of Edisto Island." The Black Edisto Island residents came prepared to detail their disappointment with the federal government's Reconstruction policies. Howard was all too aware that he had to break the devastating news that the freed people who had taken up land in this coastal region of the state had to relinquish their property claims to former enslavers. Standing before a community of freed people in a public meeting, he relayed the new policy. He then asked that the group elect a committee of three respected members of the community to send a letter of petition to the Freedmen's Bureau.[49]

The freed people took Howard's advice. Within days of the meeting, Howard received a letter from freedmen Henry Bram, Ismael Moultrie, and Yates Simpson on behalf of the Edisto Island community. The men revealed feeling as though they were "at the mercy of those who are combined to prevent us from getting land enough to lay our Fathers bones upon." They had property in "Horses, cattle, carriages, & articles of furniture," but they were "landless and Homeless."[50] In a final plea to Howard, they argued that they felt as if the administration wanted them to forgive Confederates who had beaten and exploited them, people who were endeavoring to keep them "[i]n a condition of Helplessness."[51] For these formerly enslaved people, forgiveness was not an option. They wanted economic opportunity and freedom instead.

Howard responded on October 22, 1865. His reply was, however, a paternalistic one. He wrote, "You are right *in wanting homesteads* and will *surely be defended in the possession of* every one which you shall purchase or have already purchased."[52] In seeking to assure the freed people that he understood their indignation, he seconded an ex-Confederate argument about the second-class status of freed people. The argument espoused by rebels was that African Americans needed to earn wages to purchase land, not be given land by the federal government. Though Howard wanted the freed people of Edisto Island to accept Johnson's terms of amnesty to rebels, he did not communicate an appreciation of the work that freed people had already completed in tilling the land and helping the Union win the war.

Despite Johnson destroying a crucial tool in freed people's plans for economic uplift, African Americans continued to express interest in the bank. Perhaps it was the divestment of land at this crucial moment in the months after the final battle of the war that spurred freed people to gravitate toward the bank. Because few African Americans had access to depository institutions before the creation of the military savings banks or the Freedman's Bank, bank administrators decided to open branches in cities with sizable Black populations.[53] By the end of 1865, the bank had opened branches in Norfolk, Washington, Lynchburg, Richmond, Natchez, Vicksburg, Huntsville, and Memphis. Though Black soldiers were the bank's initial customers, freed people in these cities also slowly entered these bank branches, trusting the cashiers and the institution with their money. But these branches could do little to help freed people outside of these hubs. African Americans still needed economic help. Even Black soldiers who had been mustered out continued asking white military officers to keep money for them. "Found large sums of money with some military officers which ought to have been in the hands of the freemen long since," one bank committee report detailed.[54]

Despite the rapid spread of the bank's influence in the South, freed people's expectations for the bank continued to collide with those of its administrators. Cashiers and trustees believed that though freed people were not ignorant about the benefits of saving, they were still learning from their interactions with local bank officials and agents about the fundamentals of banking. Fundamentally, depositors treated their accounts as one would a modern-day checking account, not a savings account. In practical terms, freed people would deposit money and, once they had saved a desired amount, would withdraw their money, even before earning interest on their deposits. Depositors were not concerned about earning interest; they wanted a safe place to store their money. Some bank administrators understood this. In January 1866, in his capacity with the Freedmen's Bureau, Alvord testified before Congress about his work with the bureau. He described his travels in the South, revealing that freed people were saving money "for old age, for sickness, for purchasing homesteads, and other prosperity in the future."[55] Freed people's priority, which shaped their engagement with the bank, was saving money to buy land.

The majority of the bank's administrators, however, were slow to understand freed people's economic goals. They were also slow to convey to depositors that the bank could only function successfully if depositors kept their money in the bank to accrue interest payments. If depositors withdrew their money en masse, that is, in a bank run, then the bank branch could not meet the needs of all the depositors. Administrators' failure to relay this information early in the bank's tenure resulted in a potentially disastrous run on the Norfolk branch shortly after it opened. In July 1865, the bank received word of a "recent agitation among Col. people at Norfolk," which resulted in "a falling off of the deposit and a larger demand upon that branch than they are able to meet."[56] For the bank to function, the individual branches could not keep the entirety of the deposits at the branch. According to the bank's bylaws, only about a third of the bank's deposits would be kept at the branches. Most of the deposits were sent monthly to the bank's main branch in New York City.

Despite the challenges at the Norfolk branch during the summer and fall of 1865, African American patronage helped the bank, and its branches, grow steadily in its first year. Black depositors surely hoped that the institution would provide them with a sense of economic secu-

rity at a time when they yearned for the stability that they hoped freedom would provide. As depositors poured their savings and earnings
into accounts, the bank's coffers grew. African Americans had deposited over $305,000 in the first year. "All of this money is from Freed-
men," a triumphant announcement in the *Christian Recorder* reported.
To put a finer point on the staggering amount of money that Black
people collectively deposited into their bank accounts, the depositors
were freedman who many whites believed "could not take care of themselves."[37] It was clear that the "freedmen welcomed the institution."[38] By
December 1866, the bank spread its net even wider and added an additional eleven branches, in Savannah, Mobile, New Bern (North Carolina), New Orleans, Charleston, Augusta, Baltimore, Jacksonville,
New York, Tallahassee, and Beaufort, for a total of nineteen branches
by October 1866.

The bank embarked on an aggressive advertising campaign in the
South to draw in Black depositors. In addition to targeting newspapers
in cities with large populations of African Americans, bank administrators also advertised directly to African Americans through attending
Colored Conventions and taking out ads in the associated publications.
These Black-led conventions were hotbeds of political activism in the
nineteenth century. Between the 1820s and 1850s, these events attracted
formerly enslaved and free people, including abolitionists such as Henry
Highland Garnet and such writers as Frances E. W. Harper. After the
Civil War, African Americans continued the political tradition of gath-
ering to discuss issues such as state-sanctioned violence against free
people and economic uplift. During Reconstruction, the conventions
became venues in which, as the scholar P. Gabrielle Foreman contends,
"attendees strategized about how to secure citizenship and civil liber-
ties."[39] The conventions attracted a cross section of African Americans
that included entrepreneurs, businesspeople, and those who had recently
emerged from slavery.

One of the earliest Colored Conventions in which representatives
from the bank made an appearance was in Augusta, Georgia, in April
1866, a month after the bank opened a branch in the city. At a meeting of the Georgia Equal Rights Association, its president, Captain J. E.

Bryant, announced that Augusta bank cashier C. H. Prince would work with the association as a financial agent to help members save money to resurrect the *Loyal Georgian*, a "Weekly Journal devoted to the maintenance of EQUAL RIGHTS AND PRIVILEGES of all men *irrespective of color or race*."[60] Members of the association then voted to open an account and deposit money into it on a weekly basis at the Freedman's Savings Bank of Augusta. But this was not the only mention of the bank in the association's April 1866 bulletin.

On the final page of the official published report of the Georgia Equal Rights Association meeting, the Augusta branch of the Freedman's Bank had taken out a full-page ad. It signified a partnership between the local bank administrators, who were white, and the Black members of the association. The ad encouraged freed people to open accounts, with the mottoes "Save your Money!" and "Every Man, Woman and Child should put their money for Safe Keeping and Accumulation of Interest, into the Freedmen's Savings Bank."[61] The ad announced that the branch would accept deposits of one dollar or more and that it would be open every day from 12:30 to 3:30 p.m. Beyond giving the African American attendees and readers of the convention basic information about the bank, including its location and the name of the bank cashier, the advertisement also included language designed to inspire trust in the institution. "The Deposits can be drawn out whenever the Depositor chooses," the advertisement assured. The ad ended by invoking Lincoln's legacy, a reminder to African Americans in Augusta that the bank was a savings bank "approved by the late President Abraham Lincoln."[62]

❧

ON FEBRUARY 7, 1866, a group of thirteen Black men entered the building at 1600 Pennsylvania Avenue, in Washington, DC, teeming with a mix of excitement and apprehension about their upcoming meeting. Representing the National Convention of Colored Men, the visitors to the White House were on a special mission: to advocate for the civil rights of African Americans. Included in the group were Black men who felt confident speaking on behalf of the millions of Black people in the nation who, though free from slavery, continued to face violence and poverty as they attempted to make their way in the era of freedom. Included in the group was Frederick Douglass.[63]

This was not Douglass's first trip to the White House. He had accepted three previous invitations from Lincoln to discuss various matters, from unequal pay and treatment of Black Union soldiers in 1863 to the president's request that Douglass help Black people flee Confederate states in 1864. In the first two meetings, Douglass met with Lincoln privately. Yet it may have been his third visit to the White House in March 1865, on inauguration day, that stood out in his memory. This visit surely shaped his impression of Andrew Johnson.[64]

Lincoln invited Douglass to the White House to celebrate his second inauguration on March 4, 1865. On that rainy, overcast March day, Douglass waited eagerly within the crowd of observers for the opening ceremonies to commence. He caught Lincoln's eye. At that moment, Lincoln pointed Douglass out to his vice president, Andrew Johnson, in the crowd. Upon seeing Douglass in person, even from afar, Johnson recoiled. "The first expression which came to his face," Douglass revealed, "and which I think was the true index of his heart, was one of bitter contempt and aversion."[65] Perhaps Johnson abhorred Douglass's salt-and-pepper kinky hair and brown skin. Or it's possible that Johnson did not appreciate the increasing sway that men such as Douglass had on Lincoln's political leanings. It is clear, however, that Johnson detested what Douglass stood for: Black people's enfranchisement and political rights.

When Johnson recognized that Douglass had witnessed his scorn, he "tried to assume a more friendly appearance, but it was too late; it is useless to close the door when all within has been seen." From that moment on, Douglass concluded, "Whatever Andrew Johnson may be, he certainly is no friend of our race."[66]

As the thirteen Black men walked through the halls of the president's house—a building constructed by enslaved laborers—on February 7, 1866, almost a full year into Johnson's presidential term, Douglass remembered Johnson's first impression of him. This memory surely bolstered his resolve to advocate on behalf of millions of African Americans.

As the men and Johnson met each other, this historic meeting was about to test the president's ability to play the role of a unifier. A stenographer recorded the "kindly" nature with which Johnson greeted the men.[67] Johnson then proceeded to shake each man's hand, perhaps as an initial demonstration to his visitors that he was attempting to take the meeting, and their concerns, seriously. The handshake with Douglass was likely freighted. Both may have remembered their first impressions of each other on that fateful inauguration day the previous year.

The meeting was, as one historian has argued, a "calculated performance."[68] Johnson and Douglass traded barbs, with Johnson arguing that white Americans were not ready to accept voting rights for Black men, and Douglass, with the other Black men in the background, struggling to get a word in. Johnson was headstrong and inflexible. When Douglass suggested that Black people desired to "share in the privileges" of freedom, Johnson retorted that poor whites struggled with similar economic and political challenges as free people had. When Douglass advocated for expanding the franchise, Johnson suggested emigration. The meeting ended there, with Douglass and the men standing to leave. Douglass said to his group, "The President sends us to the people, and we go to the people." Not to be upstaged, Johnson, perhaps remembering that the stenographer was recording every verbal transaction, got in the last word. "Yes, sir; I have great faith in the people. I believe they will do what is right."[69] By the end of the hour-long meeting, in which Johnson spoke for approximately forty-five minutes, the men realized that Johnson would not be the next Lincoln. If political and economic rights formed the foundation of their agenda, then they would have to look past the executive branch for support.

Less than two weeks later, Johnson made another political move. He vetoed the Civil Rights Act of 1866, a legislative measure that would go a long way toward fulfilling the desires of the Black men invited to speak with him in the Oval Office.[70] Though Congress eventually overrode the veto, Johnson sent a clear message to the nation, to Congress, and to African Americans. He would not make freed people's access to the rights and privileges of American citizenship a priority. Douglass and his colleagues may not have been surprised at Johnson's obstinacy toward advancing Black civil rights. Despite his expressed support of institutions such as the Freedman's Bank, Johnson would not use his political credibility to support African Americans.

Freed people continued to face legislative hurdles to securing their rights to American citizenship. Despite these real obstacles, the bank became a source of dignity for African Americans. It was an institution that represented their deservedness for the privileges that real inclusion, that is, citizenship, would bestow. African Americans who opened accounts took pride in their ability to work and save. They were also connecting their engagement in financial services to the goal of attaining political rights. Continuing to patronize the bank, African Americans believed, "is the way for our people to get equality of political rights."[71] One step in the direction of economic and political inclusion was a Black person influencing, as much as possible, the direction of the bank's board of trustees.

The trustees realized their intention of adding a Black trustee when they nominated Henry Highland Garnet to join the board in May 1866. The trustees perhaps believed that he would be a good fit. Garnet was an outspoken orator who had escaped from slavery in Maryland with his family in 1824. A resident of Washington, DC, he was a vocal abolitionist during the era of slavery, worked as a chaplain for the Union army during the war, and was the pastor of the Fifteenth Street Presbyterian Church. He was an influential member of Washington's Black elite, and the trustees believed that he could be a useful ally in the board's quest to court Black depositors. Also, he already had a connection to the bank. His wife was the second person to open an account in the Washington branch.[72]

The trustees, though, were left disappointed. Garnet never accepted the position and there was no explanation as to why. The bank did not make this nomination public, because if they had, depositors might have questioned why such a renowned member of the African American community rejected the offer to join the bank's esteemed board of trustees.

Despite the bank's success during its first year, its growth also aroused doubt—and violent attention of ex-Confederates—almost immediately. Reports of former Confederates attacking African Americans in cities such as Mobile and New Orleans trickled out of the South. In addition to white lawmakers in these cities imposing strict Black Codes designed to threaten Black people's ability to work, participate in party politics, and even attend Freedmen's Bureau schools, the Freedman's Bank branches also became targets of white racial violence. In the early months of 1866, after the Mobile branch was established on January 1, the "old State militia," a group "synonymous with violence and oppression toward loyal men and freedmen" during the war, had been attacking African Americans. Former Confederates marked symbols of Black uplift and prosperity as deserving of their assaults. The newly established bank branch was one such symbol.[73]

The criticisms kept coming. In July 1866, a scathing critique of the bank appeared in the pages of a Camden, South Carolina, newspaper. A writer called the bank a "swindling institution" because it was giving freed people greenbacks in exchange for hard money that African Americans were depositing.[74] Though the writer may not have been a depositor, the publication of a public message about the bank's business—and its unsavory reputation in some communities—might have reflected a larger concern about the institution's reputation.

Despite these initial concerns, African Americans steadily patronized the bank, depositing their earnings and savings, including gold and silver coins. As administrators added more branches throughout the South in 1866, the growing pains became apparent to both the depositors and the bankers seeing the gold mine that the bank could become.

PART TWO

Betrayal

CHAPTER THREE

The Trouble with Expansion, 1866–67

I consider the Freedman's Savings and Trust Company
to be greatly needed by the Colored People, and have
welcomed it as an auxiliary to the Freedmen's Bureau.

—GENERAL O. O. HOWARD, 1867[1]

Freedman's Bank total deposits, as of March 1866:
$305,167 ($5.8 million today)

Freedman's Bank total deposits, as of March 1867:
$1,624,853.33 ($33.2 million today)

THE FREEDMAN'S BANK WAS OFF TO A ROUSING START. As the Thirteenth Amendment, which officially abolished slavery, became law on December 6, 1865, freed people continued their forward march into freedom—and into bank branches. They took great pride in the bank's expansion, by eagerly patronizing offices opened in their cities. In January 1866, one of those cities was New Orleans.

New Orleans was a natural location for a branch. At the outbreak of the Civil War, it was the largest city by population in the South. It also turned into one of the war's major battlegrounds, as Union and Confederate military forces jockeyed for control over this sprawling urban center that served as an economic outlet to the Atlantic world.[2] New Orleans was a vibrant multiracial and multiethnic city, with a conspicuous free Black community during the era of slavery. Free people of color could trace their ancestry from West and West Central Africa to the West Indies, France, and Spain.[3] The racial boundaries that defined slavery in most regions of the United States evolved along different lines in Louisiana. People of African descent pushed back against legal impositions of strict categories between slave and free, and against the ways in which ideas of *Blackness* played out in slavery as an institution. The binary racial categories of Black and white that permeated much of the American lexicon around racial difference was complicated in Louisiana, in New Orleans specifically.[4]

The Free Labor Bank, the successful military savings bank established in New Orleans in 1864, increased the likelihood that the city's formerly enslaved and free community would flock to a bank branch in the city. With a large population of freed people, the city was a prime location for the bank's continued expansion. The board appointed Charles S. Sauvinet to be the New Orleans branch cashier after the first cashier resigned his post two months after the branch opened. In some ways, Sauvinet was the perfect person to represent the Freedman's

Bank in New Orleans. A free man of color and a native of the city, he represented the region's racial and ethnic diversity. Born in the ante-bellum era, he was the son of a white French immigrant from France, by way of Saint-Domingue, and a free woman of color, also from Saint-Domingue. As a child, Sauvinet lived with his mother and siblings in a home near the French Quarter built for them by his white father. His light skin, free status, and connections to a white parent of economic means meant that Sauvinet lived as a member of the New Orleans elite. He took advantage of the privileges that his status provided. He traveled throughout Europe and along the way cultivated a knowledge of various languages. He also developed a self-assurance about his status and iden-tity that spurred his willingness to challenge the racial status quo.[5]

Sauvinet had a distinguished military career during the Civil War, having served under General Butler during the Union army's occupa-tion of New Orleans in 1862 and 1863. He enlisted as a member of the Louisiana Native Guard in the early years of the war. Through his mili-tary service, he deployed his linguistic skills as a translator and his polit-ical acumen as a strategist to rally Black troops' support for the Union army's military effort. By the war's end, Sauvinet was the only man of color promoted to the rank of captain in the U.S. Army.[6]

By appointing Sauvinet as the New Orleans cashier, bank trustees followed through on a promise that Hewitt and Alvord had been mak-ing to African Americans during their travels in the South. Working in opposition to many of the trustees' wishes, Hewitt and Alvord pledged that they would hire Black personnel in bank branches who would teach and encourage African Americans to embrace financial literacy. Freed people in cities such as Washington, Beaufort, and Richmond pressed bank administrators to hire cashiers who reflected the populations the branches were serving. The same was true in New Orleans. But if a Black person were to work as a cashier, Sauvinet was the archetype of the kind of Black person whom trustees wanted to work in local branches. He was educated and well traveled, had served in the Union army, was a free man during slavery, and was biracial. He reflected the bank's target demographic. He would fulfill the goal of serving a community that looked more like him than like the cashiers at other branches.

As cashiers, men such as Sauvinet served as branch managers. Cashiers were responsible for shepherding depositors through the process of opening accounts, depositing money, and withdrawing funds. Cashiers also needed to maintain an accurate accounting of how much each depositor held in their account and how much money the bank had on hand.

Therefore, when Mrs. Ellen Baptiste Lubin entered the bank's branch at 114 Carondelet Street, on a sweltering Monday, July 2, 1866, she probably encountered Sauvinet. She may have been hearing murmurings about the new savings bank that had opened in January 1866 in the heart of the city, close to the French Quarter, for freed people. Perhaps she wanted to patronize a bank that had been touted as "among the best institutions in the United States."[7]

Lubin's experience mirrored that of other new depositors. When depositors opened accounts, they would enter a bank branch and the cashier would fill out their depositor application record. She was one of two people who opened an account that day in July 1866. To open an account and deposit money, Lubin had to provide a few pieces of information. She had to detail her name, marital status, whether she had children or a living spouse, her place of birth, place of residence, and occupation. She could have also provided her skin color, if she had a former "Mistress" or "Master," and the plantation where she had been enslaved.[8]

Lubin would have relayed this information to Sauvinet. This is what she shared. Ellen Baptiste Lubin was married and a mother to two daughters, Marguerite and Mary Lubin. They lived on Burgundy Street between Ursuline Avenue and Hospital Street in New Orleans, mere blocks from the Mississippi River. She was born in New Orleans and worked as a laundress in 1866. Lubin, however, took advantage of the opportunity *not* to give specific pieces of information. She declined to give her "Height and Complexion." She also did not mark the name of a former enslaver. There are two explanations for this omission. The first is that she could have been a free woman of color in New Orleans at the outbreak of the Civil War. Thus, when it came time to identify her mistress, master, and the plantation on which she may have been

Ellen Baptiste Lubin depositor record, New Orleans Branch

enslaved, she perhaps reveled in having "Free," meaning her free status during slavery, identified on her account. Alternatively, Lubin may have been enslaved during the war. She could have elected to not give the name of the person or people who legally owned her and her children to publicly disentangle herself from her enslavers. Moreover, though she was married, she did not add the name of her husband, Eugine Lubin, to her account. This account was in her name only, to be controlled solely by her.[9] The information that she provided to Sauvinet to open her account represented the claims that she was making to manage her own financial future.

Though we don't know how much money she deposited into her account, we do know that Lubin represented a notable segment of depositors not seen in the bank's leadership or administration: Black women. Lubin was a Black woman who had decided to participate in this new age of finance. She represented the tens of thousands of other Black women who decided to patronize the bank. To ensure that their families could reap the benefits of their hard work, a privilege many were deprived of during the period of slavery, Black women such as Lubin opened bank accounts on their own, in their own names. This was largely unheard of during the nineteenth century. But Black women took advantage of the opportunity to enter the world of finance through opening accounts, depositing money, and saving money. Not only in New Orleans but in branches that opened across the South and in cities such as Philadelphia and New York, African American women made the bold stride into freedom by taking hold of their financial futures.[10]

After registering Lubin as an account holder, Sauvinet would have then accepted whatever cash or other legal tender she had to deposit into her account. In exchange, she would have received what was called a passbook, bank book, or deposit book, depending on the branch. In these books, bank cashiers recorded depositor information, including how much the depositor had in his or her account. In her passbook, Lubin would have had an accounting of the date and amount of her deposit.

Like all other depositors, she received a bank book loaded with information about the bank. Even though each branch had a uniquely designed deposit book, in general, the Freedman's Bank passbooks were used as objects of propaganda as much as they were for accounting purposes. Each branch's bank book was distinct. Some featured a drawing on the cover. One placed Lincoln as the central figure, with one hand holding a broken chain and the other hand on a safe titled "Freed Man's Safe." With a "Lincoln and Freedom" banner under a solemn picture of the slain president, these passbooks also included smaller sketches of men whom white bank officials held in high esteem: General Ulysses S. Grant, General O. O. Howard, General William T. Sherman, Secretary of War Edwin Stanton, and Admiral David Farragut. Other bank books named the locations and cashiers of the growing list of bank branches, and dedicated two or more pages to outlining the bank's rules and regulations, including how interest on deposits accrued. Some books even included a breakdown of how much money in interest depositors would earn by depositing their wages and keeping money in bank accounts. Most had an updated list of the bank's trustees, including the executive officers. Importantly, the passbooks included a message to assure depos-

Deposit book of Charles C. Murray, Savannah, Georgia

itors, stating, "The money on this Pass Book will be repaid whenever called for with interest due."[11] This was a message on which depositors had come to rely when they became unsure about how much trust they could put in the institution and those who ran it. Trustees would revisit this message as they extolled the benefits of banking with the Freedman's Savings and Trust Company.

When Lubin exited the New Orleans branch on July 2, 1866, stepping out onto Carondelet Street, she held on to a deposit book that she surely hoped would reflect her journey to economic security. Her engagement with the bank at this moment coincided with a dramatic uptick in racial violence in regions of the South such as Louisiana. It is possible that Lubin left the bank longing to create an economic safety net to shield herself and her family from the ravages of white racial terrorism that plagued Black people in the South.[12]

Four weeks after Lubin opened her account, Sauvinet witnessed how former Confederates in New Orleans eagerly deployed violence to combat Black political uplift. On July 30, 1866, while tending to bank business, he observed a white militia brutally beat and murder a crowd of African Americans who had met to discuss revisions to the Louisiana state constitution. Sauvinet observed the skirmish, offering shelter in the bank to Black men and women evading the violence. Many did not escape alive. On that day, whites killed 34 Black people, and injured 119.[13]

Despite the continued waves of ex-Confederate intimidation, Lubin, Sauvinet, and Black people across the South were embracing a maxim that the bank had been disseminating. By opening a savings account, they imbibed the message: "ECONOMY THE ROAD TO WEALTH. SAVE YOUR MONEY!"[14] Such aphorisms about saving as a vehicle to wealth and wealth as a component of freedom were central to the bank's strategy of attracting Black depositors. Administrators, including the branches' cashiers, continued to espouse the idea that the bank would help freed people achieve economic stability, even wealth and political freedom. For his part, Sauvinet worked to ensure the success of his branch. As he did so, he was joining other cashiers who were accepting hundreds of thousands of dollars of depositors' money. Black people were absorbing the idea of bank patronage as economic self-determination.

However, changes in the bank's operation and mission loomed.

❦

A YEAR INTO THE BANK'S TENURE, capital flowed from the depositors to the bank branches and then to the bank's central office, where the bulk of the deposits were held for investment. Freed people appeared to be enriching the bank. In the summer of 1866, the bank proudly advertised that at the various branches around the country, it had accepted a total of $616,802 ($11.7 million today) on behalf of depositors. Black journalists rejoiced at this news. "All of this money is from the Freedman," a writer from the *Christian Recorder* celebrated. That freed people had raised and deposited such a staggering amount of money was something they announced with pride. The writer mused that these were people who whites believed "could not take care of themselves."[15] Depositors, bank cashiers, and trustees were also excited to witness the increasing amount of money rolling into the bank. The public celebrations, though, obscured the reality of the bank's financial situation. Between March 1865 and June 1866, much of the bank's growth came from the transfer of deposits from the military savings banks. The initial success did not tell the full story of the bank's operations.

The bank was growing too fast. In 1866, the trustees slowly noticed that it was struggling to sustain its rapid rate of expansion. The problem was twofold. First, the trustees rushed to expand the bank's footprint in cities with large Black populations. Instead of opening a handful of branches, perhaps in Norfolk, Beaufort, and New Orleans, cities that housed the military savings banks, and assessing how well they performed, the trustees moved too quickly. They did not take the time to evaluate the first branches' financial viability before spending depositors' money to open more branches across the South. The second part of the problem stemmed from the bank's investment guidelines. The Freedman's Savings and Trust Company was a savings bank. Trustees could not invest bank deposits in anything other than governmental securities, which meant that trustees were also constrained by the types of investments they could make.

Some of the trustees believed the bank's conservative investment strategy undermined Black depositors' engagement. Practically, the bank could make money and offer depositors interest on their deposits only if they kept their money in the bank long enough for the bank to make a return. More directly, if depositors did not keep their money in accounts for long enough, the bank would not see a return on its investments. And these were not short-term financial products. The maturity dates on some of the securities were five to ten years.[16] Though the bank received periodic dividend payments, these payments did not offset the cost of operation, nor the interest payments given to depositors. Therefore, even though depositors had placed over $616,000 into accounts, they also withdrew over $384,000 during the same period. This left a balance of approximately $232,000, on which the bank had to pay interest and cull out operating costs. In June 1866, fourteen months into the bank's tenure, the board agreed to pay 2.5 percent interest on all deposits over five dollars made in the previous six months.[17] It was far less than the ceiling of 7 percent as articulated in the bank's bylaws, and less still than the dividend payment of 5 percent made to depositors as of January 1, 1866.[18] But the board had the ultimate authority to set the rate of return on deposits, based on the returns of the bank's investments.

Again, the bigger problem for trustees involved the depositors' immediate financial needs. It became clear to the administrators that depositors had little financial incentive to keep their deposits in the bank for the long term. This meant that depositors were not leaving their money in the bank long enough to accrue payments from the bank's investments. Bank administrators had to work with this reality. The bank could not earn enough through its investments to cover both the interest payments and the rising expenses of operating a bank with multiple branches across multiple states. The trustees' aggression with expanding the bank's reach did not line up with the practicalities of running a savings bank that operated in several states with numerous depositors who were depositing small sums of money. The returns on government bonds were less than what the trustees had promised to depositors in interest payments. Throughout 1866, the trustees entertained opening branches in more locations, from Wilmington to Memphis to Houston. They believed that increasing the number of accounts, depositors, and money coming into the bank would help offset its expenses.

Ultimately, the trouble with the bank's expansion was that expenses piled up quickly. The bank's investments were not yielding enough of a profit. The bank was earning too little money from its investments to pay for its rapidly growing list of expenditures. The payment of cashiers at the various branches and the cost of renting building space in the cities across the nation ran up the price of offering freed people an institution in which to deposit their money. Cashier salaries, for example, ranged from $600 per year at the Richmond branch to the Beaufort branch's $2,000 per year.[19] As the months passed, cashiers continued to ask for raises.

Moreover, the bank branches were expensive to maintain. In some cities, the trustees and local bank administrators agreed to buy buildings outright. In others, the bank rented buildings and space. The most expensive office to maintain was the central office in New York. The rent on the small office in the American Exchange Bank was $1,200 per year, and the New York cashier's salary increased the price of doing business.[20] The hurdle was that the bank had little working capital. Though members of the board had loaned the bank $100 each shortly after it opened for business in May 1865, the expenses continued to increase.

Alvord felt the strain under which the bank was operating. He was also slowly crumbling under the weight of his multiple responsibilities. In addition to navigating his family life from afar, his various positions with the Freedmen's Bureau, the American Tract Society, and the bank were beginning to wear him down. In December 1865, he wrote of his difficulties. "I am struggling with my multifarious work," he revealed.[21] He had limited time and energy. And the state of his family's finances worried him. He ruminated over where he should dedicate his time and energies: to his life as a pastor or to public service. If pastoral life could have provided his family with comfort, he would have fully embraced it. "[N]obody would give me 2500 or 3000 salary as a pastor," he ruminated. "I Must continue to obtain about this sum," he revealed, "by some such side issues as I have been at for the last 20 15 years."[22] The financial anxiety from his involvement with all three entities was becoming burdensome. Perhaps this burden drove him to become even more involved in the bank's executive committee, hoping that it would pay off in the future.

Despite his financial situation, Alvord did not take his position in the bank for granted. When members of the agency committee lauded his work with both the bank and the bureau, even going as far as to say that his position in the bureau "was important to the interests of this institution," Alvord took their praise as a sign.[23] He recognized that he could fulfill his family's economic needs while also carrying out his mission to serve African Americans in both the Freedmen's Bureau and the Freedman's Bank.

To further prove his dedication, Alvord testified before a congressional committee in February 1866 on the state of freed people in the country. One of the topics he discussed, with great pride, was the "Finances of Freedmen."[24] Alvord offered members of the committee a frank but uplifting perspective on freed people's financial situation. In addition to describing the number of schools opened in southern states and the number of teachers needed to educate freed people, he detailed how "a considerable number [of freed people] had money."[25] He assured members of Congress that the bank "promises to do much to instruct and elevate the financial notions of the freedmen."[26] But, as he spoke, Alvord began to reiterate some of the paternalistic language that became commonplace among white agents of the Freedmen's Bureau. He argued that he had witnessed that most of the freed people were "[p]oor and dependent" and "there are multitudes who know nothing about thrift."[27] "Slavery prevented every forecasting of thought," he contended. "Their minds are childish and dark,"[28] he asserted. In this way, Alvord was demonstrating the pull of his responsibilities at the bureau and the bank. He regurgitated the bureau's paternalism toward freed people while celebrating their eagerness to save and invest in the bank.

Whenever Alvord heaped praise on freed people's diligence to establish a stable economic foundation for themselves, he was also proselytizing the work of the Freedmen's Bureau. For him, the bureau worked in tandem with the bank. The success of one signified the success of the other. Republican members of Congress created the Freedmen's Bureau to be the federal government's grassroots force to enact its Reconstruction policies. While a biracial coalition of bureau agents strategized to defend the new legal rights of African Americans in the South, Freedman's Bank administrators articulated a similar mission. According to the literature distributed by the bank, freed people's participation in the body politic required that they seek economic inclusion. But, instead of representing solely the bank in the congressional hearing, Alvord testified in his capacity as the Freedmen's Bureau inspector of schools and finance, not the Freedman's Bank secretary. It is possible that he was trying to navigate the political minefield that continued to characterize Reconstruction politics as he attempted to advocate for both the bank and the bureau. In the process, though, he blurred the line between the two institutions—for members of Congress and for freed people. The Freedmen's Bureau possessed governmental authority to enact its policies. The bank did not. A cabal of bankers and philanthropists controlled the bank's actions. This reality would place Alvord in a precarious position, as he continued to unite the missions of the Freedmen's Bureau and the Freedman's Bank.

Alvord's public-facing discussion of the bank and its depositors occurred during a period in which some trustees were evaluating their affiliation with the financial institution. On March 8, 1866, the bank's president, William Booth, "declined to accept the presidency," stepping down from his post.[29] Between March 1865, when he assumed the role as the bank's president, and March 1866, Booth did little to carry out the bank's mission. He failed to do any meaningful legwork to ensure that the bank would faithfully serve freed people. Instead, he functioned as a figurehead. Perhaps he believed that the bank's philanthropic mission meant that he did not need to put in the time and effort to properly steward the institution. And maybe he understood that greater change was on the horizon, and he did not want to be at the helm as it took place.[30] With little fanfare or disappointment at Booth's departure from the presidency, the board members in attendance "unanimously elected" the bank's first vice president, Mahlon Hewitt, to lead the bank.

Hewitt stepped into the bank presidency at an auspicious time. He faced important decisions about how to balance the bank's mission—to serve freed people—with trying to keep the institution afloat. Between March 1865 and October 1866, the trustees approved opening nineteen branches. Though thousands of depositors opened accounts and deposited money in their accounts, these depositors were disseminated throughout the country. Administrators were spending money to maintain a multitude of branches where depositors were saving relatively small amounts of money.[31] Though this structure fulfilled the bank's purpose, it also undermined its ability to operate.

By December 1866, the trustees entertained the idea of *not* opening new bank branches for a short period of time. They even discussed "the matter of closing agencies" in cities where branches were "virtually closed," such as Alexandria, Vicksburg, and Huntsville, in an effort aimed at "reducing expenses."[32] The ebbs and flows of bank management became apparent to Alvord, who had lofty goals but no experience in finance. During the first year, Alvord had become the bank's most vocal advocate for expansion to more cities to serve more potential Black depositors. Despite his enthusiasm, he slowly began to understand that the main reason why the bank needed to contemplate "closing agencies" was that its charter limited how trustees could invest the deposits.[33]

Though the costs of maintaining the agencies factored into the board's discussion of slowing the rate at which they approved opening new branches, the trustees were not considering the realities of Reconstruction for freed people. Though a hopeful time, Reconstruction was also a period in which African Americans had to figure out the practicalities of freedom. Where would they work? How would they earn wages? Could they reunite with their families? Could they buy land, and where? While African Americans celebrated freedom, they also confronted the reality of living as freed people with the specter of white supremacy and violence.

White Americans also struggled to cope with this new landscape of Black freedom. Instead of coming to terms with the reality of slavery's end and Black people's pursuit of full citizenship, they used violence to combat the rising tide of African American political and economic uplift.[34] The abolition of slavery did not eliminate white hostility toward Black progress. The sheer scale of white terrorism and violence toward African Americans was palpable, especially in regions of the Deep South such as Louisiana, Texas, and Florida. The pervasiveness of white racial violence may explain why bank branches in cities such as Houston and Tallahassee never experienced the same amount of success as in other regions of the South.[35] For example, as the trustees were contemplating the fate of the Houston branch in late 1866, L. S. Barnes, an agent with the Freedmen's Bureau, made an official report to his superiors in which he detailed sixteen violent murders and brutal beatings of African Americans that had occurred between August 1865 and September 1866 in a county just north of Houston. He contended that this number was surely an underestimation because freed people were afraid of retribution from white perpetrators for reporting these crimes. African Americans, he wrote, would not "report many of these things unless they see some prospect of the guilty being punished, as many of them would forfeit their lives forever."[36] The truth of Reconstruction for African Americans, a mix of celebration and vigilance, was an experience that the bank's white trustees could have never understood.

This was a stark realization for Alvord, that even the noblest of plans required a practical approach. As a result, he devised a two-part strategy after the December 1866 board meeting. He hoped that his proposition would solve some of the bank's problems. The first part of his plan involved bringing on new trustees. Less than two weeks after the meeting, on December 27, 1866, Alvord shared the first part of his proposal with Hewitt. He wanted to add two dynamic and influential people to the bank's board. He suggested that it would be a good idea, "for our reputation," to have Washington-based bankers Henry D. Cooke and William S. Huntington as new trustees. Not only were they "excellent men of high business reputation," but according to Alvord, they were "friends of the Negro."[37] The addition of trustees who lived and worked in Washington, instead of New York, was the first step in Alvord's plan. He could not have known at this time how significant his suggestion of Cooke and Huntington would be.

The second part of Alvord's proposal was just as consequential. He wanted to move the bank's main office from New York to Washington, DC. He wrote privately to Hewitt on January 21, 1867, that moving the central office to Washington, "where everything could be done at less expense & and where some of our friends, as you know, think the Charter required us to be, we might find the desired relief."[38] In addition to decreased operating costs, Alvord believed that relocating to Washington would have myriad advantages. Trustees would be better positioned to tap into a network of supporters in the Freedmen's Bureau and in other sectors of the federal government. By moving to Washington, he argued, the bank would be closer to larger populations of freed people.[39]

Though Alvord actively lobbied trustees, making practical justifications for why the bank's center of operations should move to Washington, he also had personal motivations. He continued to struggle financially. His duties with the bank and the Freedmen's Bureau strained his family's resources and began to take a toll on his health. He needed to figure out how to balance his dedication to the government's work of aiding freed people with his financial obligations as a husband and father. A move to Washington would help his financial prospects. Indeed, he would quickly exploit his unique position among some of the most profit-oriented business minds in the nation to shore up his own economic position.

In fact, Alvord had already been making plans, privately, to move his family to Washington, DC. On January 12, 1867, he opened a Freedman's Bank account for his six-year-old son, John Watson Alvord. While he could have established his son's account in the New York branch, he instead opened his son's account in Washington. He did so at the same time that he was advocating within the bank's trustee membership for the central branch's relocation.[40]

Alvord understood that his proposition needed to be approved by the other trustees. The fact that his proposal went from introduction to serious consideration so quickly was significant. Between December 1866 and January 1867, the trustees mulled over his proposal. Instead of merely pondering the merits of the suggested move to Washington, the trustees decided to openly discuss it. It is unclear whether Alvord was surprised that he garnered the support that he desired. In the end, the bank's addition of new board members *and* move to Washington would indelibly alter its ability to fulfill its mission: to help freed people realize their economic goals.

❧

THE YEAR 1867 PROVED to be a pivotal one for the bank. It started with several trustees deciding to abdicate their positions on the board. Some had underestimated the responsibility of serving as a trustee for such a high-profile institution. Others could not give much time to ensuring that the bank operated in a dutiful way. It had become clear, two years into the bank's tenure, that those in leadership positions would need to take seriously the task of guiding the bank into its next phase.[41] The Freedman's Bank had a philanthropic mission and depositors depended on the institution being guided by people who acted with financial diligence.

Alvord understood this charge, which perhaps spurred him to continue with his plan. The scheme that he put in motion in late 1866 started to play out on January 10, 1867. This next phase began with the nomination of a man whose influence would indelibly shape the bank's direction. When Alvord introduced Washington banker Henry D. Cooke's name at the monthly board meeting, his nomination represented the transformation on the horizon. With seemingly little hesitation, the trustees hastened Cooke's candidacy and he sailed through the confirmation process, earning the board's nomination.[42]

Who was Henry D. Cooke? Who was the man who had elicited such enthusiasm from Alvord? Henry D. Cooke was the lesser known, but no less influential, brother of Jay Cooke, an Ohio-born titan of finance in mid-nineteenth-century America. Though Jay Cooke had catapulted himself to national prominence, it was Henry Cooke who took advantage of his brother's financial acumen to build a political and economic legacy for himself in Washington, DC.

Trained as a lawyer, Henry Cooke did not have a mind for, nor an interest in, the law. Instead, he desired a life of adventure—and risk. He had his first taste of the world of finance and politics when he traveled with his brother-in-law William Moorehead on a political expedition to Chile in 1846. Moorehead was serving as an American consul in Chile and Cooke accompanied him as an attaché, learning about high-stakes politics in the process.[43] While he lived in Valparaiso, Chile, Cooke witnessed the dynamic nature of global trade that occurred as ships from around the Atlantic and Pacific docked in the port city to replenish their supplies. He also gained valuable information about the discovery of gold in Chile, and farther north in California. He decided to move to California in 1848, setting his sights on his next venture: a steamboat company. During his time in Chile, he realized that travel from New York to San Francisco could be expedited. At the time, the most efficient way to travel from America's east to west coast was by sailing around the horn of South America. He was among a group of investors who believed that Panama would be the perfect country through which to travel for easier access to America's Pacific coast from cities on the eastern seaboard. Such proposals became even more exciting with the discovery of gold in 1848. But his dreams of streamlining travel from the east coast to the west did not come to fruition quite yet. After his time in Chile, he ventured to America's west coast. He lived in San Francisco in 1851 when the city was devastated by a fire. His home, and his hopes to build a financial future based on innovative travel and gold, were destroyed.[44]

Cooke returned to his hometown of Sandusky, Ohio, having lost the small fortune he accumulated during his time in California. He regained his footing by 1856. With his brother's largesse, Cooke became the owner and editor of the *Register*, a Sandusky newspaper, in which he wrote editorials about politics and the burgeoning Republican Party. He used his journalistic experience in Sandusky to purchase the *Ohio State Journal*, a newspaper in Columbus, the state capital. It was in Columbus, writing for and running two newspapers, that he continued to cultivate relationships with influential politicians. For example, he began covering the rise of soon-to-be political stars such as then Ohio governor Salmon P. Chase.[45]

The Civil War changed Cooke's trajectory. It sent him on a path away from journalism and barreling toward the world of finance. His brother convinced him to join his new business, selling government bonds to investors in the United States and abroad in support of the Union's military campaign. By December 1861, Henry Cooke joined his brother as a partner and agent in his company, Jay Cooke & Company. Henry took advantage of the opportunity to employ his business and political skills. Each of his life circumstances—from his time in Chile to the loss he experienced in California and his success as a journalist and newspaper owner—had helped him develop a very particular understanding of the relationship between economic and political capital. He brought this knowledge with him to his work with Jay Cooke & Company, the first investment bank in the United States—and the most successful seller of government bonds during the Civil War.[46]

Henry Cooke prided himself on his network of allies among powerful lawmakers and political appointees from Ohio, including Senator John Sherman (brother of General William T. Sherman), General Ulysses S. Grant, and Salmon P. Chase.[47] He put these relationships to good use during the war. Politicians such as Lincoln and Chase relied on

Jay and Henry Cooke to help them embark on an aggressive campaign to raise money through bond sales to help finance the Union's war efforts. Though the Cooke brothers used the language of patriotism in their bond sales, their involvement in selling government debt was not entirely altruistic.[48] They and members of the Lincoln administration understood that raising funds through selling debt was an efficient strategy to win the war—and to outmaneuver the Confederacy economically.[49]

The success of the bond sale and the work of Jay and Henry Cooke during the war ultimately helped the Union. Jay Cooke & Company raised approximately $1.5 billion ($27.8 billion today) for the federal government.[50] In the process, the Cooke brothers became millionaires.

Henry Cooke continued to serve as the president of Jay Cooke & Company's Washington branch, First National Bank. He also served as the bank's de facto lobbyist, using his friendships to expand his business interests. He was a major player in the world of high-risk finance *and* politics. Some considered him to be "in some respects the most talented man in the Cooke family."[51] The brothers reaped millions of dollars in profits from selling American debt to investors. Their success in helping the Union fund the Civil War put them in the good graces of the Lincoln administration. They continued to build on the political capital they cultivated during the war. After the war's end, they leveraged their connections to expand Jay Cooke & Company's footprint in the banking industry. The company gained the first charter from the newly created Office of the Comptroller of the Currency (OCC) to operate a commercial bank nationally. With the OCC signing off on Jay Cooke & Company's new enterprise, Henry Cooke made Washington, DC, his political playground when he ran First National Bank.

Henry Cooke evolved into a political animal. He had become adept at cultivating relationships with members of Washington's political elite, especially Republicans who sought to push their political agendas through Congress during the first years of Reconstruction. He also continued to grow his and his brother's businesses, making First National Bank one of the most successful banks in the nation. In fact, Jay and Henry Cooke had no qualms about using their personal connections to expand their business empire. When it came time to open First National

Bank under the new banking guidelines in 1863, they exploited their relationship with the nation's first comptroller, Hugh McCulloch. They were the first to receive a national charter from the OCC, to operate the First National Bank of Philadelphia. The bank's Washington branch, under Henry Cooke's control, was number twenty-six.[52] Henry Cooke crafted a strategy that combined using his political connections and knowledge of finance to invest in a diversity of businesses. In addition to running Washington's First National Bank, Henry Cooke also served as the vice president of the National Life Insurance Company *and* he sat on the board of directors of the National Safe Deposit Company, which was housed in a building adjacent to the Treasury Department.[53]

The Cooke brothers' success put them in a unique position. But one brother installed himself in Washington, DC, over New York or Philadelphia, to take advantage of proximity to political and financial power. It was Henry Cooke who made good use of his political connections to diversify Jay Cooke & Company's investment portfolio—and to infiltrate the Freedman's Bank.

A TUG-OF-WAR BEGAN between the faction of the bank trustees desiring to remain in New York and those, such as Alvord, who wanted a new future for the bank in Washington, DC. Despite this tension, on February 7, 1867, Cooke's nomination was up for a vote. If any trustees expressed apprehension about the nomination, no one announced it in the meeting's official record. What did appear in the record was overwhelming approval for Cooke's place on the board. He received a unanimous positive vote from the trustees. He quickly accepted the trustee position. And there was no question as to the role that he would play—and the committee on which he would sit. Cooke would serve on the finance committee. What's more, he would be the committee's chairman.

Cooke's appointment was not the only shift in the bank's administrative structure. In fact, Alvord was enacting the second part of his grand plan. In the same February 7 meeting that would transform the bank's financial mission, Alvord introduced the radical idea that he had been pondering. He proposed that the trustees approve of moving the bank's central office from New York, America's financial center, to Washington, its political one.[54]

On March 14, 1867, the trustees assented to Alvord's proposal. A month later, on April 16, they voted in favor of moving the central office to Washington, DC, declaring that it "is newly declared to be the Principal office of the Company."[55] When the central office decamped to Washington at the end of April, the bank's focus began to slowly shift.

Instead of the bank's fundamental mission being to serve the financial interests of freed people, its move to Washington represented the process of pivoting away from that goal—and away from the very people the bank was founded to serve. The Freedman's Bank would instead begin catering to the politics of the Washington machine. That is to say, bank administrators such as Alvord began to acquiesce to the political influences represented by the bank's new appointees. The transition from New York to Washington inaugurated a new era in the bank's priorities. No longer would the trustees and bank officials operate primarily by the bank's philanthropic mission. The twin influences of big finance *and* high-level politics began to chip away at the bank's benevolent foundation.

As Cooke made the transition onto the board, the bank lost another trustee. This time, the bank's president, Mahlon Hewitt, stepped down. On April 16, at the end of the final board meeting in New York's American Exchange Bank, Hewitt gave the trustees in attendance a summary of his time affiliated with the Freedman's Bank. More pointedly, he detailed the reasons for his departure. He mentioned that for the past year "there had been no growth." "It was that feature," he revealed, "that excited my anxiety for its future."[56] He recognized that the bank could not sustain itself without steady, even if incremental, progress. He was unsure about the bank's future success if the trustees did not find ways to earn a greater profit on depositors' investments. He hesitated to offer specific ideas on how they should move forward. He did, however, communicate his discomfort with how the bank was being run, even under his stewardship. It is possible that he was aware of the ways in which new board members would reshape—and even undermine—the bank's original mission. Perhaps the newest trustees signaled to Hewitt that he needed to end his affiliation sooner rather than later.

The bank's readjustment did not stop with the trustees. Its shifting economic priorities also included an official hiatus from opening new branches. While the trustees were figuring out how to handle the expansion of the bank through new branches in cities with high Black populations, and determining how to pay depositors, the expansion briefly slowed. The new finance committee began to reorganize the way that it conducted business. Under Cooke's guidance, the committee began making plans to exploit the slush fund of Black depositors' money sitting idle in branches across the country.

Soon after Cooke joined the board, he recognized that he could dictate the actions of the board's most influential committee. By the time of his appointment in the spring of 1867, the finance committee needed to be reenergized; it was in shambles. There had been no official meetings between September 18, 1865, and June 8, 1867—an almost two-year gap. The committee was ripe for the taking.

Cooke's sphere of influence extended to the appointment of more trustees. The month after he accepted the board's nomination, he wielded his authority to gather support for the nomination of a new trustee who, if approved, would surely join him on the finance committee. William S. Huntington, a cashier at Cooke's First National Bank and the treasurer of the National Safe Deposit Company, joined Cooke on the board and the finance committee. Some considered Huntington to be "a henchman of Cooke," which meant that he was a man whom Cooke could use to cosign his aggressive and risky business ventures.[57]

Cooke pushed for more. He did not stop with the addition of Huntington. His influence continued with the bank's actuary. D. L. Lambert, who had been serving as the actuary and recording secretary, resigned on May 1, 1867. In a move that would reinforce the influence of a coterie of bankers, Cooke maneuvered to appoint an actuary of his own choosing, a colleague named Daniel L. Eaton, also known as DL, to fill the role on May 2, 1867.

D. L. Eaton was a Maine-born, Washington businessman with connections to both congressional Republicans and a small but powerful cadre of Democrats. Around the time of his appointment as the bank's actuary, he established D. L. Eaton & Company in early 1867. His company manufactured a special brick used in the construction of buildings in Washington, DC. The most prominent building project for which Eaton's firm provided brick was Howard University. In fact, Eaton benefited financially from the personal relationships that he forged with influential members of the DC elite, namely Union general O. O. Howard. Eaton and Howard likely knew each other from their time at Bowdoin College, where Howard graduated in 1850 and Eaton graduated a year later.[58]

On March 2, 1867, Congress approved General Howard's proposal to establish an institution of higher education in Washington for African Americans. Beginning in the spring of 1867, General Howard was enveloped in the daunting task of erecting a university for African Americans that would bear his name. It would come to be known as Howard University, one of the first group of Black colleges and universities founded in the nineteenth century.[59] He tapped Eaton to provide the university's building material, a patent brick.[60] Howard University was one of several building contracts that Eaton secured during the years that he would serve as the bank's actuary.

In establishing his company, Eaton went into business with a small group of investors. He did not select these investors at random. In fact, each shareholder in D. L. Eaton & Company worked for the Freedman's Bank as a trustee *and* worked for the Freedmen's Bureau in some official capacity. As investors and business partners Eaton counted Alvord, Charles H. Howard (brother of General O. O. Howard, commissioner at the Freedmen's Bureau, elected as bank trustee in April 1867), John Kimball (bank trustee as of November 1867 and a Freedmen's Bureau superintendent of schools), Eliphalet Whittlesey (Freedmen's Bureau commissioner in North Carolina and bank trustee as of November 1867), and Dwight Bliss (bank trustee as of November 1867 who worked for the bureau in the construction of Howard University). Each person invested about $12,000 ($245,000 today).[61]

As Eaton was growing his business, through taking advantage of his political connections, he surely recognized that a position in the Freedman's Bank could be beneficial to his prospects. Not only would he be responsible for evaluating risk in the bank's portfolio, he would also have inside information into the bank's finances. He quickly capitalized on his relationship with Cooke, and perhaps with other members of the board. Though he accepted the position as the bank's actuary on May 2, 1867, this was not his first engagement with the Freedman's Bank. In fact, he—perhaps colluding with Cooke and Huntington—made a decision that had the potential to sully not only his reputation but also the bank's good name.

※

IT HAPPENED ON APRIL 19, 1867, two weeks before Eaton accepted the position as bank actuary. His nomination for and subsequent acceptance of the actuary position on May 2 should have immediately raised red flags among the trustees.[62] Maybe they were unaware of the scope of his early involvement with the bank.

Three days after the board approved the move to Washington, DC, D. L. Eaton received the bank's first loan—an illegal loan. Eaton entered into an agreement, perhaps negotiated by Cooke and Huntington, to borrow $1,000 from the bank.[63] The terms of the loan were favorable to him. His loan would reach maturity on April 19, 1875, which meant that he would have seven years to pay back the money that he borrowed. He would be responsible for paying a total of $1,433, paying an interest rate of 6.2 percent. Eaton, however, had to offer collateral to secure the $1,000. He secured his loan with one of his Washington properties.

The moment when the finance committee executed the loan, and Eaton accepted the terms, marked a deviation. With this loan, the bank began to veer into dubious financial territory. Moreover, when Eaton welcomed the trustees' offer to serve as the bank's actuary, the person within the bank's administration responsible for assessing the riskiness of its investments, the bank was heading in an untenable direction.

Eaton accepted the nomination to serve as the recording secretary and actuary already having received the bank's first illegal loan. He not only owed the bank, he also was responsible for ensuring that administrators made prudent financial decisions. His job involved mitigating investment risk. Ultimately, Eaton made haste to use his position in the bank, and within the finance committee, for his own economic needs.

Eaton's illegal loan was not the only one. A second illegal loan, also finalized in 1867, went to Charles D. Bailey, the bank's treasurer. Bailey received a $7,000 loan, secured by 480 shares of Young Men's Christian Association (YMCA) stock and approved by the finance committee.[64] He made payments on the loan so that it was eventually reduced to $2,600. The committee made this loan from the bank's "available fund," which bank administrators were supposed to use to offset operating costs—not to lend.

The bank's illegal foray into lending was not accidental. The calculated movement of trustees off the board, the strategic voting of cunning trustees onto the board, and the central office's move to Washington were harbingers of the bank's advance into illicit activity. These actions occurred as freed people were fighting to attain political and economic rights.

Perhaps in a vote of confidence, in May 1867, the trustees elected Alvord as the bank's next first vice president, positioning him to influence the bank's direction even more—and to continue to profit, both morally and economically, from his involvement with the bank.[65] Though previous vice presidents had not taken on much responsibility, Alvord was intent on performing differently in the position. He would be more visible and more engaged. Because the executive committee members earned small salaries, accepting the vice presidency, and moving up the ranks, meant that he would be able to put his family in a more stable financial position. Alvord's financial security, though, came at a cost. He was becoming compromised. He was beginning to put his own economic future ahead of the interests of the freed people he had sworn to serve. His introduction of Cooke to the board, Cooke's influence over Huntington and Eaton, and his investment in Eaton's company would prove to slowly erode the bank's benevolent mission.

⚜

BY THE END OF 1867, African Americans had placed $1,624,853 ($33.2 million today) into the bank's vaults, most of it sent to the bank's new central office in Washington. Cashiers such as Charles Sauvinet in New Orleans and others in cities throughout the South were accepting hundreds of thousands of dollars of Black people's money. If anyone had doubts about the ability of formerly enslaved people to support themselves through hard work and diligence, then these numbers should have put those doubts to rest. With each dollar deposited, each dollar saved, and each account opened, African Americans proved their place within the fabric of American society. Many depositors patronized the bank to heed the call to demonstrate that they deserved the privileges of American citizenship. The Black newspaper the *Christian Reporter* argued that opening bank accounts and depositing money with the bank was "the way for our people to get equality of political rights."[66] The connection between economic power and political influence was important for Black people. The deposits proved freed people's willingness to work and earn wages—and a willingness to accept the fragile bargain of buying their way into the body politic. They did so facing violence from whites who were rebuffing the political and economic progress of Reconstruction.

Some depositors did not hesitate to withdraw their money and spend it in any way they saw fit. This reality shocked and frightened whites, who continued to grapple with African Americans as freed people. In August 1867, thirty-six Black soldiers who served in the Union army in Texas returned home to Greensville County, Virginia, withdrawing a combined amount of $3,800 from the local Freedman's Bank branch upon their arrival. A Greensville resident wrote to a Richmond, Virginia, newspaper, alerting readers that the men "intend to float around the city for several days before going home."[67] Not only did these men have money to spend, but their presence as freed people with the autonomy to move around as they wished scared white residents.

For African Americans such as Lubin and Sauvinet in New Orleans, citizenship was bound up in a host of privileges, important among which was the freedom to pursue economic opportunities at their disposal.[68] Yet African Americans were living and working within a system that defined freedom for them in limited ways. They were learning that liberation in Reconstruction America also meant the willingness to take and evaluate risk. Risk-taking was a hallmark of engagement in this new era of capitalism, democracy, and finance.[69]

The bank's messaging to depositors, however, was not about risk, it was about inclusion. To continue drawing in depositors and their money, the bank embarked on an extensive marketing campaign throughout the South, especially in cities with large and newly enriched Black populations. They targeted African American newspapers in big southern cities, hoping to attract Black depositors to their branches.[70]

The bank had been making a concerted effort to connect depositors' contributions to American citizenship. In a calculated advertising campaign with the Freedmen's Bureau, it continued to spread the message of thrift, hard work, and saving money. The *New York Dispatch* ran an article on August 19, 1866, titled "Bankable Colored People." It chronicled the New York branch opening its Bleecker Street location in July 1866. "We are glad," the writers unveiled, "to see the interest taken by rich men in the money of the negroes." With a heavy dose of paternalism, tinged with the writers' underestimation of Black people's eagerness to bank, the writers declared, "When the freedmen learn how to 'save,' they will be pretty nearly intelligent as white folks, and when a thousand or more combine to make a fortune for bankers, they will almost deserve to be recognized as 'citizens.'"[71] The writers' racial animus oozed through the piece. Despite low expectations from white Americans, however, African Americans were actively connecting citizenship to their patronage of the bank.

The trustees took notice. Through illegally borrowing depositors' money, they had started to chip away at the bank's moral underpinnings. With the addition of Henry Cooke and his allies, and the central office's move to Washington, the bank would expand in the coming years. But its core would slowly erode from the inside out.

CHAPTER FOUR

A Change in Priorities, 1868–70

We call upon every male and female to deposit their little
earnings. . . . Remember, you are poor—save your money. You
want homes—save your money. You want education—save your
money. You want to live comfortably—save your money.

—*THE TRI-WEEKLY STANDARD*, JUNE 20, 1868[1]

Freedman's Bank total deposits, as of March 1868:
$3,582,378.36 ($76.1 million today)

Freedman's Bank total deposits, as of March 1869:
$7,257,798.63 ($161 million today)

IN FEBRUARY 1868, THE BLACK RESIDENTS OF RALEIGH had reason to rejoice. A Freedman's Bank branch would open in their city. The bank would complement the work of freed people, who were building their own businesses, founding churches, and establishing schools. Raleigh's Black population had steadily increased in the years after the war's end, as African Americans from rural regions of the state moved there to take advantage of the city's opportunities for educational and economic uplift. The branch would be in the center of this growth. To be opened at 9 Fayetteville Street, the branch was located mere blocks from Raleigh Institute, the future home of Shaw University, the first historically Black university founded in the South.[2]

The Raleigh branch, however, was special. Joining William J. Wilson as a Black cashier was thirty-seven-year-old minister George W. Brodie. When Brodie accepted the position as the branch's cashier, he had agreed to work toward the bank's stated goals of encouraging freed people to save money and build wealth. Though he was a well-known minister and civic leader with the local AME church, his financial acumen was untested. Despite his lack of experience as a banker, his appointment reflected the economic potential of Raleigh's Black population.[3]

Meanwhile, as Raleigh's Black community reveled in Brodie's appointment, Washington, DC, was in turmoil. The halls of Congress buzzed with political tension, which extended through the city and propagated across the nation. On Monday, February 24, 1868, in a vote of 126 to 47, members of the House of Representatives did what no other Congress before them had done: impeach the president. From that moment, President Andrew Johnson would be the first American president to be impeached.

The impeachment proceedings marred the end of Johnson's presidency. He could do little to redeem himself politically. What's more, the end of his term was near. Venerated Union general Ulysses S. Grant was elected president in November 1868, as Johnson, wounded from the sting of his impeachment, vacated the White House.[4]

For Republicans, the impeachment was not only about expelling Johnson. It was a show of political strength. The process of bringing the president to trial for behaving in ways that were "unmindful of the high duties of his office" represented Republicans' efforts to demonstrate that they would use any strategy to ensure the realization of their political agenda. They wanted to pass legislation to reform the nation.

In reconstructing the country after the end of a violent war, Republicans, as a party, would also continue this push in support of the Freedman's Bank as the institution continued to expand and evolve. But while the party, especially the radical wing, championed the political potential of freed people, in the coming years it would also put freed people in the crosshairs of its political plans. Just because Republicans' agenda included advocating for African Americans' political rights, including the passage of the Fourteenth Amendment in July 1868, it did not reflect the same level of concern with freed people's economic rights. African Americans in cities such as Raleigh hoped that Republicans, especially those who worked in the Freedman's Bank, would take their fight for inclusion seriously. The fact that African Americans were assuming more prominent roles in the bank, though, did not mean that they could completely extinguish the nefarious interests that had begun to take hold.

🌿

AMID THE SHOWDOWN between the legislative and executive branches over Johnson's future as president, the Freedman's Bank was undergoing a shakeup of its own. In a move that was three years in the making, John Alvord was elected president on March 12, 1868. When he transitioned into the position as the bank's president , he was made responsible by the board for guiding the bank's trustees and administrators, who were engulfed in the process of making the bank's full transition to Washington. Alvord's ascendance to the role of Freedman's Bank president was not surprising. In many ways, he had been the bank's most vocal advocate, even risking his family's economic stability to fulfill his calling to bring savings banking to African Americans. As he accepted the role as president, he was facing challenges that would determine the bank's future. His biggest potential hurdles, and potential opportunities, concerned the reshuffling of the board of trustees and reconceptualizing of the bank's fundamental mission to serve freed people. Alvord's tenure as president would test his faith in the ability of the nation's banking system to serve African Americans.

The chaos caused by Johnson's impeachment, the election of Alvord as the bank's new president, and the central office's move from New York to Washington, DC, overshadowed one of the bank's major changes. An addition that, surprisingly, did not garner as much attention—or much press coverage—was the appointment of the bank's first Black trustees.[5] The trustees had finally fulfilled a promise that people such as Alvord had made to Black depositors on their travels throughout the South in the first stage of the bank's opening.

One of the bright spots in the bank's transition to Washington was that the board could connect with the city's visible and politically active Black population. The city was home to a significant number of educated, well-connected, and ambitious African Americans. To make political inroads into the city's prominent Black community, trustees, perhaps encouraged by Alvord, began to tap into Black Washington to encourage the bank's first group of Black trustees to join the board in 1867.[6]

The first Black men elected as trustees were Walker Lewis, Bishop Sampson Talbot, and Rev. D. W. Anderson.[7] Anderson and Talbot served as pastors at prominent churches in the city, Talbot at the African Methodist Episcopal Zion Church, and Anderson at the Nineteenth Street Baptist Church. Walker Lewis worked as a messenger for the Treasury Department.[8] Their roles would be determined by the committees on which they served. In some ways, they were window dressing, helping the bank to bolster its status in Black communities. In other ways, they would attempt to help steer the bank in new directions.

One of the most influential of the new Black trustees joined in November 1867. Dr. Charles B. Purvis, a medical officer in the Union

C. B. PURVIS.

Dr. Charles B. Purvis, 1887

army during the Civil War, was a physician and one of the first professors of medicine at Howard University's medical school. Born free in Philadelphia in 1842, Purvis was the son of prominent abolitionists Robert Purvis and Harriet Forten Purvis. After graduating from medical school at Western Reserve College in Cleveland in 1865, he proudly accepted a position at the new Howard University. A professor of obstetrics, he also worked as a surgeon in the Freedmen's Hospital. Being a member of a prominent Black family and serving as a physician in an important institution such as Howard University made Purvis the most high-profile African American to serve on the board.[9] He was not active on the board during his first few years, as he was serving as the acting assistant surgeon of the army. Neither he nor the other Black trustees were fully aware of the goings-on of the bank's board, the finance committee in particular.

With the bank's relocation and the addition of new trustees, the finance committee continued to inch the bank into illegal territory in 1868. Perhaps the political frenzy of Washington and Congress aided their goal of expanding the bank's mission. The idea that the bank could transition from being a savings bank to being a commercial bank was certainly on Eaton's mind as he took the daring step of introducing an idea that would fundamentally alter the charge of the Freedman's Bank.

On February 3, 1868, Eaton wrote a letter to Maine senator Justin Morrill encouraging him to consider introducing legislation that would allow the bank to expand its investment portfolio. This expansion involved lending. He argued to Morrill that the bank was operating at a deficit, meaning that its expenses exceeded its income. The expenses amounted to $43,000 while the income came out to $42,000.[10] According to Eaton, the bank's operating costs and projected expenses were untenable in the long term.

He targeted Morrill because of his reputation as a supporter of broadening access to educational and financial opportunities to members of American society with fewer economic resources. Eaton was strategic in his lobbying efforts. The piece of legislation for which Morrill was best known was the Morrill Act of 1862, which provided land grants for the creation of institutions of higher education across the nation.[11] For this reason, Eaton argued that by expanding the bank's operational and investment portfolio to formally include lending, the bank would be able to help freed people in new ways. He expressed a hope that the bank would be in a position to offer freed people loans to buy land, providing them with the necessary access to credit. He worked to convince Morrill that the bank's intentions were ethical because Eaton likely recognized that such a change would have monumental consequences for the bank's future—and for his personal financial ties to the institution.

Three months later, the full board considered a similar proposal. On May 14, 1868, the board met to discuss whether they, as a governing body, would be able to use money reserved in the bank's "available fund" to loan, "as opportunities may offer under the direction of the finance committee."[12] They debated whether it would be feasible, and admissible under the bank's charter, to set aside "a sum not to exceed fifty-thousand Dollars."[13] The proposal suggested that the bank could lend to people who had adequate collateral and that the loans were "not to exceed one half the value of the property on unincumbered real estate."[14] Instead of simply forbidding discussion of this proposition, as he should have done as the newly elected bank president, Alvord allowed for the proposal to be sent to the finance committee for consideration. Despite the reality that the proposal violated the bank's bylaws, the finance committee took it under consideration. Eaton presented the idea to the committee on June 16. Cooke, as the committee's chairman, made the final determination about whether the bank should make a *formal* foray into lending.

On June 26, Cooke wrote to Eaton of his decision. "I am clearly of the opinion," Cooke detailed, "that the power to make such loans is *not* given by the clause in the 6th section of the act of incorporation to which you refer."[15] He continued by clarifying that the bank's "available fund" was to be used to "meet 'current payments.'"[16] He then concluded that the available fund was not to be used for loaning—that is, for risky investments and speculation. He ended his letter, "I think a careful reading of the clause will justify this interpretation."[17]

Cooke's perspective in the letter was clear. The existing charter did not legally allow the bank to lend. As he penned his response to Eaton, Cooke perhaps sought to ensure that he was on the record as rejecting Eaton's proposal that lending from the bank's available fund was not within the guidelines and was illegal, as outlined by the bank's charter. Without acknowledging that Eaton himself had received an illegal loan, which by this point had been disbursed, with Eaton a year into a seven-year repayment plan, Cooke (and by extension Eaton) was on record as having been clear about not running afoul of the charter.

But this conversation did not stay between these two members of the finance committee. In fact, the letter *did* alert board members outside of the finance committee about the possibility of using the bank's funds to engage in speculation. The seriousness with which Alvord took this proposal, going so far as to have the finance committee consider the practicality (and legality) of the proposition, suggests that the board was taking a step in the direction of finding innovative ways to profit from the bank's investments.

Lending, however, was not the only avenue that the board considered. One of the largest investment opportunities of the Reconstruction era was in railroads. The federal government began subsidizing the construction of an expansive, and expensive, railway line that would connect the Atlantic and Pacific coasts. Congress ratified the Pacific Railway Act in 1861, which provided land grants and authorized a government bond issuance to fund the construction of the railway. The first railway was close to being completed when the Freedman's Bank began buying government-issued bonds in February 1868.[18]

On February 13, the board agreed to buy railroad bonds to add to their investment portfolio. They agreed to authorize Eaton and Cooke to flip $300,000 in governmental securities to railroad bonds.[19] This was the first time that the bank made a formal investment in anything other than governmental securities—besides the illegal lending to bank administrators. And the bond broker, that is, the seller of these government-issued bonds, was none other than the "Banking house of Jay Cooke."[20]

Henry Cooke likely offered his vigorous support of the proposal to buy railroad bonds. As he did during the Civil War, when the Union needed to raise capital to continue the fight against the Confederacy, he and his brother Jay were the go-to men to help raise capital for the construction of America's railroad infrastructure.[21] The Cooke brothers continued their service as sellers of government bonds. They were arguably the nation's most ambitious and successful agents. They exploited their reputation and their connections to a vast network of investors to find buyers for the government's newest investment product.

In another conflict of financial interest, it was Henry Cooke who likely facilitated the bank's purchase of railroad bonds. And it was the same Henry Cooke who benefited from the sale, since, as the broker, he reaped a percentage of the bonds that he sold. As of June 1868, the finance committee agreed to "invest in Pacific Railroad bonds of Government issue" to diversify their investments.[22] This addendum, "of Government issue," made the purchase still comport with the congressionally approved bank charter, but it was nonetheless a riskier investment than other governmental securities. However, the purchase of railroad bonds still did not offer the immediate returns that the finance committee members had hoped for. They believed that they needed to take yet another step to cover the bank's increased overhead.

In some ways, luring in more depositors was one key to the financial puzzle. Depositors continued patronizing the bank in 1868, with bank deposits totaling $3,582,378 by the year's end. In 1868, freed people added $1,957,525 to accounts across twenty-four branches.[23] With the steady growth in deposits, from $1.6 million by the end of 1867 to $3.5 million in 1868, depositors made the case for opening and maintaining more branches.

Bank directors pushed the messaging to African Americans in the South to keep their deposits rolling in—and to encourage depositors to keep their money in the bank for a sustained period. In fact, the bank's literature, including bank books and advertisements, consistently invoked ideas of patriotism. The relationship between banking and citizenship became central to the bank's propaganda to Black depositors. In a November 1869 convention in Washington, DC, on the experiences of "laboring people of color throughout the United States," bank representatives gave an update about the bank's growing prosperity. Echoing the messages that Alvord and Hewitt disseminated on their earlier tour of the South, by investing in bank accounts African Americans were, essentially, supporting the nation economically. Because "these savings . . . are loaned to the United States, *ie*, invested in their stocks and bonds," African Americans were indirectly loaning money to the federal government.[24]

Despite depositors' continued enthusiasm, the trustees decided to slow the bank's expansion in 1868 and 1869. With branches opening in Raleigh (NC), Macon (GA), and St. Louis (MO) in 1868, and one opening in Chattanooga (TN) in 1869, the trustees were being more judicious in their expansion plans. Perhaps this was because they were attempting to strike a balance between their interest payments to depositors and the costs of maintaining the increasing number of branches.

The reality was that the bank was barely staying afloat. Despite the positive press that the bank received in Black newspapers around the country and at Colored Conventions, the board could not keep up with the rising costs of operation. The expenses of the various branches and the new central office in Washington ballooned the bank's budget. In particular, the New York branch was in trouble. Because of "its inability to compete in that city with other similar institutions," trustees were forced to consider shutting down the branch in America's financial center.[25]

The bank's struggles reflected the ebb and flow of finance in the mid-nineteenth century. The fundamental rules of capitalism influenced how the bank functioned in the marketplace, and how depositors' money would be affected without proper guidance and stewardship. Members of the finance committee understood better than most the underlying tenets of capitalist production. They may have heard of and read a Prussian economic philosopher named Karl Marx, who had published his treatise on the political economy of capital the previous year. In fact, Marx and his collaborator, Friedrich Engels, had been writing articles in the *New York Daily Tribune* on American and British economic policy. Between 1852 and 1862, they wrote 487 articles on a range of topics, from political corruption in England to the Civil War's disruption of the global cotton trade.[26]

According to Marx, for capital to grow, it had to circulate within the market. That is, merely saving money was not going to produce profits. Money had to be invested. And investment required risk.[27] This meant that for the bank to be profitable, and to theoretically pay higher returns to the bank's depositors, it needed to make money on the deposits sitting in accounts. The quickest way to do so was through making loans and diversifying how and where the trustees made investments. Therefore, the finance committee rationalized amending the bank's charter.

The upheavals with the Johnson impeachment, the election of Ulysses S. Grant to the presidency, and the continued fights in the southern states over freed people's political and economic power worked in the trustees' favor—but not necessarily in the depositors' best interests. With Congress's attention elsewhere, there was no formal examination of the bank's business. There was no regulation, no oversight. Since the bank opened for business in March 1865, Congress had not conducted a single official examination of its finances. As the bank expanded to attract more depositors and as it opened more branches in more locations, its administrators operated as if there would not be interference from lawmakers. The administrators, along with the branch cashiers, conducted business as usual without meddling from Congress or from the OCC.

Despite the bank's fiscal concerns, in 1869 the trustees decided to make a monumental gamble with its crumbling finances. This revolved around the bank's transition to Washington. It became clear, at least to the trustees, that they needed a new office. The finance committee, for example, had been meeting in the offices of the First National Bank. Seeing that Henry Cooke was First National Bank president, the meetings took place there to be convenient for Cooke and because the bank lacked its own location in Washington. By 1869, after the central office had fully made the transition from New York to Washington, the trustees decided that they were entitled to more than a simple office. The Freedman's Bank deserved its own building. In June 1869, the board decided to find "a proper building site for a Banking House."[28] After months of visiting locations, negotiating with agents, and determining how much they should spend on a lot and building, the trustees agreed to put a bid of $80,000 for a building on the corner of 16½ Street and Pennsylvania Avenue. The board agreed to the location, the price, and the terms of sale, all finalized by Henry Cooke.[29] Not only would the bank's central office—and with it the focal point of the bank's business ventures—be in Washington, but administrators approved buying and renovating a building designed to reflect the economic promise of freed people specifically, and African Americans more broadly. By the end of the year, the central office of the Freedman's Bank would be a prime piece of Washington, DC, real estate—adjacent to both the Department of the Treasury and the White House.

The bank's purchase immediately attracted scrutiny. A critique appeared in the *New York Times* in October 1869. The writer recognized that the institution was a "success" and that the "amount of deposits, which reach nearly $1,500,000, is a respectable fact." However, the board's decision to spend such a large amount of money on a building of "no real necessity" was not a prudent one. "[T]he statement that the Company has given $80,000 for land upon which to erect a handsome bank building at Washington," the writer castigated, "does not convey a favorable impression."[30] The deposits of free people did not deserve to be spent on such an extravagance, according to the writer. Despite the criticisms, the board moved forward with making the Freedman's Bank building one of the most spectacular in the city.

The critique reflected a real conundrum that the bank's administrators and trustees faced. How could they finance an expensive new central office building—not simply an *office*—as concerns loomed about paying cashier salaries, renting office space in the various branch locations, and paying depositor dividends? Though the trustees celebrated the purchase, perhaps as a reflection of their own desires to display political capital, the building represented the trustees' aspirations more than the reality of financial success. The purchase, however, preceded an event that would invariably alter the bank's trajectory—and its legacy.

ᴥ

PERHAPS BECAUSE OF the purchase of a new and expensive central office location, the repeated requests from cashiers to increase their salaries, or the overall growing cost of the bank's operations, the board was convinced to reconsider the issue of loan making. The official reexamination occurred in December 1869, the year's final meeting. Nine of the board's members attended, including Alvord and Eaton. The final topic of discussion for the year was "securing legislation for power to loan money on other security than Government bonds."[31] Though Alvord did not require the topic to be discussed further, at least in an official capacity that year, the reintroduction of this topic—that of generating profit through offering loans instead of merely investing in government bonds and securities—was poignant.

By the beginning of 1870, the board had already begun setting aside money, likely in anticipation of congressional approval of their change in policy. They used the provision of establishing an available fund to allow for lending. First it was $100,000, as of January 1870. Then, a month later, the board approved that an *additional* $600,000 be put aside to loan.[32]

Between December 1869 and March 1870, the bank's representatives shifted their attention to lobbying members of Congress. The finance committee, specifically Cooke and Eaton, deployed their connections within the worlds of banking and politics to embark on a mission that would inexorably alter the bank's trajectory. They utilized their political capital to spread the word among congressmen and senators that they wanted to make a significant, and potentially lucrative, change to the bank's fundamental mission.

The target was the bank's charter. Specifically, they wanted to revise section 12, which stipulated that "no President, Vice-President, Trustee, officer, or servant of the corporation shall, directly or indirectly, *borrow the funds* of the corporation or its deposits."[33] Cooke saw the millions of dollars in deposits just sitting in accounts. He decided to wield his connections to Washington's political elite to convince members of Congress to amend the bank's charter. He wanted Congress to allow the bank to make business loans—and to permit trustees to borrow money at low interest rates. Cooke moved forward with the belief that the millions of dollars held by the bank could be used to fuel economic activity through making interest-accruing loans. What he did not reveal were his personal reasons for wanting to expand the bank's investments.

The finance committee argued that the depositors were not receiving as much interest on their deposits as they could be. Government bonds were not giving as high a return as a more diversified investment portfolio would. On the surface, this was economically sound reasoning. Treasury bonds were a safe investment with steady, albeit low, returns.

Support for amending the charter was spreading. Even General O. O. Howard, who would join the board in 1870, argued that Black depositors deserved to earn higher interest on their deposits. By diversifying the bank's investment portfolio to include bank loans to "qualified" borrowers, the bank would be acting on behalf of their depositors to ensure that they would receive higher and more competitive dividend payments.[34]

The proposal was to amend the charter such that a third of deposits would be kept in an "available fund" for operating expenses and another third would be invested in "stocks of any state or of any incorporated city of the United States." The amendment would come in with the final third, which would be available for investment "in real estate & in bond and mortgage on real estate double the value of the loan."[35]

For anyone receiving a loan, the real estate collateral had to be at least double the value of the loan. The amendment would therefore require the bank's underwriter, Eaton in this case, to ensure that borrowers could secure the loan by real estate twice the loan's value. So a borrower who wanted a $1,000 loan from the bank had to prove that he (or she) possessed real estate worth $2,000. While this proposal had the potential to bring more capital into the bank to help offset the increasing operating expenses, the amendment would also restrict who could even qualify to be a borrower. According to the amendment proposal, only those who held property would be eligible for a loan from the bank. Ultimately, the proposal would benefit those with access to capital. The bank's trustees argued that congressional approval of the amendment would allow the bank to loan millions of dollars of freed people's money to people who already had it. The trustees were seeking a charter amendment that would ultimately benefit those who already had wealth. Under the proposed amendment, most of the bank's Black depositors would not qualify to borrow money from the bank that they helped enrich.

❦

CONGRESSMAN BURTON COOK, a Republican from Illinois, introduced H.R. 1594, to amend "An Act to Incorporate the Freedman's Savings and Trust Company" on March 21, 1870.[36] Though most members of Congress appeared to be supportive of the proposal, a few did not trust that the bank's trustees were making a prudent economic decision on behalf of the depositors.

On April 1, the bill received the Senate's full consideration. Senator Sumner, the most vocal supporter of the Freedman's Bank and one of the more radical Republicans who advocated for Reconstruction policies in favor of freed people, began the debate with a simple statement. "I hope there will be no objection to that [the amendment]."[37]

The amendment's passage through the Senate did not go as smoothly as Sumner had hoped. One of the plan's most vocal opponents emerged as Senator Simon Cameron of Pennsylvania. Cameron had served as Lincoln's secretary of war in 1861 and 1862. He was known to be an ardent supporter of the abolitionist movement in the antebellum era. He did not trust that the bank's trustees had the depositors' best interests in mind, arguing that gambling with the deposits was risky at best, a bellwether of destruction at worst. He spoke up, defying Sumner. Cameron argued that "no wisely-conducted bank will allow its money to be loaned upon real estate, where it can never be collected immediately." He continued, "There is nothing so unsafe, so changeable in its charter, and so easily to be inflated in a board of directors as real estate." He finished his comments by asking that the Senate reject the charter amendment.[38]

Cameron's skepticism did not dissuade Sumner. In response, Sumner took Cameron's comments as an opportunity to speak again on behalf of the bank's trustees. He stated that because the proposal required that mortgages be secured by real estate twice the loan value, this amendment would further protect the bank—and in theory protect the depositors. "The corporation would be at the last moment responsible," Sumner assured. He continued by highlighting his trust in the trustees and in their underwriting processes. He expressed his confidence in "those who make the loan," arguing, "I assume that they are sufficiently intelligent not to get a bad security." He hoped that his faith in the bank's trustees and administrators would convince senators such as Cameron to sign off on the amendment. Sumner then concluded, "Is that not enough, provided these men are competent for their posts? If they are incompetent then everything will go."[39]

Senator Cameron was not deterred. He retorted that he understood "human nature in the aggregate." He was not convinced that the bank's benevolent mission would keep the trustees from tapping into the bank's reserves. In fact, he argued that these same trustees would probably be the first in line to "borrow upon bond and mortgage secured by their own real estate." Perhaps Cameron had been privy to private information about the bank's actuary borrowing money illegally from the bank two years earlier. Or maybe he understood the allure of savings bank deposits to bankers who were simultaneously running—and were invested in—commercial and investment banks.

Cameron believed that Sumner's trust in the bank's trustees was misguided. He argued that if Sumner fully understood what he knew, that banks across the nation had been engaged in malfeasance, in which "directors borrowed the money either for themselves or their friends, and gave real estate as security," then he would not be so eager to lend support to the charter amendment.[40] According to Cameron, the best of intentions, even the bank's charitable mission, would not keep entrepreneurial, perhaps even greedy, capitalists from pilfering the bank if the opportunity presented itself.

Though Cameron was the first person to go on record as opposing the amendment, he was not the only senator who questioned the amendment's soundness. Senator Roscoe Conkling, a Republican from New York, intervened. In addition to recommending that the real estate security for bank loans be more than double the value of the loan, he suggested a more stringent restriction. He recommended that bank directors not be able to borrow money from the bank, or be able to borrow only under very specific circumstances. In a daring statement, Conkling argued, "There should either be an inhibition upon the directors against borrowing altogether, or else the loans made to them should be confined to very narrow limits."[41] If those provisions were not included in the amendment, Conkling declared, then he agreed with Cameron.

George Henry Williams added his voice to the cadre of senators who opposed the amendment. A radical Republican from Oregon, Senator Williams stated that considering the recent troubles that both savings and commercial banks had had, "every precaution should be taken to prevent loss to the poor people for whose benefit these institutions are organized."[42] He had not heard any argument that would convince him that amending the charter would be a good idea. By allowing the bank's trustees to gamble and speculate with freed people's money, they would indirectly increase the amount of risk that freed people were assuming. Williams argued that allowing the trustees to invest in unstable securities, that is, bank loans, would undermine the bank's raison d'être.

After Cameron and Williams voiced their objections, Senator Samuel Pomeroy of Kansas sought to reshape the tenor of the discussion. He highlighted the basic economics of the Freedman's Bank's finances. The bank was a simple savings bank and its founders agreed to pay the depositors an annual rate of 5 percent on their deposits. But, while depositors were supposed to have received 5 percent interest, the bank's investments in government securities did not yield enough to cover interest payments and the bank's operating expenses. "The only reason why the corporation desire [*sic*] to change their securities is that they cannot afford to pay their depositors five per cent and at the same time be confined to Government bonds at four and a half or five per cent," Pomeroy explained.[43] The bank's directors were stuck. They promised depositors a relatively high rate of interest on their deposits, but the bank's investments in low-risk securities, combined with the high cost of operations, meant that it was consistently operating at a deficit. According to Pomeroy's rationale, the bank's directors needed to find ways to make their investments more profitable for the very people that the bank was founded to help.[44]

Sumner pushed for the bank amendment to pass, and his urgency was palpable to his fellow senators. In a political move that he hoped would shore up enough support, he highlighted section 12 of the bank's charter to underscore for detractors the bank's credibility. In what was surely a declarative statement, Sumner read aloud for the Senate chamber, "That no President, Vice President, Trustee, officer, or servant of the corporation shall, directly or indirectly, borrow the funds of the corporation or its deposits ... except to pay necessary expenses, under the direction of the Board of Trustees."[45] This move should have convinced members of the Senate that the proposal was sound. After all, Congress had already approved this stipulation in 1865. But Cameron readied a rebuttal. "You will find that in the charter of every corporation that has broken up in the country," he countered. "It is always put in."[46] Cameron proved to be the most vocal opponent of the amendment. He had little faith that the Freedman's Bank trustees and administrators would *not* use the deposits for their own investments. And those who would suffer if the bank failed were not the trustees but freed people. "Remember," he stated, "that this money belongs to thousands of people all over the country, freedmen and others."[47] Cameron was beginning to bother other senators with this vehement and vocal objection. His comments became so intolerable that the vice president, Hannibal Hamlin, intervened. "The Senator from Pennsylvania will suspend his remarks," Hamlin interceded.

Discussion continued on April 28. Senator Cameron took the opportunity to express his dismay. "I think it will in the end probably destroy the institution," he pronounced. His perspective, in addition to those of Williams and Conkling, was a prescient one. In the Senate chamber, they were putting the potential for internal malfeasance on public display. And his concern was well founded. Despite the new regulatory infrastructure, neither the OCC nor Congress had examined the bank. This oversight would prove to be problematic.

The bill ultimately passed. Regardless of Cameron's objections, the House version of the bill was ratified on May 3, 1870, paving the way for a complete reorganization of the bank's mission.[48] Members of Congress approved the amendment because the language suggested that the bank was going to engineer ways to protect the depositors' investment in the bank if borrowers failed to pay back both the loans and the interest. By requiring collateral twice the value of the loan, Congress was trying to ensure that the depositors' money and investments would be safe. The amendment, as written, would compel borrowers to relinquish their real estate collateral to the bank if they failed to pay back their debt obligation. In theory, the bank and, importantly, the depositors would mitigate the risk of lending money to borrowers by having the legal ability to recoup the borrower's real estate if the borrower defaulted. The amendment was a theory, an exercise in testing borrowers' economic behavior. That behavior would soon be evaluated.

WHILE AFRICAN AMERICANS continued to see their investment in the bank as a symbol of their trust in the benefits of banking, white administrators saw an opportunity. At the December 1869 meeting of the National Colored Labor Convention in Washington, the bank's presence was front and center. The only business to take out a full-page advertisement in the official publication of the convention's proceedings, the Freedman's Bank assumed an important place in the convention's agenda.

"SAVE YOUR MONEY!" and "Every Man Can Become Rich if

He Will!" featured prominently on the advertisement. These messages conveyed to the Black men and women in attendance, and those reading the publication afterward, that depositors would become rich not just by saving money but by depositing their "five and ten cent pieces" into bank accounts "where they will be safe."[49] In addition, the ad championed the convention's support of the bank by announcing, "The great National Labor Convention of Washington endorsed the Banks by an unanimous vote."[50] It is possible that having Dr. Charles Purvis in attendance, the bank's most prominent Black trustee, helped underscore the bank's commitment to helping Black depositors. At the same time, the bank continued to connect saving money with land accumulation and wealth. "Any man who saves only ten cents a day for ten years," the ad promised, "and buys land with his savings so made, will be RICH."[51] The challenge for African Americans, however, was the omnipresence of violence. Could African Americans rely on the federal and state governments to protect their property rights?

One of the main themes that connected the five-day event was African Americans' economic power. Though the convention's chairman, George T. Downing, celebrated the passage of the Fifteenth Amendment, he recognized that the legislative triumphs of the past four years—with the Thirteenth, Fourteenth, and Fifteenth Amendments— were important but also symbolic. In effect, the Republican Party's radical wing was limited in what it could do to secure Black people's rights. On paper, the Reconstruction amendments formally ushered African Americans into the body politic and made important headway in constructing a biracial democracy. But in practice, Black people continued to struggle with the everyday vestiges of slavery. More decisive action was necessary. Black people, along with their white Republican supporters, needed to shift to focusing on "financial policy." According to Downing, as workers, African Americans were becoming more knowledgeable and demanding of their elected officials, expecting legislators to work on their behalf. They were also coming to realize that "being united, they can be an influence equal to capital."[52] In some ways, this is how the bank was positioning itself.

When the list of committees was announced, the Committee on

Savings Banks was a prominent one. The committee's chairman, William J. Wilson, offered the report. He was uniquely positioned to give a comprehensive analysis of the committee's findings and recommendations. Wilson, an African American man, worked as the cashier of the Freedman's Bank's Washington branch. He held one of the most prominent public-facing positions with the bank. In the branch's most profitable years, he claimed that he serviced from 150 to 200 depositors per day, handling $6,000 to $20,000 in deposits every business day. He held a good deal of influence. Wilson's words held sway.[33]

In his report, Wilson argued for the expansion of savings banks in the South to serve freed people who had "just escaped from the shackles of slavery."[34] "[T]he way to a better condition," he announced, was "the free school, the open Bible, the Savings Bank."[35] He celebrated freed people's embrace of these principles, saying that by March 1869, the bank had $7,257,798.63 in deposits and "to-day the aggregate of all the deposits is over ten millions!"[36]

Wilson issued a stern warning about the depositors, however. There had "been constant and heavy drafts from these aggregations," which meant that depositors were depositing and then withdrawing money frequently. The bank encouraged freed people to open accounts to save for the purchase of land. Freed people believed that landownership would help them secure economic stability. This was the message that the bank was also disseminating. Therefore, when depositors had accumulated enough in their bank accounts to buy what they really wanted, which was land, it made sense that they would then withdraw the money from their accounts. Though Wilson may not have agreed with this point of view, he must have recognized that depositors required liquidity—quick and easy access to their money.

Wilson's observation about depositors' financial habits was a topic that the bank's administrators struggled to understand. The depositors wanting quick and reliable access to their money continued to be a hurdle for the bank. Depositors hesitated to leave money in their accounts for a long enough period to accrue interest *and* long enough for the trustees to invest the deposits. Wilson revealed the differing weights that the depositors and administrators put on the benefits of saving and investing. Essentially, this aspect of Wilson's report reflected an asymmetry between depositors' needs and the trustees' goals. Bank trustees and administrators wanted freed people to continue investing in the bank, while depositors used the bank to save money and invest in land. Depositors cared less about interest payments than they did about what they could use their savings to acquire. To depositors, land was tangible. Land would help them build a stable economic foundation. As the advertisement stated, land would make them "RICH." Accrued interest was not tangible. Accrued interest was not land.

The depositors prioritized wealth that they could see and bequeath. Emerging from slavery, an institution in which enslavers and slave traders considered them to be property, the formerly enslaved conceptualized *investing* differently than the men who founded and ran the bank and its branches. For newly freed people, cash was king. Cash could be used to buy land, purchase machinery and materials, or even relocate. Cash could buy medicine, clothing, and food. Saving would help freed people achieve the practical goals of buying what they needed and wanted. Investing, on the other hand, was obscure—it was numbers on a page. What freed people desired, what they really wanted to help them transition during this unstable period of freedom, especially in the southern states, was money and property. If the bank could help them save, then they would be patrons. But once the bank satisfied their economic goals by providing them with a secure place to store their precious earnings, they would withdraw their money to buy what they really wanted, which was land.

The bank had been advertising in Colored Convention publications, in Black newspapers, to Black church congregations, through the Freedmen's Bureau, and to prominent members of Black communities across the nation since March 1865. The bank's own advertisement in the December 1869 National Colored Labor Convention publication connected saving money to buying land to becoming rich. Therefore, on that day in December 1869, ten months after the passage of the last of the Reconstruction amendments, Wilson's message illuminated one of the bank's central problems: the depositors' goals did not line up with the evolving goals of the bank's administrators.

Despite the tone of Wilson's comments to the convention's attendees, he ended his report lauding the bank and encouraging Black people's continued patronage. "But though the deposits have reached one-and-a-half millions of dollars," he announced, "your committee think [*sic*] that such amount but poorly represents the savings of the colored people within reach of the influence of this company."[57] Wilson believed that freed people possessed the economic strength to enrich both themselves and the bank even more. He closed his remarks by praising the bank's trustees. The first person he honored was the person whose goals for the bank were probably the most misaligned with those of the depositors: Henry D. Cooke.

It was at this time that Cooke and the finance committee, with Alvord's blessing, was beginning to finalize their plan of expanding how the bank handled the investing of depositors' monies. Meanwhile, bank administrators did not hesitate to take advantage of their messaging to depositors to continue depositing money into their accounts. When the trustees in December 1869 decided to make the push to "secure legislation for power to loan," they proceeded down a precarious path.[58] With the millions of dollars that freed people were putting into accounts in bank branches across the country, and with a plan in place to expand the bank's investment portfolio, the trustees pushed the bank's priorities in a new direction.

By May 1870, a few months after the National Colored Labor Convention, the Freedman's Bank would turn from being a simple savings bank to being a lending behemoth.

CHAPTER FIVE

A Lending Bonanza, 1870–72

Colored men, women, and children, remember that your life-
long enemies in this community are striving to break down the
Freedman's Bank. You have by your good sense shown that you can
save money, and erect the finest building in the South, continue
to show good sense by not allowing the ex-dealers of your bone
and sinew to frighten you from the support of an institution that
is a powerful instrument in the work of your advancement.

—*NEW NATIONAL ERA*, OCTOBER 24, 1872[1]

**Freedman's Bank Total deposits, as of March 1870:
$12,605,781.95 ($292 million today)**

A WAVE OF CELEBRATIONS ERUPTED IN BLACK COMMU-
nities across the nation in early 1870. From Camden, New Jersey, to
Nashville, Tennessee, African Americans took to the streets and organized day-long fêtes to mark a historic moment in their fight for equal
protection under the law. The reason was the ratification of the Fifteenth Amendment on February 3, 1870, which expanded voting rights
to Black men.[2] Black activists such as Frederick Douglass, who had
been dedicating his political capital to advocating for Black men's suffrage rights, lauded the amendment's passage. But even he continued
to have a sobering outlook on the practicalities of voting rights for a
people still grappling with the everyday challenges of white racial and
economic violence.[3]

For many African Americans, though, the expansion of the franchise was reason enough to celebrate. Many used this event as motiva-
tion to invest in their economic futures by opening Freedman's Bank
accounts. Perhaps that was why Robert and Betsey Harris, of Richmond, Virginia, brought their eleven-year-old daughter, Mary Susan,
and their six-year-old-son, Charles, to the bank's Richmond branch on
February 5, 1870, only two days after the Fifteenth Amendment's ratification. This trip was a family affair. Robert Harris had opened his
own account two days earlier, on February 3, perhaps inspired by his
newly endowed voting rights.[4] But on this day, he and his wife were not
at the Richmond branch for themselves. They were opening accounts
for their children. Though neither Robert nor Betsey could read or
write, Mary Susan had been learning how to read, the first person in
her family to take advantage of the opportunity to gain crucial literacy
skills.[5] By having an account of her own, Mary Susan would also begin
to gain an important education in financial literacy. It is possible that
she could read a bit of the contents of her deposit book, because her parents listed her and her brother's occupation as "going to sch[ool]."[6] The

Harris family took steps in early February 1870 to demonstrate the type of behavior that bank administrators had been encouraging. Whether they knew it or not, Robert and Betsey Harris were passing on to their children lessons in self-sufficiency. The education that Mary Susan and Charles were receiving as they entered the bank, and watched their parents interact with the bank cashier, was as important as the lessons they were being taught in their classrooms.

Members of the Freedman's Bank's finance committee were not as concerned with African Americans' celebrations of Black men receiving voting rights in February 1870. They were not concerned about families such as the Harrises beyond their willingness to deposit money into their accounts. Instead, men such as Cooke and Eaton focused on how to expand the bank's business—not for the depositors, but for themselves. How could they use the millions of dollars in deposits that freed people were putting into Freedman's Bank accounts for their own investments, their own ventures? They wanted to keep using Black people's deposits as their personal slush funds. The bank continued advertising to Black men and women, pleading that they continue to "Save! Save! Save!"[7] With Congress's approval of the charter amendment on May 6, 1870, after months of lobbying, Cooke, Eaton, and Huntington wanted to keep the deposits rolling in as they embarked on a new plan. They were ready for the bank to fully make the transition, to cease operating as a simple savings bank. On that day, the Freedman's Savings and Trust Company officially became a commercial bank. The lending spree legally began.

On the surface, the congressional debates about allowing the trustees to expand the Freedman's Bank investment portfolio gave the administrators the veneer of having operated within the law. The reality was that the finance committee, given cover by the board of trustees, had already entangled the bank's deposits—and Black people's money—in shady business deals. In efforts led by Cooke and accelerated by Eaton and Huntington, this cabal had been preparing for the charter amendment's ratification for over two years. From Eaton writing to Senator Morrill in February 1868 to the finance committee urging the board to set aside money in 1869 for lending, Cooke, Eaton, and Huntington had been exploiting their knowledge of the political landscape in Washington to pave the way for the amendment. The bank, and the depositors' money, had been made ready for the trustees' coming plunder.

African Americans such as the Harris family, with Mary Susan and Charles taking their first brave steps into their financial futures, were unprepared for what lay ahead. These children would be the victims on whose backs the trustees would continue to build their wealth. Mary Susan and Charles Harris would succumb to the avarice of Gilded Age capitalists.

THOUGH THE BANK'S administrators in Washington had already dabbled in illegal lending three years earlier, the finance committee had fast-tracked the approval of several dubious loans in the two months *before* the amendment went into effect. In early 1870, Congress's prospective approval of the charter amendment generated a sense of anticipation within the finance committee. By May 6, Cooke, Eaton, and Huntington had mired the bank even more deeply in unlawful business activities, in the amount of almost $85,000.[8]

Three weeks before Congress officially approved the charter amendment, Cooke, Eaton, Huntington, and finance committee member L. R. Tuttle gathered for the monthly committee meeting at the "Banking House of HD Cooke" on April 13. They discussed a series of transactions that the committee had approved over the previous five weeks. In anticipation of a positive Senate vote for the amendment, the finance committee accelerated the bank's investment in lending.

They threw open the coffers for specially selected borrowers. Over a monthlong period, between March 3 and April 2, the committee approved fifteen loans, averaging one loan every two days. The borrowers were handpicked by the finance committee and came from a very small group of people within Washington, DC. Three borrowers in particular parlayed their connections with the bank's trustees into an additional source of funding for their business enterprises.

One was the real estate appraisal firm of Kilbourn & Latta. Owned by real estate brokers Hallett Kilbourn and James M. Latta, the firm was as well known in Washington, DC, as the men who owned it.[9] Through their real estate brokerage, which they established in 1865, Kilbourn and Latta sold prime pieces of real estate to discerning and wealthy buyers in the nation's capital. As of December 1867, they advertised that they "had upon their books for sale upwards of 200 HOUSES, ranging in price from $1000 to $100,000 each."[10] Kilbourn and Latta appealed to the Freedman's Bank finance committee for not one but three loans. They subsequently received loan payments on three separate dates, on March 7, March 30, and March 31, for a total loan amount of $7,200.[11]

Kilbourn and Latta built their reputation, and their business, on their knowledge of the city's landscape of upscale properties. It is possible that they appealed to the finance committee for a loan because they were about to embark on an investment opportunity in Washington, DC, real estate. On March 16, they published an advertisement in the *Evening Star*, a Washington newspaper, under the header "Business Chances," announcing that they had "$70,000 To Invest in Good Real Estate Paper at moderate rates."[12] They were making a statement that they had a sizable amount of capital ready for investment. Perhaps a portion of their $70,000 investment was made up of the loan they received, illegally, from the Freedman's Bank that same month.

The loans that Kilbourn & Latta received were not their only interaction with the bank in 1870. After the amendment took effect in May 1870, the trustees realized that they needed help appraising the value of properties that borrowers would use as collateral for loans. Therefore, in June 1870, the board brought Kilbourn & Latta into the bank's business even further by hiring them as real estate appraisers. They would "be consulted in cases where the Actuary or the Finance Committee are not acquainted with the value thereof." Because of their knowledge of the local real estate market, Kilbourn & Latta consulted the finance committee on "cases where that is doubt or question as to value" of a prospective borrower's real estate collateral.[13] The board had no official discussion of the obvious conflict of interest in hiring the duo. Despite being indebted to the bank, Kilbourn and Latta used their expertise and connections to extract even more money from the bank—and from the depositors.

The second questionable borrower was architect and civil engineer Thomas M. Plowman. Between March 3 and April 2, Plowman received three loan disbursements, on March 3, March 12, and April 2. He received a total amount of $7,750, which he likely funneled into his business, Starkweather & Plowman, with his business partner Norris Starkweather. Plowman exploited a direct connection that he had to the bank to procure the loan. He and Starkweather had been working with Cooke on a construction project in Georgetown called Cooke's Row, a venture that Cooke hoped would transform the neighborhood west of the White House and the Capitol. Beginning in 1867, Cooke had broken ground on Cooke's Row, with Starkweather & Plowman designing the row of four duplexes, called "cottages," on Q Street NW.[14] Plowman served as the project's builder, and in February and March 1869 he received several payments from Cooke for work done on the cottages.[15] It was their Cooke's Row project that paved the way for Cooke to approve Plowman's appeal to the bank for a series of loans in the spring of 1870. And Plowman's borrowing was not his only connection to the bank and its trustees. As of June 1870, Starkweather & Plowman would receive a contract from the bank's trustees to be the official architects of the bank's new building on Pennsylvania Avenue.[16]

The third borrower, the one who received the largest loan, on March 3, 1870, was the Maryland Freestone Mining and Manufacturing Company, also known as the Seneca Sandstone Company. The finance committee approved the company borrowing $12,000. As with Starkweather & Plowman and Kilbourn & Latta, the representatives of Seneca Sandstone Company were well acquainted with members of the finance committee. Unlike with the other two borrowers, Henry Cooke had a direct investment in the success of the Seneca Sandstone Company—and therefore the success of the loan, despite its illegality.

Cooke's involvement with the Seneca Sandstone Company began in 1867. He was the third member of a group, which included J. L. Kidwell and H. H. Dodge, that purchased the company, which included a 614-acre plot of land in Maryland located on the C&O Canal that housed a stone quarry. The stone harvested from the quarry was previously used in the construction of the Smithsonian Castle and would be used to build Howard University.[17] According to Dodge, his reason for investing in the company and the quarry was that the property was considered to be "very valuable for the excellent quality of the stone."[18] The stone's quality and the quarry's value, however, did not keep Dodge interested in maintaining his stake of the business. By 1869, he had decided to divest himself of his investment and sold his shares of the company to Cooke.[19] With Dodge out of the picture, Cooke held the company's controlling interest. It was at this time, with Cooke as the Seneca Sandstone Company's majority shareholder, that the company received the $12,000 preemptive loan from the Freedman's Bank—negotiated and approved by Cooke.

The conflict of interest did not stop Cooke from enriching himself and the company's other shareholders. And this loan would not be the company's last from the bank, nor would it be the largest. This loan was only the beginning of the financial relationship among H. D. Cooke, the Freedman's Bank, and the Seneca Sandstone Company.

Between March 3 and April 2, the bank made an astounding $41,155.66 in loans.[20] These three loans alone made up 41 percent of the loan volume issued illegally to borrowers between those dates. Furthermore, Eaton, in his capacity as the bank's actuary and finance committee secretary, did not record any information about the loans' terms, such as the dates of maturity or interest rates. In addition to the $41,155.66, the bank had loaned out another $43,225.01 before May 6, for a total of $84,380.67 *before* the charter amendment received congressional approval.[21] Therefore, of the $84,380.67 that the finance committee illegally approved before the charter amendment took hold, almost half that amount was loaned in the two months before Congress gave its approval for the bank to expand its business.

The finance committee's preemptive lending in the spring of 1870 had common features. The borrowers represented the network of businessmen and bankers connected to Cooke, Huntington, and Eaton. Likely encouraged by Cooke, businessmen in Washington began to see the Freedman's Bank as ready-made for lending. And Cooke, in conjunction with select members of the finance committee, determined who was creditworthy. The borrowers were largely businesses and businessmen involved in the construction of buildings around Washington, DC. From Kilbourn & Latta as real estate agents to Plowman as an architect and civil engineer and the Seneca Sandstone Company as a manufacturer of building materials, the set of loans that the finance committee approved before Congress ratified the amendment related in a direct way to the building up of the District of Columbia. This trend would only continue over the next three years. And above all, the person that united all these businesses was Henry Cooke.

Kilbourn, for example, hosted a meeting at the offices of Kilbourn & Latta on January 12, 1870, to discuss "a plan for a change in the municipal government of this district."[22] The group he represented was proposing to Congress "An Act to Provide for the Territorial Government for the District of Columbia." He hosted an assembly of well-connected businessmen to discuss efforts for Congress to consider and ratify what would be known as the Organic Act of 1871, which would transform the District of Columbia into an independent territory, with congressional representation and a governor. Kilbourn's efforts paid off, because Congress passed the bill on February 21, 1871, which combined Georgetown and Washington to create the District of Columbia. The Organic Act also created a Board of Public Works, on which many of the bank's affiliates and business partners would serve.[23]

Kilbourn's efforts also provided him with a substantial boost to his social capital by entrenching him even more within Henry Cooke's ever-expanding network. When the time came to decide who would take on the herculean effort of managing the District of Columbia, to serve in the position of governor, as stipulated by the Organic Act of 1871, Kilbourn's committee held sway with President Grant. Therefore, Grant, with "special trust and confidence," nominated his friend, none other than Henry Cooke, to be the first territorial governor of the District of Columbia on February 28, 1871.[24] Kilbourn's lobbying surely played a role in Grant appointing Cooke—and Cooke eagerly accepting the position.

Controlling the Washington branch of Jay Cooke & Company, serving as an executive of various businesses, including the Seneca Sandstone Company, maintaining relationships with members of Congress, *and* controlling the multimillion-dollar deposits of freed people with the Freedman's Bank were not enough for Cooke. He added to his empire by inserting himself even more into the arena of Washington politics. He leveraged his political and financial relationships to secure an important, and highly visible, public position in Washington when President Grant appointed him to be the District of Columbia's first territorial governor.[25]

In a letter to Cooke officially nominating him to the position, Grant wrote that he believed in Cooke's abilities and integrity. With congressional support, Grant used his political power to endow Cooke with even more authority. The successful politicking by men such as Kilbourn helped bolster President Grant's decision and Cooke's political position. Being the first governor of Washington, DC, elevated Cooke's status. Not only would he wield control over political life in the district, but he would also not hesitate to use the position to enrich himself and his partners even more, as he had been doing with his position in the Freedman's Bank. The tight-knit network of businessmen and politicians that revolved around Cooke would shape the ledger of borrowers from the Freedman's Bank.

Less than two weeks after Congress approved the charter's amendment, the bank's board of trustees convened. Only nine members attended, despite the meeting's important goal: to officially accept the new changes. The amendment, in its approved form, read:

> And to the extent of one-half in bonds or notes, secured by mortgage on real estate in double the value of the loan; and the corporation is also authorized hereby to hold and improve the real estate now owned by it in the city of Washington, to-wit: the west half of lot number three; all of lots four, five, six, seven, and the south half of lot number eight, in square number two hundred and twenty-one, as laid out and recorded in the original plats or plan of said city: *Provided*, That said corporation shall not use the principal of any deposits made with it for the purpose of such improvement.[26]

The amendment included two major details. First, it stipulated that borrowers needed to be in legal possession of real estate valued at double the amount of the loan. This meant that the bank's trustees needed to come up with a system to evaluate the collateral that borrowers used as security. The second part of the amendment referred to the bank's new Washington, DC, central office. According to the amendment, Congress allowed the trustees to use bank funds to renovate the bank's new building, as long as they did not draw from money held in depositors' accounts. The trustees could, for example, use the interest payments from borrowers to finance the building renovations. The two parts of the amendments were designed to work together. If the bank made money from this new *legal* foray into lending, then it would earn money on the interest that borrowers paid to afford renovations of the new building. Left out of the amendment's language, however, was the benefit to the depositors. That is to say, how were the depositors profiting from this new arrangement? Would they receive higher interest payments on their deposits through this drastic change to the bank's mission?

Theoretically, the borrowers should have benefited from the bank's new investment strategies. They should have been receiving more regular and higher interest payments on their deposits. But as the trustees took the official step into lending, with Congress's approval, they redirected the financial benefits that were supposed to flow to the Black depositors. Instead, as the March 1870 loans showed, the finance committee, with the board's full support, put Black depositors' priorities on the back burner.

The board also established a set of rules that would, in theory, guide the bank's new lending criteria. There were four main guidelines. First, the board agreed to "clothe the Finance Committee with power to Act under the amended charter."[27] This meant that the finance committee would "report their action in all matters touching the investment or loan of money to the Board of Trustees for confirmation at its regular monthly meetings."[28] Cooke and the finance committee were essentially given the leeway to loan out as much money as they desired, with little oversight. Second, anyone who applied for a loan outside of Washington, DC, would be subject to the approval of the board, instead of just the finance committee. This provision was supposed to limit the types of loans that the bank made, and to whom. Third, the finance committee had the power to decide the terms of the specific loans. This provision gave the finance committee carte blanche to determine how much money the bank, and therefore the depositors, would make from lending. The fourth guideline was, "No loans to be made for longer time than one year."[29] This guideline was designed to limit the amount of risk that the bank, and therefore the depositors, assumed.

The board's instructions gave the finance committee almost total control over the bank's loan making. And the board ceded control to Cooke. This independence was risky, if not dangerous, in his hands. He was given the reins to dictate the terms of the bank's lending policies, including which borrowers would be given priority, the amount that they could borrow, and, importantly, the interest rate on their loans. Ultimately, the board's new loan procedures freed Cooke to exercise almost complete command of the bank's finances.[30]

After Congress ratified the bank's charter amendment, the finance committee was eager to begin its foray into lending. Between June 8 and July 14, the bank loaned $174,158.75 to borrowers.[31] There was no information circulated in newspapers or periodicals about the new lending policies. Instead, all the advertisements from the bank continued to focus on depositors, encouraging them to open accounts and save money. By the fall of 1870, the finance committee opened the lending floodgates. It wasn't a trickle; it was a tidal wave.

🙜

UNDER COOKE'S INFLUENCE, the finance committee had begun to accept applications for loans from close affiliates of bank trustees. But neither Cooke nor the other finance committee members had created a formal application process. And without formality, there was lending chaos. Eaton, for example, readily accepted applications primarily for loans from white members of the Washington elite.

As Black depositors continued to pour millions of dollars into their accounts, hoping that their dreams of political and economic freedom would be fulfilled, the controlling members of the Freedman's Bank began to steadily ignore the depositors' needs. Despite the trustees' shift to focusing on lending, freed people hoped that their investments would aid their ascendance into a new era of liberty.

One man who decided to patronize the bank and helped bolster the bank's presence in his community was Robert Smalls. Smalls rose to national prominence for his gallant actions during the Civil War. On the evening of May 12, 1862, the twenty-three-year-old snuck aboard and commandeered a Confederate ship docked in Charleston Harbor. The Confederate soldiers responsible for manning the ship left it unattended for the night, leaving the ammunition, the firearms, and eight enslaved people on board. Deploying navigation skills he had honed as an enslaved boy, Smalls took control of the ship under the cover of night. Early the following morning, he steered it with the enslaved people onboard to a fleet of Union vessels stationed outside the harbor. His daring act secured him his freedom. He also garnered an official commendation from the Union army and a $1,500 award from the federal government for his wartime heroics.[32]

Smalls remained in South Carolina after the war's end, building on the notoriety he gained during his service in the war. On March 14, 1870, he walked along Bay Street, in Beaufort, South Carolina. As he strolled past the shops and homes that dotted the unpaved thoroughfare, he passed facades weathered by the mayhem inflicted by the war. He sauntered past fellow residents, both Black and white, perhaps contemplating how different Bay Street had looked a mere five years earlier, as the Civil War and legal bondage were coming to an end.

The remnants of slavery—and its violent end—lingered on Bay Street. Houses and shops once owned by ex-Confederates lined the gravel-filled road. Beaufort was a bustling port city in its heyday and was home to the nation's richest families during the first half of the nineteenth century. These slaveholding families built generational wealth through investing in South Carolina's major export: Carolina Gold rice. They tapped into national and international banking networks to finance their investments in rice cultivation. Beaufort's enslavers formed relationships with bankers as far away as New York and London from whom they requested lines of credit to buy enslaved people. They forced the hundreds of thousands of enslaved laborers to grow the rice that propelled the region's slaveholding capitalists to economic prominence.[33] Smalls surely remembered the ships docked in the Beaufort harbor. He most certainly recalled the enslaved laborers who, like himself, loaded rice onto vessels headed to New York, New Orleans, and Liverpool.

In the early decades of the nineteenth century, the port city's hustle and bustle reflected the wealth of white enslavers, slave traders, and merchants—people whose families had called Beaufort home for generations. But these people would not have been able to put their wealth on display without the rice and cotton cultivated, harvested, and prepared for transport by enslaved people. These white families poured capital into maintaining slavery as an institution, relying on enslaved labor to build their fortunes in the process. Smalls was owned by one of the families.

His enslaver, Henry McKee, owned not only a cotton plantation in Lady's Island, a five-mile journey down the Beaufort River, but also a stately home in Beaufort.[34] Smalls lived most of his childhood in McKee's Beaufort home, located at 511 Prince Street. McKee finished the residence in 1840, the year after Smalls was born. Smalls's mother, an enslaved woman named Lydia Polite, worked inside the McKee household as a domestic servant, and Smalls lived with her on Prince Street in a small cabin behind the home until he was twelve years old. In 1851, McKee instructed Smalls to leave Beaufort, and leave his mother, for Charleston, where he found work as a waiter at the Planter's Hotel, one of the most luxurious hotels in the city. From there he worked odd jobs at Charleston's harbor, where he perfected his familiarity with the harbor's geography. This knowledge would change his life less than a decade later.[35]

Memories of the sectional conflict and his remarkable quest for survival might have snuck into Smalls's thoughts as he walked to his intended destination. Maybe as he strolled from his home to Bay Street, he was thinking back on his election in 1868 to the South Carolina General Assembly, as a member of the state house of representatives from Beaufort.[36] Smalls was one of the first African American men to serve in the South Carolina General Assembly. Later he would be one of the first African American men elected to the U.S. House of Representatives.

Perhaps, on that day in March 1870, Smalls was contemplating one of the most significant purchases of his life, the house on Prince Street where his mother toiled for their enslaver, located about a half mile from his destination. In 1864, with the money that he earned from the U.S. government for capturing and delivering the Confederate ship to the Union, he bought the home in which he and his enslaved mother lived for between $600 and $650. The home's owners, a family called the De Trevilles, who purchased the home from McKee in 1851, abandoned it during the Union army's occupation of the South Carolina Low Country. This presented Smalls with an unprecedented opportunity. During a government auction of abandoned Confederate properties in January 1864, Smalls had the financial resources to purchase not only a home but the house in which he grew up, the home of his former enslaver.[37]

Yet one might wonder whether, as he fixed his eyes on the intended destination, an ecru building with a two-story portico that housed the Freedman's Bank Beaufort branch, Smalls was enthusiastic about taking this next step to solidify his economic status as a free man, a homeowner, and an important voice for African Americans in the Carolina Low Country. He marched up the small flight of stairs that led him to a simple lobby. Having lived through the unpredictability of slavery, Smalls must have felt a mix of anticipation and apprehension as he opened the door to enter the bank.

He likely met with the branch's white cashier, Nelson R. Scovel. The board of trustees approved Scovel's appointment as the Beaufort branch's cashier in the summer of 1868. Scovel was as ambitious as Smalls. Because there was no other financial institution in Beaufort, the branch was popular not only among the region's prominent Black population but among white businessmen and merchants as well.[38] Scovel was making a name for himself in Beaufort, as a representative of the bank and an advocate for the expansion of banking in the region.

It is likely that the two men knew each other. By the time Smalls encountered Scovel to open his account on that day in March 1870, he had already been spreading news of the Beaufort branch and Scovel's good work.[39] Smalls sat on a committee, an advisory board, that helped

ensure that bank administrators and the branch's cashier heard community feedback about the bank's work. The Beaufort branch was one of
the more successful in the network of Freedman's Bank offices. By early
1870, approximately two thousand Black families had purchased land in
the Sea Islands off the South Carolina and Georgia coast with money
that they saved in the Beaufort branch.[40] The freed people of Beaufort
took great pride in their economic accomplishments, and the office in
Beaufort was, for bank trustees such as Alvord, a shining example of the
bank's outstanding work. For Smalls, opening an account was the next
step in his support of the bank and its mission.

There is no information about how much Smalls deposited into his
account on that day in March 1870. Yet there is a record of his race,
listed as "Black," his residence, which was Beaufort, South Carolina,
and his occupation, a member of South Carolina's House of Representatives. As with the tens of thousands of other depositors, he hoped
that his investment in the bank would help him sustain his swift rise
from enslaved man to politician representing African Americans just
out of enslavement. At this point in his relationship with the bank, he
was unaware of the hundreds of thousands of dollars flowing out of the
bank to borrowers.

Little did men such as Smalls know that the bank's trustees were
invested in plots to use the depositors' money for their own potential gain. The millions of dollars that continued to be deposited into
regional bank branches were being sent by sometimes untrained cashiers
to the bank's central office. And the bank's finance committee became
committed to enriching themselves, at the expense of freed people.

⁓

BLACK DEPOSITORS SUCH AS Robert Smalls and borrowers such
as the Seneca Sandstone Company continued to patronize the bank,
each with their own justifications for engaging with the financial institution. Depositors were relying on the bank to help them reach their
financial and their political goals. Saving money to purchase land continued to be freed people's primary objective. Borrowers expressed a different intent. The Freedman's Bank, by late 1870, enticed businessmen

in and around Washington, DC, because of the finance committee's eagerness to relax the bank's recently amended lending policies.

Meanwhile, Alvord, as the bank's president, had abdicated some of his responsibilities to the bank, instead choosing to dedicate time to his Freedmen's Bureau work. In 1870, just as the bank was undergoing the transformation of its structure and mission, Alvord took time away from Washington to continue his travels around the southern states observing the bureau's work. He hoped that his conversations with leaders of Black communities throughout the South would spur people such as Smalls to open accounts. Alvord reveled in the freed people's economic successes. In a January 1870 correspondence to General O. O. Howard, Alvord stated that he appreciated freed people's hard work to realize their goal of purchasing land. They made deposits in the bank not just to demonstrate their deservedness of citizenship but also because they believed that purchasing land would help them be more secure in their free status.

During his travels to South Carolina, for example, he witnessed hundreds of Black men save enough money in Charleston and Beaufort to "enabl[e] them to make large purchases."[41] He was incredibly proud of the positive attention the bank was receiving in the press. "In 1865, the Freedman's Savings Bank of Washington, D.C. received less than $1000 a day, and during 1869, the daily deposits amounted to $14,000," a Charleston newspaper lauded in March 1870.[42] As of November 1870, the bank had expanded to thirty-three branches, with almost 44,300 depositors. The average deposit amounted to $284. Bank patrons had deposited over $12.6 million in the bank. With their savings, they were purchasing land, homes, agricultural equipment, and seed and, importantly, were paying laborers to work their land.[43]

Alvord's lofty message about freed people's success in using the bank to save money to buy property obscured his lack of engagement with the bank's everyday operations. In fact, he signed his correspondences with Howard "J.W. Alvord, General Superintendent of Education," not as the president of the Freedman's Savings and Trust Company. He had been taking time away from his duties as the bank's president, during a pivotal chapter for the bank, to travel in his position with the Freedmen's

Bureau. His myriad responsibilities, both as the general superintendent of education for the Freedmen's Bureau and the bank's president, meant that he was spreading himself too thin.

Despite his distractions, Alvord had made a series of lucrative financial decisions. Over the previous five years, he had been successful in shoring up his family's economic situation. He invested in D. L. Eaton & Company, which had been engaged steadily over the previous three years in providing building materials to Howard University. His investments had paid off. In 1860, when his family lived in Massachusetts, his assets were valued at $3,000. By 1870, after he moved his family to Washington, his assets were worth $31,000, an almost tenfold rise.[44] Alvord had been privileging his bureau responsibilities and prioritizing his own financial stability. He had not been dedicating his full attention to running the bank. He had allowed millions of dollars of freed people's money to flow into the finance committee's hands.

Alvord's travels in the South on behalf of the Freedmen's Bureau provided Cooke with the opportunity to fill the void. By 1869, he had been placing advertisements in newspapers announcing the bank's financial success. In past announcements, the bank president's name would have been included. But in a March 1869 ad in Washington's *National Intelligencer*, Cooke's name, in addition to those of William Huntington and Lewis Clephane, all members of the finance committee, took center stage. Alvord's absence allowed for Cooke to exert even more influence. It became a real problem for the trustees, and for the depositors, by the fall of 1870.[45]

In October 1870, as freed people's deposits cascaded out of the bank to various borrowers in Washington, the board demanded Alvord's full attention. They requested that he make the bank his priority. The board made a formal appeal, "requesting the President of the Bank J. W. Alvord Esq. to devote his whole time and energies to the Bank work."[46] Alvord had accepted the role two years earlier knowing what the responsibilities as bank president required. Though he was not trained in the intricacies of banking and finance, he did witness the work of his two predecessors. He observed the challenges that they faced. Perhaps that rationale explained the trustees' support for his candidacy in 1868. But the mere fact that the board made an official request to Alvord—two years after his appointment—illuminates the seriousness with which some of the trustees took his absence and lack of attention.

Either because of his truancy or his blind faith in the intentions of the Cooke-led finance committee, Alvord simply went along with the bank's change of priorities. The bank now had a new mission: to lend money to the friends, colleagues, and business partners of the bank's trustees, in particular, to associates of the finance committee. Without his official disapproval, the message that Alvord was communicating was one of acceptance, even acquiescence, to this new mission.

It is likely that a few of the less outspoken trustees were privately urging Alvord to establish his presence in Washington because they witnessed the outsize influence of the finance committee on the bank's affairs. By 1871, the bank's business was consolidated in the hands of Henry Cooke, William Huntington, and D. L. Eaton. They hijacked the bank's mission and by 1872 had transformed it into a lending power-house. Though Alvord, as president, had the official authority to dictate the bank's agenda, he demonstrated that he was not up to the task. He did not possess the gravitas necessary to properly steer the bank. Instead, by not exercising his authority as its president, he acceded to the finance committee's whims. Alvord yielded at one of the most important moments in the bank's history.

❧

THE DRAMATIC TRANSFORMATION in priorities created an increased sense of instability among the bank's trustees and administrators. The trustees did not have a clear sense of how much money the bank had been loaning out to borrowers. In fact, Eaton, as actuary, and General George Balloch, as treasurer, could not keep track of how much they were lending.

Though the bank made hundreds of loans between 1870 and 1874, the majority were made between 1870 and 1872. In this two-year period, a handful emerged as examples of the ways in which the board operated as a lender to well-connected white members of the Washington economic and political establishment. More specifically, the borrowers who received the highest number of loans and the most money in loans from the bank had personal connections with Cooke, Huntington, Eaton, or other members of the board of trustees. The loan terms did not conform to those outlined in the charter amendment, the borrowers asked for and received loan-repayment extensions, and sometimes the borrowers secured their loans with little or no collateral. Members of the board of trustees also received loans, subverting the charter amendment. In short, the finance committee, as well as cashiers at local branches, made risky loans that jeopardized the tens of millions of dollars that freed people had been depositing into their bank accounts. Though many of the loans failed to comport with Congress's guidelines, a handful would prove to be the bank's undoing.

J. V. W. VANDENBURG

The debtor that owed one of the largest amounts to the bank was a man named J. V. W. Vandenburg, a contractor with Washington's Board of Public Works. A congressman in the 1880s derided Vandenburg as a "pet of the District government—a sort of *protégé* and favorite contractor for the grand public improvements and put in execution by the board of public works."[47] Vandenburg relied on his relationship with D. L. Eaton to secure almost $150,000 in loans from the bank.

Vandenburg did most of his business with Eaton, which eliminated the hurdles that he might have faced if he dealt with another trustee—or another financial institution.[48] He would sometimes only have to wait "several days" before he "got his money" from the bank. For the loans that Vandenburg received, Eaton was supposed to have accepted only real estate as collateral. But, running afoul of the amendment, Eaton accepted "some Government bonds" from him, as well as "auditors [*sic*] certificates from the Board of Public Works for the District of Columbia."[49] Vandenburg used proof of work done for Washington's Board of Public Works to demonstrate that he was a creditworthy borrower. Even though, according to Vandenburg, the Board of Public Works had no money and was struggling to pay contractors and builders for work completed, he received certificates from a board of managers that directed the city's Board of Public Works to prove that he was being paid by the city for work completed.

Again, the network was small. Henry Cooke served as the head of the Board of Public Works. As governor of the District of Columbia, Cooke was an ex officio member, but as governor he was responsible for the city's construction projects. And that was not all. The person who approved Vandenburg's contracts was the Board of Public Works' vice president, Alexander R. Shepherd, a man who had carved out his own financial relationship with the bank and the trustees. On August 28, 1870, the bank's board of trustees accepted the bid of A. R. Shepherd and Brothers, a city contractor, to install heating in the new bank building. The company's principal was Alexander R. Shepherd. In a clear conflict of interest, the board had approved a series of loans amounting to at least $44,500 for Shepherd between May 1870 and September 1871.[50] Ultimately, Vandenburg's financial dealings exemplified the cozy relationships forged among the bank's trustees, members of the Washington city government, and businessmen in Washington, DC.

In addition to his individual borrowing, Vandenburg used his investments in his own business to borrow even more money from the bank. He served as the treasurer of the Abbott Paving Company, an enterprise that contracted with the Board of Public Works to lay concrete pavement in Washington.[51] Through Vandenburg, the Abbott Paving Company received five loan disbursements between September 1872 and December 1872. In this four-month period, the company, with him as the treasurer, received $97,216 from the bank.[52] In total, he received $122,000 from the bank, of which only $68,000 was recorded by the finance committee in the official record.[53]

His professional relationship with Eaton was so lucrative that Vandenburg offered him a "half interest in a $100,000 contract for sewer-pipe." Eaton did not put in any money, "incurred no risk or responsibility, and had no trouble about it except to sign receipts for his share of the profits." The conflict of interest did not deter Eaton from accepting Vandenburg's largesse. Indeed, Vandenburg provided him with this financial windfall as "a gratuity," a kickback for helping him procure almost $150,000 in low-cost (almost no-cost) loans from the bank.[54]

HOWARD UNIVERSITY AND GENERAL HOWARD

One of the relationships that proved to be the most controversial for the bank's lending portfolio was the one between John Alvord and General O. O. Howard. In early 1870, for example, Alvord and Howard corresponded frequently in their positions with the Freedmen's Bureau. Alvord was traveling throughout the South, observing the work of bureau agents helping freed people secure economic and property rights. Howard was the head of the Freedmen's Bureau, founder of Howard University, and supporter of the Freedman's Bank and of Alvord as the bureau's superintendent of education and the bank president. The reciprocity between the two men extended to the relationship between the bank and the bureau. A May 18, 1871, comment in a Louisiana newspaper summed up the relationship perfectly: "Among the great advantages springing from the establishment of the Freedmen's Bureau, none eclipses the establishment of the Freedmen's Savings Bank."[55]

It comes as no surprise, therefore, that Howard appealed to Alvord and the bank for financial support in helping him build what would become Howard University. For this reason, one of the more prominent series of loans went to Howard University, negotiated through General O. O. Howard and the university's treasurer, George Balloch.

Between December 31, 1870, and January 28, 1871, Howard University received the first loan disbursement of $8,000.[56] The second loan to the university, for $3,500 and finalized in June 1871, was negotiated by Balloch, who was doing double duty as Howard University's treasurer, one of its trustees, *and* a bank trustee and finance committee member.[57] These first two loans did not attract scrutiny. Instead, it was a third set of two loans that immediately sent up red flags.

During the summer of 1871, General Howard applied for a loan from the bank for $40,000 at an 8 percent interest rate. The finance committee considered the application, and the proposed terms, and chose to offer him a 10 percent interest rate. His application for this loan had been with the finance committee for several months, as they determined whether the university—and Howard—would receive the bank's largesse. In some ways, the committee's additional consideration was surprising. After all, in June 1871, the finance committee approved lending $111,538.69 and, in July 1871, approved $75,118 in loans to borrowers.[58] And General Howard and Balloch had more than enough in collateral to secure the loan. By 1871, the land on which Howard University would reside was valued at approximately $1 million.[59] Despite the committee's increased scrutiny, by September 1871, the finance committee decided to approve, at an unspecified interest rate, the $40,000 loan, which Howard received on October 11, 1871.[60]

The second loan would prove to be even more controversial. Interestingly, the finance committee approved extending the terms of the $40,000 Howard University loan a year later, in September 1872. In the fall of 1872, General O. O. Howard negotiated another loan for the university, for a larger amount. On October 22, 1872, Howard University received a loan from the bank in the amount of $75,000.[61]

The loans, and Howard's affiliation with the bank, were quickly mired in controversy, both within the board and externally with Democratic members of Congress. Howard officially joined the board of trustees on March 10, 1870, two months before the charter amendment went into effect, but then resigned a month later. The trustees said that he had not paid back a personal loan that he received from the bank when he was nominated and elected to the bank's board. Then the board revoked his election.[62] According to a letter from George Whipple to Alvord, the rationale was that Howard's election to the board set a bad precedent, because the trustees "did not like to have it seen that they had ever voted upon a candidate while in one of the funds."[63] Considering the borrowing behavior of other trustees, this logic was unexpected. The trustees' hesitancy with having General Howard on the board likely reflected a growing consternation among moderate Republicans and Democrats in Congress with the Freedmen's Bureau's work and Howard's management of the agency.

While on the surface, this seems to have been a valid use of the bank's funds—to loan money to an educational institution founded with the mission of educating the nation's Black Americans—the financial reality of the loan was more complex. Howard used the money from the loan to help build the university and medical school. He contracted with Seneca Sandstone Company to supply the building materials and with D. L. Eaton to furnish other construction materials and services, an unsurprising connection with the business network in Washington.

❦

COOKE, EATON, AND the finance committee's approval of loans to businessmen and institutions such as J. V. W. Vandenburg, General Howard, and Howard University was just the tip of the lending iceberg. Potential borrowers flooded the bank with applications, drawing on their connections to members of the finance committee, to receive loans from the Freedman's Bank in both very small and very large quantities. The largest single loan, for $175,000, went to E. H. Nichols and R. M. Pomeroy, on behalf of the Union Pacific Railway. Nichols worked as the treasurer of Union Pacific and Pomeroy served as an investor in the railroad venture.[64] The finance committee made the loan, which they issued in August 1871, for a one-year term, at 10 percent interest, "paid semiannually." Trustee Edgar Ketchum was responsible for ensuring that the "papers, vouchers, securities" that Nichols and Pomeroy submitted were sufficient.[65] Moreover, Nichols and Pomeroy did business with Jay Cooke & Company, which suggests that Cooke and Huntington negotiated the loan's terms on their behalf. The connections between the trustees and borrowers were clear. In fact, the finance committee's lending practices suggest that borrowers had a better chance of receiving a loan from the bank if they had a business relationship with members of the board of trustees. But this unofficial policy applied only to white borrowers.

Even the Young Men's Christian Association (YMCA), which operated out of a building in Washington, took out loans for $33,000, approved by Eaton.[66] This was one of the more unsavory transactions that Eaton negotiated. The YMCA was a segregated organization in the

1870s, even though the first Black YMCA was established in Washington in 1853. So, as the YMCA accepted a loan from the bank, raised from the deposits of African American people, the organization was actively sustaining a racially segregated institution.[67]

The finance committee did not have a standard policy regarding how they would handle loan repayment or default. They would often extend the life of loans or change the interest rate of certain loans. When borrowers defaulted on their financial obligation to repay, the committee was slow to secure and sell the borrowers' collateral. At times, the collateral was worthless. One example was a loan that Eaton made to one F. H. Gassaway in March 1872 for $3,300. At the time of the loan, Gassaway worked for Huntington and Cooke as a clerk of First National Bank. He put up fifty shares of Metropolis Paving Company stock and "other securities" as collateral.[68] By the time that the finance committee called in Gassaway's loan in March 1873, the sale of the "other securities" brought the loan balance down to $1,100–$1,200. By the summer of 1874, Gassaway was in default and the remaining collateral, the Metropolis Paving Company shares, "had no market-value" and the bank could not recoup what remained of Gassaway's loan.[69]

Not only did the finance committee members prioritize lending to people in their personal and professional networks, but Eaton and Huntington were approving loans to borrowers using stocks and bonds as collateral, not real estate. Per Congress's approval of the bank's restructuring, loans made by the bank had to be secured by real estate, not stocks or bonds. The finance committee quickly ignored this regulation. What's more, Eaton had begun to make loans without consulting the committee.[70] Perhaps the committee members believed that because they had the final say in evaluating the individual borrowers themselves, based on their own personal and professional relationships with prospective borrowers, they did not need to abide by Congress's stipulations for how borrowers would show their creditworthiness. Perhaps they believed that they could trust Eaton's vetting.

The finance committee's speed with lending suggests that protecting freed people's money came second to their interest in using African Americans' deposits for their own ventures. Not only did Cooke,

Eaton, and Huntington, in collusion with the rest of the finance committee, disregard the lending rules for borrowers, but they also ignored an important stipulation in the charter amendment. It was an issue that a handful of senators introduced during the congressional debates about the bank's charter amendment in 1869—the possibility that bank trustees would use the bank's deposits for themselves. The fears of Senator Cameron of Pennsylvania were realized.

In addition to ignoring Congress's lending guidelines, the number of trustees who received loans between 1870 and 1872 was staggering. In direct contravention of section 12 of the charter, at least six of the trustees took out loans. Eaton, Cooke, Huntington, Balloch, George Stickney (Eaton's nephew and the bank's assistant actuary), and W. P. Drew were all on record as having borrowed money from the bank.[71] Some offered collateral in the form of bonds, not real estate. Others, Huntington for example, received a $5,000 loan on May 15, 1871, with no collateral. Though he paid it back less than a month later, on June 9, the loan and the loan terms were clearly illegal.[72]

Of all the loans that the finance committee made, white borrowers accounted for 80 percent of the loan volume, while they were only 8 percent of the account holders.[73] Of the bank's loan volume, almost 30 percent went to people involved in real estate while approximately 24 percent went to people who owned or managed businesses.[74] The borrowers and bank trustees were a tight network of people who comprised politicians, public servants, businessmen, and even Freedman's Bank employees themselves.

Most of the bank's lending went to borrowers in Washington, DC. This informal policy meant that the depositors, the vast majority of whom did not bank at the Washington branch, did not have access to the bank as borrowers. While the finance committee expanded the lending of millions of dollars to white men with connections to the trustees, including the trustees themselves, the Black people who were supplying the capital that the bank loaned to white borrowers could not rely on the bank for lines of credit.

Of the small number who did, they were Black churches and a handful of Black organizations. In November 1870, for example, the cashier of the Norfolk branch appealed to the board to approve a loan for $3,000 for "a colored church in Norfolk."[75] Eaton subsequently approved the loan. The handful of Black churches in Washington that received bank loans benefited from their proximity to the central office and to the bank's personnel. The pastors and bank stewards used their social capital to encourage Wilson, the Washington cashier, to advocate on their behalf with Eaton. The Fifth Street Baptist Church and the Fifteenth Street Presbyterian Church each borrowed $10,000. The Nineteenth Street Baptist Church received a loan of $4,500.[76] At least two Black churches outside of Washington were lucky enough to tap into their local branches for loans. The Zion Baptist Church in Portsmouth, Virginia, received $1,300 from the Norfolk branch and the Dallas Street Church in Baltimore borrowed $2,500 from the Baltimore branch.[77] Though these loans suggest that local bank cashiers were trying to expand access to the bank's resources, it is clear that Black applicants who represented these organizations were heavily scrutinized by bank administrators, in a way that white applicants simply were not.[78] One Black trustee, Dr. Charles Purvis, revealed that the finance committee was responsible for accepting applications, evaluating, and approving the loans before news of the loan making went to the entire board. Instead, with Black applicants, the applications went directly to the entire board first. "Loans upon colored churches, and those little properties across the river here, and many applications for loans from the South," Purvis disclosed, "were always submitted to the board of trustees."[79]

One of the only Black institutions that received a loan was the Douglass Institute in Baltimore. Approved in June 1872, the $10,000 loan went to a Black political and educational organization founded in the city where Frederick Douglass spent his teenage years, before his escape to freedom.[80] Perhaps Douglass himself served as an intermediary between the Black representatives of the institute and Eaton or Huntington. As an early supporter of the bank, and of the messages that the bank continued to advertise about Black wealth-building and thrift, Douglass's name held sway among Republicans in Washington, perhaps even with certain trustees. It is possible that the institute received the loan because of the regard that certain members of the Freedman's Bank board, Alvord for example, had for Douglass.

By this time, Douglass had transitioned fully to Washington, DC. He had taken up his next challenge, as the publisher of the *New National Era*, a newspaper for Black people in the nation's capital. He had been encouraged by friends and acquaintances that the position would bolster his visibility on issues that were important to him.[81] Chief among them were voting rights for Black men and the protection of Black people's civil rights by the federal government. In 1870, when he accepted the position, Douglass was commuting between his home in Rochester, New York, and Washington, DC. But an untimely fire at his home in Rochester extinguished his plan to live in two places. His full-time move to Washington inaugurated a new phase of his foray into political life. Douglass, as the editor, and his sons, as the publishers, invested in the newspaper, making it the premier venue for the region's African American reading population.

Douglass consistently reported on the Freedman's Bank business in the *New National Era*. From giving monthly financial snapshots of how much the bank had been accepting in deposits to publishing the bank's aphorisms about saving, Douglass became one of the bank's most outspoken advocates. The newspaper's first issue, published in January 1870, detailed the "remarkable statistics" of the Freedman's Bank. Between 1870 and 1874, the *New National Era* ran at least two articles about the bank in every issue.[82]

Douglass's support of the bank extended beyond the advertisements and updates that his newspaper ran. First, he became a depositor. He opened an account on January 3, 1871, placing $1,500 in the Washington branch.[83] And on January 12, George Balloch nominated him as a bank trustee. By early March 1871, the trustees approved his nomination with little fanfare. Douglass begrudgingly accepted the appointment, arguing that he "had reluctantly consented" to "become one of its trustees."[84] This decision brought him into an even more intimate relationship with the trustees and the institution.[85]

As Douglass became more involved with the bank, as a supporter, depositor, and reluctant trustee, he published a story that bank administrators surely hoped would send an important signal to depositors and borrowers alike. One of the central stories in the December 14, 1871, issue of the *New National Era* was of the bank's newly finished central office on Pennsylvania Avenue.

·ᘳᘰᘮ·

AS MONEY BEGAN to surge out of the bank into the hands of white borrowers in Washington, by the summer of 1870, the board came to the realization that they did not have enough money to renovate the prominent new building on Pennsylvania Avenue that they had purchased the previous year. Initially, the board did not want to spend more than $60,000. They amended the budget in July 1870 to a hefty $100,000.[86] In the end, through drawing from the bank's deposits instead of using money in the "available fund" for the building's construction—another illegal move—the bank's new building cost a shocking $313,218.26, which included the cost of the prime location, the labor for renovations, and the materials.[87] The trustees argued that they wanted the new central office to convey the wealth generated by freed people. The building certainly attracted Black people's attention.

On December 7, 1871, the bank made its official transition from 507 Seventh Street to its gleaming new home, a "magnificent banking palace" at 1507 Pennsylvania Avenue.[88] The five-story building overlooked the White House and the Department of the Treasury. One observer wrote, "There are few banking houses in America equal to it," a reference perhaps to not only the scale of the building and the stunning architecture but also the money that freed people put into the bank, giving it the veneer of success.[89]

The building's first floor was dedicated to the bank's depositor business. The "cashier's room," as it was labeled, welcomed visitors who entered the building to open accounts or make deposits. With a "beautiful solid marble counter, paneled and moulded . . . surmounted by black walnut desks, guarded by railings of the same material," the new building represented the economic achievements of the tens of thousands of freed people who put their money and their trust in the

*Freedman's Savings Bank Building, Pennsylvania Avenue and
Madison Place NW, Washington, DC, ca. 1890*

bank. It also came furnished with a vault, "protected by a massive metal door . . . secured by a ponderous combination lock." The vault contained "an immense safe, constructed to resist fire and burglars."[90] In sum, the bank's newest building was spectacular.

And it should have been. With the steady increase in the trustees' expectations for what the central office could (and should) be, the trustees had augmented its operating budget dramatically. The bank stood out for its opulence. Despite the sumptuous materials that the architect and builders used, marble and black walnut, some believed that the bank was a gaudy representation of freed people's economic promise. Frederick Douglass was one of them.

Douglass remarked upon seeing the building for the first time: "With the usual effect of sudden wealth," he wrote, "the managers felt like making a little display of their prosperity."[91] One of the costliest and most "splendid" buildings in the city, the central office was fashioned with "all the modern improvements."[92] "The magnificent dimensions of the building," according to Douglass, "bore testimony to its flourishing condition. . . . I felt like the Queen of Sheba when she saw the riches of Solomon."[93] Yet, what he observed was supposed to represent a shining beacon of economic hope for the millions of Black people in the United States. The building was supposed to be a physical manifestation of freed people's hard work and dedication. By 1872, the bank boasted over seventy thousand accounts opened, with freed people depositing a total of $31.6 million between 1865 and 1872.[94]

By early 1872, Douglass had no idea that the bank was hurtling toward insolvency. But what lay ahead—for the depositors, the trustees, the cashiers, and him—would upend their perspective on the Freedman's Bank and the banking industry writ large.

6313

No.   Record for Fred'k Douglass, Senior

Date of Application.   January 3, 1871

Where born,   Talbot County, Maryland

Where brought up,

Residence,   Rochester, New York

Age,

Complexion,

Occupation,

Works for

Wife,

Children,

Father,

Mother,

Brothers,

Sisters.

Freedman's Bank depositor record of Frederick Douglass, Washington, DC, branch

PART THREE

Collapse

CHAPTER SIX

A Bank Examination
and a Bank Failure, 1871–73

The GREAT NATIONAL SAVINGS INSTITUTION,
established by the authority of the United States Government,
for the benefit of the Freedmen, knows no distinction of race
or color, and offers its great advantages to all classes alike.

—*NEW NATIONAL ERA*, JULY 3, 1873[1]

Freedman's Bank total deposits, as of March 1872:
$31,260,499.97 ($804 million today)

ON JANUARY 9, 1872, FOUR MEMBERS OF THE FINANCE committee met at Henry Cooke's office at First National Bank in Washington, DC, located across the street from the Department of the Treasury and a block away from the Freedman's Bank's new central office. Cooke, Huntington, Alvord, and LeRoy Tuttle, a bank trustee who also served as the assistant treasurer of the United States, attended. As the four men made their way through the meeting's agenda, which included the $23,715 in loans that they approved, Alvord perhaps wondered why Cooke had called this meeting in his office.[2] The finance committee had held their previous meeting at the bank's new building. After spending over a quarter of a million dollars on the property and renovations, the trustees designed the luxurious central office for these types of gatherings. It is unclear whether Alvord understood that this finance committee meeting would proceed unlike the previous ones.

Though the four men discussed the loans that the bank made for the month, they also needed to deal with an issue involving Cooke, Huntington, Jay Cooke & Company, and Cooke's newest investment opportunity: the Northern Pacific Railroad (NPRR). The men were likely scrutinizing, in the privacy of Cooke's bank, an official notice in the pipeline from the board. The next day, on January 10, the bank's attorney, William J. J. Stewart, a fellow trustee, put the finance committee, specifically Cooke and Huntington, on notice. Stewart demanded that the finance committee compel Jay Cooke & Company, and Henry Cooke by proxy, to pay back the money that the investment bank had borrowed from the Freedman's Bank. Stewart required that Jay Cooke & Company repay the loan by February 8, 1872.[3] The meeting on January 9 and the subsequent letter on January 10 would bring the bank's operations to an inflection point—and ultimately erode Alvord's tenure as the Freedman's Savings and Trust Company's president.

The loan that the finance committee would discuss in January

1872 illuminated broader problems between the Freedman's Bank and Jay Cooke & Company. These problems had started, in earnest, a year earlier. On February 7, 1871, Henry Cooke approached members of the finance committee with a proposition. He wanted to borrow $50,000, through Jay Cooke & Company, using NPRR bonds as collateral.[4] But this move was only one step toward his larger goal. He wanted the bank to purchase NPRR bonds, using Jay Cooke & Company as an agent. Despite Congress's requirement that all loans be secured by real estate collateral, not bonds or company stock, the finance committee and some of the trustees decided to follow Cooke's lead.

Cooke used his well-honed powers of persuasion to lobby trustees to support his plan. Exploiting relationships and leveraging social capital to finalize business deals was a common strategy for him. He regularly negotiated deals among himself, his business partners in Washington, DC, and investors looking to profit from Henry and Jay Cooke's newest ventures.[5] The brothers and their team had a visible, and alluring, track record. They had been wildly successful during the Civil War at raising money for the Union in its most pressing time of need. Together, the brothers and their band of bond agents raised approximately $1.6 billion for the Union.[6] Henry and Jay Cooke cultivated a powerful set of friends and allies in the process.

Therefore, it surely came as no surprise to the trustees when Cooke introduced the idea of the Freedman's Bank buying Jay Cooke & Company's NPRR bonds. Henry Cooke had personal motivations for proposing that the bank invest in this new and exciting project. He, his brother, and their banking partners would profit from the transactions because the NPRR project was Jay Cooke & Company's newest undertaking. Having witnessed the construction of the Union Pacific and Central Pacific Railroads, which began in 1862 and connected the Missouri River to the California coast, investors in the late 1860s began to see railroads as a novel financial opportunity. They wanted to expand this government-sponsored technological and commercial enterprise by connecting more regions of the United States by rail.[7] Congress issued a charter for the Northern Pacific Railway Company to begin construction in 1864. The plan for the NPRR was straightforward, to unite the

Great Lakes and the northern Pacific coast by rail. But raising capital was difficult and slow going. By 1869, managers of the NPRR were in dire straits. They needed more money. For this reason, they pursued Jay Cooke and his partners. Seeing the Cooke brothers' financial success in the early 1860s, they wanted Jay Cooke & Company to jump into the railroad fray, to help them raise capital for this potentially lucrative project. Jay Cooke decided to use the capital that he and his brother accumulated with their company to invest in the new railroad project. In December 1869, Jay agreed that the company would become the project's bond agent, with Henry taking a prominent role in securing investors and bond purchasers.[8] Together, the two agreed to sell $100 million in NPRR bonds. In the process, Jay Cooke & Company secured 60 percent of the company's stock. With this financial move, the Cooke brothers were demonstrating their bona fides as Gilded Age capitalists.[9]

In some ways, Henry Cooke's proposal to the finance committee was not unprecedented. The finance committee had already started to accept railroad bonds as collateral for loans (flouting the parameters outlined by Congress). Financiers, even the federal government, invested heavily in the promise of transcontinental travel through the construction of the transcontinental railroad network. Though Cooke had been buying government-backed railroad bonds as a part of the bank's investment in government securities, he had also been buying railroad bonds not backed by the federal government—including bonds of companies that included him and his brother as investors.

With the NPRR venture, the Cooke brothers deployed the same tactics that they used during the Civil War to sell government bonds: raising capital from investors in Europe and appealing to the American people's sense of patriotism to help fund the railroad construction effort.[10] Therefore, when Henry Cooke pushed his proposal to the Freedman's Bank trustees of holding $50,000 worth of bonds in February 1871, he was not hiding the fact that he would be profiting from the exchange. The trustees understood that he would benefit financially from the sale.

A month later, in March 1871, Cooke achieved short-term success. On March 9, the finance committee instructed Eaton to "affect [sic] the sale" of NPRR bonds "as quickly as possible."[11] Cooke surely felt a sense of relief, as the finance committee's full approval was a major step in his efforts to raise money for Jay Cooke & Company's railroad investment.

But when Cooke looked to the full board to finalize the transaction, his plan did not go as he had hoped. The first person to question his enthusiasm about the bank's investment in his railroad bonds was Edgar Ketchum. Ketchum had been serving as the bank's secretary and, since the bank began its foray into legal loan making, had taken on the responsibility of questioning the bank's investment portfolio. In effect, he approached the finance committee's suggestions with a dubiousness that reflected his increasing dislike for men such as Cooke. Around the time of this potential transaction, Ketchum was one of the trustees who had begun to scrutinize the finance committee's dealings with Jay Cooke & Company.

Ketchum was a well-respected member of the bank's board. He had a reputation as a stalwart public servant and lawyer who brought a reasoned approach to the unpredictable worlds of politics and finance. In a 1902 remembrance, writer Milo T. Bogard celebrated Ketchum, noting, "If one had been asked to indicate the ideal public official of that period, the man who par excellence commanded the regard of old and young, whose name was a synonym of integrity, for conscientious fidelity to every obligation, and the complete performance of duty without sensational accessories, Edgar Ketchum would have inevitably come to mind."[12] Ketchum served under Lincoln as the collector of internal revenue, after Congress passed the Revenue Act of 1862, which mandated the collection of income taxes to help fund the Union's war effort.[13]

Ketchum had strong ties not only to the bank but to the idea of banking for freed people. His son, Lieutenant A. P. Ketchum, served as the treasurer of the South Carolina Freedman's Savings Bank, the military bank in South Carolina founded in August 1864 for members of the U.S. Colored Troops. For these reasons, Ketchum was primed to interrogate Cooke's proposal—and to uncover Cooke's reasoning behind asking for the bank's potential investment.

Shortly after the finance committee approved the transaction with Cooke, Ketchum, along with fellow trustee William J. J. Stewart, made

official an inquiry into the finance committee's loan making. Specifically, Ketchum and Stewart expressed skepticism that Cooke's proposal
would be the best investment for the freed people's deposits. When the
finance committee made its report, including Cooke's proposition, in
the April 1871 meeting, Ketchum was ready for a fight. He made a series
of motions, meant to introduce doubt about Cooke's financial acuity
among the trustees, with the goal of weakening Cooke's influence.

First, he started with Cooke's other investments. Ketchum suggested that the company not loan to any borrower that offered "Mining
and Manufacturing stocks or bonds" as collateral.[14] Ketchum's rec-
ommendation to restrict taking these stocks or bonds as security was
a direct attack on Cooke and Huntington, who owned the Maryland
Freestone Mining and Manufacturing Company and the Seneca Sandstone Company. Ketchum was communicating to them that he did not
believe that their companies' stock was a worthy form of collateral for
bank loans. Even further, he requested that loans using such collateral
be "called in as soon as it may be."[15]

Ketchum's assault continued—and he maintained his focus on
Cooke. Ketchum doubted the viability of the finance committee's
acceptance of $50,000 in NPRR bonds as security for Cooke's loan. He
argued that the "road is but begun and is of vast extent in line and operation and may not be able for years to pay any interest out of its earnings."[16] According to Ketchum's logic, if the trustees were required to be
proper financial stewards of depositors' money by making prudent decisions about investments, then NPRR bonds were not the best venture
to pursue. The railroad was years from being operational, which meant
that the bank's investment would take years to pay meaningful dividends. The trustees could not, in good faith, make such an investment
with any more of freed people's money. Ketchum did not believe that
the trustees could entrust Cooke with any more of the bank's deposits.
He was too big of a financial risk.

Yet, by 1871, it was clear to Ketchum and the other trustees that
Henry Cooke was not afraid of risk. Through Jay Cooke & Company,
he had been the beneficiary of not only the Freedman's Bank's business
but the broader market for both government-sponsored and privately

sponsored sales of railroad bonds. Railroad construction was a promising, albeit a speculative, venture. Cooke was looking to intertwine the Freedman's Bank business even more tightly with his own, especially considering the millions of dollars that freed people were depositing into their accounts. For example, whenever the finance committee approved selling government bonds to fulfill the bank's financial needs, be it to ensure that individual branches had enough cash on hand to satisfy depositors' withdrawal needs or to pay the increasing cost of operating the bank and its branches, Jay Cooke & Company would facilitate the sale—and take a percentage of the entire transaction. Therefore, Cooke himself, and his brother's bank, reaped the financial benefits of acting as the bank's bond agent. For Cooke, his engagement with the bank was merely an extension of the work that he and his brother had done for the federal government during the Civil War. But instead of the customer being the federal government, the customer was the Freedman's Bank and, by extension, freed people.[17] The reality that he was placing large-scale financial bets, gambling with African Americans' money, was perhaps not important for him. Indeed, as one historian has argued, "Lacking both integrity and financial acumen . . . Henry Cooke was a born public relations man, and not a very honest one at that."[18]

Despite Ketchum's criticism, Cooke had valuable allies, who listened as he defended his position. Their support, however, required Cooke to submit a "special report," which suggests that not only was Cooke ready to employ his lobbying skills, but he wanted to fully convince the board of his trustworthiness as an investor. First, he acknowledged that he supported Ketchum's proposal to restrict the collateral that borrowers offered to secure their loans. But he argued that his case was "exceptional," and then proceeded to roll out a robust defense of the bank accepting Maryland Freestone Mining and Manufacturing Company bonds and NPRR bonds as collateral.

He addressed the mining company first. He maintained that it was a "well known and solvent company" whose "stocks and bonds are both well-known and have ready sale in this market."[19] He did not stop there. Cooke also invoked a group of people he rarely discussed: African Americans. In a move that he likely deployed to connect his financial rapacity to the bank's mission, he proclaimed, "It employs constantly about three hundred colored men in its works and in this city: and it is, in these respects an institution kindred with the bank: their interests are mutual."[20] He hoped that by associating the mining company with the livelihood of Black workers in Washington, the trustees would see that the bank's investment in the company complemented the bank's fundamental mission of supporting freed people. To drive home his point, he emphasized, "Those who from week to week and month to month watch over and strive to direct the best use of the freedmen's money in the bank, are those who also afford them this field of valuable and profitable labor."[21] According to Cooke's logic, the bank's investment in the mining company meant investing in freed people's economic futures. For him, funding this venture meant supporting the very people the bank was founded to help.

For the NPRR bonds, Cooke celebrated that as of February 1871, the bonds were performing better in the marketplace, "more than on the best investment in [government] bonds," according to him.[22] He also acknowledged the main question that the committee might have been asking. Was the investment safe? Cooke posed the question but equivocated in answering it. Instead, he confirmed that the trustees could rest easy knowing that they could "redeem [the bonds] on demand anytime within one year from date of purchase at same rates we gave for them." In addition, to Ketchum's claim that any dividend they would receive from the bonds would be years off, Cooke offered a salve. The railroad had "already six hundred miles of road in operation" and "nearly three hundred miles of track have been laid." And the government had been supporting the project by providing the company with millions of acres of land on which to build the railroad's infrastructure. In fact, he revealed, "the Company is endowed by [the] government with a grant of land amounting to over 50 millions of acres," and the government had purchased over $150 million of land in the process.[23] Cooke's goal was to convince the trustees, Ketchum and Stewart most of all, that he could be trusted with freed people's money.

In the end, Cooke had to offer assurances for the transaction to be completed. On May 30, 1871, the finance committee agreed to the transaction only *if* Jay Cooke & Company offered a guarantee. To protect the bank's investment, Cooke had to agree that if the finance committee required that he pay the $50,000, he would have to do so immediately.[24] Cooke accepted the terms in June 1871.

With the trustees signed off, and the transaction finalized, Cooke had officially exchanged NPRR bonds for Freedman's Bank cash. What the trustees did not know was that he had exaggerated the positive financial aspects of the bank's investment. Neither Henry nor Jay Cooke had succeeded in attaining the government's full financial support for their railroad project. Though the federal government had purchased the land for the railroad project, the brothers had not secured the government's investment in the railroad bonds. In addition, their fundraising efforts lagged. They had not been raising the capital necessary to ensure that the NPRR could sustain its growth. With the board's execution of this loan, using NPRR bonds as collateral, Cooke tied the bank even more closely with Jay Cooke & Company. Despite the shakiness of the bonds' value, he won this round against Ketchum. But his luck would soon run out.[25]

Ketchum changed tactics. He decided that Cooke's machinations, especially the cozy relationship that he cultivated between the finance committee and Jay Cooke & Company, and the bank's investment in NPRR bonds reflected a broader problem within the bank. The board had been ignoring the clear conflicts of interest present in so many of the transactions that they had completed since the charter amendment's approval in May 1870. Therefore, Ketchum believed that his charge was clear: to act as a backstop, to prevent the less risk-averse trustees from gambling with the freed people's deposits. His next step was an important one. He proposed a rule that would govern those who worked for the bank. He recommended "that no loans ought to be made to individuals or to a corporation through any trustee of this bank, having any pecuniary interest in such loan."[26] The rationale behind Ketchum's intervention became clear in the ensuing months.[27]

The NPRR project was struggling. By late 1870, the Cooke brothers had been having a hard time raising capital to fund the railroad.[28] This was the reason why Henry Cooke turned to freed people's deposits in the Freedman's Bank, to help sustain their investment in the railroad project. So, when Cooke received the loan from the bank in the spring of 1871, this infusion of capital was less of an investment and more of a bailout.

Ketchum's continued interrogation of Cooke's business approach in 1871 resonated among the trustees; on January 10, 1872, the board of trustees communicated to Cooke that they wanted him to return the money that Jay Cooke & Company had borrowed.[29] The bank was calling in its loan—and calling Cooke's bluff. Cooke had until February 8 to finalize the transaction. William J. J. Stewart reiterated this call at the next day's board of trustees meeting.[30] Led by Stewart, the trustees urged Cooke to "return said bonds taking the cash therefore in accordance with the terms of said guarantee."[31] Staking out a return in the market for government bonds, which were having a higher-than-usual rate of return, Ketchum and Stewart once again focused on Cooke.

The following day, on January 11, 1872, the board reinforced their mandate to Cooke. He needed to pay back his loan. It is unclear whether Ketchum and Stewart believed in the financial arguments they were making about the market for railroad bonds. These arguments ultimately did not matter. What mattered, instead, was that the two men were making an example of Cooke. They did not want the other trustees, nor other bank administrators and cashiers, to think that they could raid the bank without consequences. Cooke had spent the past five years expanding his financial influence inside the bank and in Washington, DC. The series of events that led to this moment in early 1872 would be a turning point for Cooke's relationship with the Freedman's Bank. In turn, Ketchum and Stewart hoped that other trustees were paying attention.[32]

Over the next month, the board, specifically members of the finance committee, forced Cooke to decide. By early February, they outlined two options as a last resort. The first option was for him to "take back the bonds" and "pay cash as per guarantee." This was the outcome that Ketchum and Stewart desired. The second option was for the bank to let Cooke "renew the guarantee," meaning, renegotiate the loan terms. In opposition to the rest of the board, the finance committee wanted

Cooke to extend the life of the loan, to be offered and to have him accept an amended agreement. "The committee would recommend in view of the fact of the increasing demand for the bonds + the desirableness to this Co. of the investment," committee members wrote, "that the Board reconsider the vote instructing the Committee to cash the bond." They argued that their logic was guided by financial principles, that bonds were offering 2.5 percent better returns than cash. The railroad bonds, they asserted, were "the next best bond in the market."[33] The finance committee wanted to extend Cooke a lifeline.

Their efforts to rescue him ultimately failed. He needed to uphold his guarantee to pay his loan "on demand." The facade started to crumble. Huntington was the first casualty. On February 6, when the finance committee met at the Freedman's Bank offices to discuss Cooke's final options, perhaps forecasting an inevitable skirmish between himself and the trustees over the NPRR bonds and the bank's relationship with Jay Cooke & Company, Huntington resigned.[34] He officially stepped down from his position with the Freedman's Bank, ending a tenure in which he had facilitated millions of dollars in loans flowing into the hands of his friends and colleagues. Eaton did not transcribe Huntington's rationale for vacating his place on the board of trustees, but the corruption that infiltrated the connection among the Freedman's Bank, Jay Cooke & Company's loan, and the NPRR bonds was clear. Perhaps Huntington recognized that he would not come out of this debacle unscathed. Or maybe he decided to end his affiliation with the bank to preserve a sense of dignity. In the end, Huntington departed first, but he was not the last.

Cooke resigned two days later, on February 8. The board thanked him for his "valuable services" to the Freedman's Bank, and this farewell ended what by this point had become a five-year raid on freed people's deposits.[35] It is unclear whether Cooke resigned in protest of the board's increasing scrutiny of his financial dealings, or if he stepped down to prevent the board from taking a deeper dive into his investment strategies. Nevertheless, his resignation illuminated that a cadre of trustees had led the bank, and the depositors, away from the bank's original mission.[36]

The fallout from Cooke's and Huntington's resignations, in addi-

tion to the increased problems with the NPRR bonds, also affected
Eaton. He stayed on for a few months, but ultimately resigned in July
1872. With his resignation, the board expressed gratitude, offering "the
thanks of this Company . . . for the faithful manner in which he has dis-
charged the duties of the said office."[37] This note of thanks shrouded
Eaton's unabashed self-interest and dedication to Cooke and Huntington's agenda. Eaton had served his role as a faithful servant, not of the
bank and the depositors but of Cooke and Huntington. He proved willing to support any of their financial gambits. Together they bilked the
Freedman's Bank, and Black depositors, using the institution as their
own slush fund. Therefore, once his two co-conspirators vacated their
positions with the bank, there was nothing left for Eaton. He did not
want to continue his affiliation under a new regime—especially one that
would more closely scrutinize him and his decision-making. Eaton's
influence, however, did not completely disappear. His nephew, George
W. Stickney, swiftly took his place as bank actuary.

Stickney assumed the position of actuary in August 1872, jumping
into his uncle's role. Per Congress's rule, he was supposed to have posted
a bond to officially take the position. Put more plainly, he needed to
have "skin in the game." The law required that much. But he did not, no
bank administrator or board member required him to, and he began his
work as the Freedman's Bank actuary with no fiduciary responsibility to
the depositors, much like his uncle.

Though the era of the Cooke-Huntington-Eaton triad ended in
mid-1872, their influence remained. Soon, the public would have a
clearer sense of how much the bank was tethered to these influential
members of the Freedman's Bank finance committee.

❧

THE NPRR AND JAY COOKE & COMPANY debacle compelled
the bank's trustees to do an internal audit, to assess the conflicts of
interest inherent in the finance committee's loan making. Between 1870
and 1872, the trustees were in open defiance of section 12 of the charter,
which stipulated that no officer, trustee, or administrator with the bank
could "borrow funds of the corporation."[38] In these two years, the trust-

ees were increasingly making loans to themselves, sometimes offering no collateral or borrowing without paying interest. For example, Huntington borrowed $5,000 on May 15, 1871, and paid back the interest-free loan almost a month later, on June 9. He did not offer collateral and there was little documentation about the loan's terms. George Balloch, the bank's treasurer, obtained several loans over this period that amounted to $56,000. Again, the finance committee did not record the terms of the loan, meaning time to maturity and interest rates.[39] It was clear that a select number of trustees and administrators believed that the freed people's deposits were ripe for the taking. Since most of the deposits from around the country were being sent to the Washington office for safekeeping and investment, the millions of dollars that African Americans had been depositing into their accounts, across thirty-four branches spread throughout the South and mid-Atlantic, funded the bank's increasingly corrupt lending spree in Washington.

In early 1872, the board finally took a course of action to remedy the finance committee's rapacity. Possibly spurred by the revelations about misdeeds by Cooke, Huntington, Eaton, Jay Cooke & Company, and select members of the finance committee, the board made the bold, and necessary, step of forming a committee on inspections. "The numerous branches of this company, their distance from the principal office, their liability to errors of employees, and conspiracies from without, make the department of inspect of utmost importance," read the mandate that Alvord and the board approved on January 19, 1872.[40] The inspector would be responsible for traveling to each bank branch to examine the branch's accounting and to help train, and in some instances retrain, the cashiers in how to accurately keep track of the deposits.

By 1872, the bank's inspector at the helm of this massive task was Anson M. Sperry. Sperry served as the bank's second inspector, having succeeded Samuel L. Harris in 1871. He had been an eager supporter of the bank since its inception. But his support was first and foremost with the Black depositors, Black soldiers above all. In the final year of the Civil War, Sperry worked alongside Alvord as a field agent with the army, collecting Black soldiers' wages to deposit into the military savings banks, then to deposit into the newly created Freedman's Bank in the spring of 1865. During this time, he relocated to Texas, where Black soldiers entrusted him with over $120,000 in their earnings to store in Freedman's Bank accounts. Sperry saw firsthand how Black soldiers desired a financial institution to suit their new financial needs, which spurred him to officially accept an appointment with the Freedman's Bank as an agent in September 1865. Sperry agreed to do an important job, "to obtain deposits + take allotments from Negro troops and Freedmen."[41] He served in this grueling role, which demanded near constant travel throughout the Southern states, until 1871 when the board nominated him to serve as the bank's internal inspector.[42]

The 1872 examination would be Sperry's most challenging assignment yet. He worked with the examining committee on the eight-month-long audit, and the committee's results revealed startling discoveries. On October 11, 1872, the committee's report made it clear that the bank—that is, the finance committee—had not been comporting with Congress's guidelines when lending the bank's money to borrowers. Furthermore, borrowers were not paying back their loans and the finance committee had been amending loan terms. Specifically, the committee found that forms of collateral were not sufficient, such as stock of the YMCA and Metropolis Paving Company, bonds of the city of Sacramento, and of course, Northern Pacific Railroad bonds.[43]

The scope of the bank's problems required swift and direct action by the board. But instead of the trustees using this inspection as a lens through which to gain a new perspective into their own mishandling of deposits, they shifted blame. The report targeted the cashiers at the Jacksonville, Vicksburg, Beaufort, and Washington branches as operating with gross negligence, in direct contradiction of the bank's amended charter. The examination found that cashiers at these branches had been making loans and using for their own purposes deposits that they should have been sending to the central office in Washington, DC. The cashiers had been "exercising in fact the functions of a National Bank." In the final line of the report, the examination committee declared, "This abuse should be corrected and stopped without loss of time."[44]

The reality was that the cashiers' actions with freed people's deposits began with the bank's central office and the bank's trustees, in Washington, DC. The internal examination was supposed to have been an opportunity for the bank's administrators, cashiers, and trustees to reflect on whether they were doing their due diligence in protecting depositors' money. Instead, the trustees used the internal review to chastise the cashiers and administrators of the Beaufort, Washington, Jacksonville, and Vicksburg branches for not complying with "the rules and regulations of the Corporation." The cashiers were supposed to have "transmitted the funds received on Deposit to the Principal office," but the committee's rationale only highlighted the cupidity of the bank's trustees.[45] Instead of examining how the problems stemmed not from the branches or the depositors but from the central office—from the trustees—the committee made the cashiers bear the responsibility for the "abuse." And the report's final line highlighted this blame.

Moreover, the report also conveyed an implicit message. It was that John Alvord, as the bank's president, had not been exercising the type of leadership required to properly steward the bank and maintain depositors' trust in the institution. The examination committee's report recognized what had devolved into an inevitable problem, one that the bank's founders had failed to fully appreciate when the bank opened in March 1865. Without strong leadership by people who would prioritize African Americans' financial needs, the bank came to be guided by men who did not care enough about freed people's economic security. The bank required a principled leader who would consistently work to protect freed people's deposits. And by 1872, Alvord was failing at his responsibilities to the bank's depositors. Moreover, with Alvord as president, the bank slid even more into unsustainable territory.

Despite the results of the internal investigation, bank administrators and cashiers eagerly welcomed new depositors. Even as the finance committee continued to approve unsecured loans to the business partners and cronies of the bank's trustees and administrators, the bank continued to funnel $1,500 annually to newspaper advertising in cities with high African American populations. Philadelphia was one of those cities. William Whipper, the cashier of the Philadelphia branch, announced to the city's 1,349 depositors in October 1872 that "the success of our branch has induced the Trustees to resolve to furnish us with a NEW BANKING HOUSE in a location more suited for our accommodation and development." Whipper wanted the number of depositors to reach 2,000, "so that we can enter the *new building* with a CAPITAL that will make our future success absolutely certain." He argued that the bank provided "security and protection to the aged, strengthens and sustains those in middle age, and forms the most *practical educator* of youth of both sexes." He asserted that the bank lifted "thousands from poverty and degradation." And, he proclaimed, "[the bank] will form the proudest monument in the history of modern civilization."[46] Whipper was intentional with his language. The maxims he deployed were designed to bring more Black depositors and more capital to the bank.

The bank's problems, however, had little to do with attracting depositors. African Americans continued to deposit hundreds of thousands of dollars into their bank accounts. And capital continued to flow from the thirty-four branches to the central office in Washington. In fact, by March 1872, the total amount of deposits accepted by Freedman's Bank branches was $31.2 million. The bank's main problem was the lack of internal and external regulation.

It was clear that Congress had not followed through on its responsibility to monitor the bank. Trustees began to withdraw their money, close their accounts, and step down from the board. Bank administrators could not stem the tide of bad press that had begun to leak in newspapers across the country about the bank's potential mismanagement—and its inevitable effect on African Americans. Members of Congress decided to finally intervene, exercising their prerogative to mandate the Office of the Comptroller of the Currency to step in. On January 20, 1873, the bank underwent its first examination. Congress finally authorized the comptroller of the currency, John Jay Knox, to scrutinize all the savings banks incorporated in Washington, DC. Congress's charge reflected one of Knox's priorities as comptroller, a position he had held since April 1872. Knox believed in transparency. Therefore, he advocated for the OCC to conduct more regular examinations of national banks. This was the best way to ensure banking stability. The first institution to undergo an audit was the Freedman's Bank.[47]

Knox was known in Washington and New York as an astute and

disciplined economic mind, with expertise in banking and monetary policy. In his capacity as the nation's comptroller, he entrusted Charles A. Meigs, a bank examiner from New York City, to conduct the audit.[48] Meigs interrogated the bank's books, including the loans that the finance committee made through the bank's central office and the loans that cashiers were making at the Vicksburg, Beaufort, Jacksonville, Memphis, and New Orleans branches. His charge was to get a full sense of the bank's stability (or instability), not just for Congress but also for the approximately seventy thousand depositors scattered across the South and mid-Atlantic. Meigs formally submitted his findings to the Senate's Committee on Finance on February 3, 1873. His report painted an unflattering picture of the bank and highlighted its shady financial dealings.

Meigs showed that the bank was involved in widespread malfeasance, with the trustees, administrators, and cashiers operating in opposition to the bank's charter. One of the more egregious missteps that he uncovered was the financing for the bank's new central office. According to Meigs, the trustees' purchase of the building and the luxurious improvements made to the edifice were "clearly a violation of their charter."[49] The new building was just the beginning of Meigs's criticism.

Despite the over $4 million in deposits, the bank's Washington branch had only $24,422.05 in cash on hand, while the bank had $93,032.25 deposited in First National Bank. Even after Henry Cooke's resignation, the trustees continued to do business with his bank. And in terms of lending, the numbers were even more startling. The bank had over $2.5 million in outstanding loans. The problem, according to Meigs, was that "a large portion of these loans have been made upon security not equal to twice the value of the loan, as required by law."[50] Instead, the finance committee accepted too many forms of collateral, from stocks and bonds to "approved claims on the board of public works." Meigs declared that the trustees had been making loans that did not comport with the rules outlined by Congress and as expressed in the approved charter amendment. In fact, he went as far as to levy the charge against the bank's trustees and officers that "it was not the intention of the act of incorporation to authorize investments of this character."[51] In his concerns about the bank's lending practices, he offered the bank a stern warning. "Many of the loans are of a character that should not appear upon the records of a savings bank," Meigs declared, "and will finally result in some loss to the institution, but the probable amount of such ultimate loss it is very difficult to determine at this time."[32]

Practically, Meigs's observations revealed that the bank's trustees and administrators had not been operating the bank with depositors' best interests in mind. He demonstrated that the bank was becoming overleveraged—meaning that it was close to not having enough cash on hand for when depositors wanted to withdraw money. The finance committee had been allowing applicants to borrow too much, to the detriment of the depositors and their financial needs.

Meigs completed his report by offering a set of recommendations for the bank to regain a sense of stability—for the depositors' sake. He recommended a three-pronged approach. First, Congress needed to step in to establish the interest rate that the depositors would receive. Until this time, the trustees had voted on depositors' interest rates, which varied over the years, but hovered around 6 percent. Meigs explained, "[I]t is believed that the undesirable loans held by the bank have been made, to a large extent, from the desire of the trustees to invest as speedily as possible the funds of depositors at high rates of interest." Second, the charter needed to be amended "to prevent investments being made except upon securities of well-known marketable values." Meigs recognized that the trustees had been making very risky investments while offering depositors an unsustainable interest rate on their deposits. He was forecasting that, left unchecked, the bank would be unable to recoup the money flowing out to borrowers, while fulfilling the cash needs of depositors, which included interest payments on their deposits. Third, he recommended that Congress require the bank "to accumulate a surplus to provide against future losses."

Meigs concluded his official report by stating that the act under which the bank was originally organized "was drawn without sufficient consideration" and that the bank's acts of incorporation needed to be repealed. A new act of incorporation was sorely needed. But all was not lost. He believed that the bank could be redeemed. "With proper legislation and necessary restrictions," he offered, "the bank would be able to correct the mistakes already made, to retrieve its present and prospective losses, and be enabled to continue a business of great usefulness to the class of depositors for whose benefit the institution was organized."[33]

As an aside, perhaps to lessen the blow of his findings, Meigs did admit his belief in the institution and in the men at its helm. He lauded the institution's work on behalf of freed people, arguing that the Freed-man's Bank was of "incalculable importance" to the future of the nation. "The executive officers are, in my opinion, men of the most undoubted integrity of character," he admitted, "devoted to the best interests of the institution, working for small compensations, and have educated themselves to the practical knowledge of the business of a savings bank to a degree that promises a prosperous future for the institution."[34] He acknowledged that the bank had grown rapidly because of freed people's increased interest in the benefits of savings. The quickness with which the bank expanded, however, caused its administrators to make "errors of judgement." But Meigs believed that the trustees, administrators, and cashiers were not likely to make the same mistakes because "the light of past experience" would "guide them in the future."[35] He expressed con-fidence that they could properly steward the thirty-four branches and seventy thousand depositors into a new era of prosperity.

Knox, in his capacity as the comptroller of the currency, publi-cized Meigs's findings. A March 1873 article in the *Christian Reporter* announced the state of the bank's finances to Black readers. But the information distributed did not give a full account of Meigs's conclu-sions. "The security upon which the loans were made is considered by the comptroller and the examiner," the reporting argued, "with few exceptions, as good for the amount loaned. There is nothing in the reports which conveys the impression that the bank cannot respond to the demands of the depositors."[36] The goal was to not dissuade Black depositors, and prospective depositors, from patronizing the bank and their local branches.

In March 1873, the bank's administrators, Alvord principally, wanted to quell any doubts that the bank could not satisfy the depositors' needs. The trustees wanted to avoid a dreaded bank run. They even tried

to convince Black depositors that they could still have trust in the institution. A March 1873 report explained, "The examiner states that the
executive officers are in his opinion men of the most undoubted integrity of character, devoted to the best interests of the institution, who
have educated themselves to a practical knowledge of the business of the
institution which promises a prosperous future for it."[37] Such messages,
however, did not fully reestablish depositors' trust in an institution that
remained susceptible to the unpredictability of the financial market.

⤴

MIDMORNING ON SEPTEMBER 18, 1873, traders in the New
York Stock Exchange paused in bewilderment. A hush fell over the trad-
ing floor. This halt in the flurry of buying and selling departed from
the usual commotion. The silence lasted only a moment. Then voices
began to crescendo as some brokers hurriedly exchanged information,
eager to fully understand the drastic change taking place in the market. Others rushed out of the Stock Exchange onto Broad Street, falling
over one another in a dash to their offices, anxious to disseminate the
breaking news. A bank had failed. The general sense of disbelief at the
morning's dramatic turn spread like wildfire throughout New York's
financial hub.[58]

Reports of the bank failure circulated quickly. News dispatches
telegraphed from New York soon reached Washington, DC. By midday,
journalists were preparing the evening's summaries. By 1 p.m., spectators in Washington, DC, observed it in real time. The first Washington casualty succumbed. The comptroller of the currency closed First
National Bank. The note posted on the bank's door read: "The First
National Bank of Washington, D.C., has found it necessary to suspend
business to-day."[59]

Meanwhile, in Philadelphia, a crowd gathered outside one of the
nation's most prominent banking offices on Third Street, in the heart
of the city's financial district. Those who wanted to enter the building
found the entrances shut and locked. The crowd continued to swell.
Soon the murmurings turned to gasps as a brave employee fastened a
note to the building's front door. It read:

We regret to be obliged to announce that owing to unexpected demands on us our office has been obliged to suspend payment. In a few days we will be able to present a statement of our affairs to our creditors until which time we must ask for their patient consideration. We believe our assets to be largely in excess of our liabilities.

Signed, Jay Cooke & Co.[60]

A bellow of surprise echoed throughout the crowd. On that day, Jay Cooke & Company, the nation's most recognizable investment bank, declared bankruptcy.[61]

It is rare to trace an economic downturn to one single event, spurred by the actions of one company. But this is what happened on September 18, 1873. There were immediate fears about the effect that Jay Cooke & Company's failure would have on the government's deposits, especially First National Bank, which held deposits of the Department of the Treasury. "Just how much money is held by First National Bank cannot be ascertained, either from the bank or Treasury officials," a news item from Washington's *Evening Star* detailed. The bank "always had the credit of keeping a considerable amount of government funds on hand."[62] The public's fears about the relationship between the Department of the Treasury and Jay Cooke & Company were well founded, especially considering the cozy relationship between the Cooke brothers and high-ranking members of the Treasury Department—relationships cultivated in part by Henry Cooke.

Henry Cooke was likely ill-prepared for the fallout from Jay Cooke & Company's bankruptcy. First, he resigned as governor of the District of Columbia on September 10, a mere eight days before Jay Cooke & Company failed. In his resignation letter to President Grant, he wrote, "I am urged to take this action by the fact that the combined demands from my private business and my public duties have been so exacting that I am no longer able to meet both or either of these demands as thoroughly as I could wish."[63] He conveyed a veiled message about his struggle to balance the various facets of his professional responsibilities. Perhaps he also struggled to face the real consequences of his brother's bank not meeting the financial expectations of its investments, most prominently in the NPRR project. The *Evening Star* proposed this rationale as an explanation for the bank's failure. "It was asserted by some," the reporting surmised, "that the large amount of gold required to be purchased by the Cookes at high rates to pay the interest on the Northern Pacific railroad bonds contributed to the result."[64] The information circulated by various news organizations reiterated this connection, that the Cookes' problems stemmed from financing the NPRR.

As news of Jay Cooke & Company's bankruptcy filtered out across the mid-Atlantic, Cooke had already plotted his escape from Washington to Philadelphia. He abandoned the cashier and assistant cashier of First National Bank, leaving them to handle the onslaught of journalists pestering them about the bank's status. The assistant cashier was "quite overcome when interrogated" by the press and the cashier was forced to convene with Knox to figure out a next course of action. By noon on September 18, Cooke had boarded a train bound for Philadelphia, supposedly "not aware of the anticipated suspension" of First National Bank.[65] Henry Cooke may not have predicted the suspension of Jay Cooke & Company's operations. But his actions suggest that he did, in fact, foresee the need to dedicate his full attention to the company's business interests.

News of the bankruptcy sprinted to news outlets across the country. By the evening of September 18, reports reached the West Coast, with the *San Francisco Evening Bulletin* reporting, "Our dispatches to-day announce the failure of Jay Cooke & Co., the well-known bankers and managers of the Northern Pacific Railroad."[66] The bank's failure was a bellwether of greater change to come in the financial markets. On September 25, reporters detailed how ten other financial houses in Philadelphia had failed.[67] Even in the Cookes' hometown of Sandusky, Ohio, the hometown newspaper, the *Spirit of Democracy*, offered a sobering assessment of the Cookes' situation. "The number of individuals who will be embarrassed, if not utterly ruined, by this failure," the writer concluded, "is very large."[68]

In the end, Jay Cooke & Company stopped interest payments to investors who purchased NPRR bonds. The bond sales had failed to generate enough capital to sustain the bank's business, especially its investment in the unfinished NPRR. By September 1873, the bank could not meet its financial obligations. Its failure reverberated in the wider market, as other financial institutions called in loans, causing an immediate contraction in the credit market. And for the first time in its history, the New York Stock Exchange ceased operations, on September 20, and stayed closed for ten days.[69]

The Panic of 1873 had begun. It would become one of the most destabilizing financial events in American history, most certainly in the nineteenth century. This financial panic revealed, first and foremost, the fragile nature of the American economy, even despite the safeguards put in place by the Lincoln administration during the Civil War. It also reflected the increasingly interconnected architecture of the financial sector. An economic panic that began in Europe in May 1873 exposed the extent to which the American economy relied on the stability of European financial markets.[70]

The *New York Times* offered a particularly poignant summary of the immediate implications of Jay Cooke & Company's failure. "Fortunes that have been years in accumulating are lost in a few hours. And the worst feature of the matter is," the writer charged, "that the loss is not confined to those who have taken their risks knowing what they were, but falls with the greatest weight on hundreds, and perhaps thousands, who have put their money into the stocks affected for purposes of legitimate investment."[71]

Jay Cooke & Company's collapse affected the Freedman's Bank immediately. The bank's connection to the company was widely known, especially in Washington. When the *Evening Star* reported on the bankruptcy on September 18, the Freedman's Bank was necessarily included in the conversation. The first pieces of information offered a positive spin. "It has been rumored that the Freedman's Savings Bank was a heavy loser by the suspension," the report noted, "but this is a mistake." According to the statement, the Freedman's Bank only had $800 on deposit with Jay Cooke & Company and the First National Bank. Perhaps the writer did not know about the complex relationship between the two institutions—or that Henry Cooke had been borrowing extensively from freed people's deposits in the Freedman's Bank to fund the NPRR.[72]

News of a bank run soon trickled out. On Friday, September 19, and Saturday, September 20, the Washington branch of the Freedman's Bank was forced to pay depositors $20,000 and $65,000, respectively. Depositors, fearful of not having access to their funds, stormed the bank's beautifully appointed office building, demanding to withdraw their money.[73] The Black press wondered about the seemingly interconnected relationship between Jay Cooke & Company and the bank. A writer for the *Christian Record* asked, "[H]ow came our own Freedmen's Bank to suspend?"[74]

The trustees and executive committee scrambled to fulfill the depositors' immediate demands for cash. At the time, the Washington branch held about $800,000, a combination of cash and bonds. The trustees met several times over the next week and decided on how to get quick access to the bank's capital reserves. They authorized Alvord to travel to New York to sell the bank's bonds to willing purchasers. Alvord, however, had a hard time finding buyers. He took $100,000 worth of bonds on his trip, each bond worth $1,000. One trustee, Dr. Charles Purvis, argued that the quantities were too expensive to sell. "It was hard to sell these bonds, because they were of a thousand dollars denomination," Purvis contended, and "if they had been $100 bonds, we could have sold them readily."[75]

The failure of not only Jay Cooke & Company but also other financial institutions devolved into a nationwide economic panic that caused depositors to quickly withdraw their money from their local branches. Freedman's Bank depositors were no different. Cashiers in each of the branches struggled to fulfill the depositors' needs because people began withdrawing their money in droves. In mid-October, for example, depositors again flooded the Washington, DC, branch, looking to extract their money and in some instances close their accounts. Some branches required thirty-day or sixty-day notice for depositors to withdraw money.[76]

By the end of 1873, the bank needed money. The trustees decided on a temporary strategy. To ensure that the branches had enough capital on hand to fulfill depositor demands, the actuary and treasurer began to discuss how to shutter unproductive branches. For this reason, in December 1873, the board initiated the process of closing branches in Lynchburg, Atlanta, Montgomery, Columbia, and Raleigh.[77] In addition to closing branches, Stickney, as the bank's newest actuary, began selling securities to recoup the bank's losses. He decided to sell some of the collateral held by the bank to offer some liquidity to depositors. One asset that he attempted to leverage was one of the bank's more controversial holdings: the YMCA building on Ninth and D Streets in Washington, DC.[78] While the process of selling assets and lowering the bank's operating costs temporarily quieted depositors, these steps did little to bring stability to the institution.

On January 24, 1874, Charles Meigs, operating on direct orders from the comptroller of the currency, conducted a much-needed examination. He reported that the bank held $3.12 million in assets but $3.33 million in liabilities. The bank was in dire straits. If all the depositors attempted to withdraw their money, the bank would not have enough cash on hand to fulfill the demand. In fact, depositors would receive only ninety-three cents on the dollar.[79]

In response, Knox ordered a second, more robust, examination on February 14, 1874. This time, Meigs would have help. He led a small group of fellow bank examiners, including his colleague J. A. Talmadge and three other assistant examiners, A. M. Scriba, Thomas Williams, and W. D. W. Barnard. Together they acted on Knox's charge to take the previous year's examination a step further by authorizing an examination of a select group of bank branches. It was a large, and necessary, undertaking. Meigs's damning set of reports had spurred Congress, the Department of the Treasury, and the Office of the Comptroller of the Currency to finally intervene. Between February and April 1874, the five men fanned out across the mid-Atlantic and the South, visiting branches in New York, Baltimore, Norfolk, Richmond, Louisville, Lexington, Little Rock, Memphis, St. Louis, Wilmington, Beaufort, Jacksonville, Charleston, Savannah, Augusta, Atlanta, and Macon.[80] These seventeen branches—half of the bank's locations—represented a cross section of the bank's depositors. From big cities such as New York and Richmond, to smaller branches in Augusta and Wilmington, the examiners had an opportunity to gather information and construct a fuller picture of the bank's overall health, especially amid the national financial crisis.

These examiners worked alone, spending two to three weeks at each branch, plowing through the cashiers' accounting, assessing their bookkeeping strategies, and evaluating the branch's physical status. The examiners accumulated a stunning amount of data. Some of it was financial information, such as the total that the branch took in deposits and the amount missing from the final accounting that the examiners did of the branch's books. The examiners also interviewed the branch cashiers, asking them questions about their accounting strategies and how they managed their branch. In addition to the data that they gathered, the examiners also offered more subjective observations about the physical state of the branches, the competence of the cashiers, and, importantly, the perspective of the depositors.

The experiences of examiner W. D. W. Barnard serve as an example. Barnard traveled to St. Louis, Missouri, to evaluate the city's branch in March 1874. He cracked open the branch's accounting records, spoke with the cashier, and even talked to depositors. According to his examination, the Black patrons of the St. Louis branch had deposited $861,736.42 into their accounts. The cashier, W. N. Brant, made the location a stable and successful branch by keeping the books "up and well kept." After evaluating all the written material and considering his interviews with staff and depositors, Barnard authored his official examination on March 13. Instead of merely writing a financial report of the branch, he decided to add a bit more detail to his official finding.

Barnard's personal reflections highlighted the depositors, and how much they had impressed him with their financial acumen, their drive, and their investment in the bank branch. They had taken great pride in the money that they had deposited into their bank accounts. Barnard, perhaps surprised, observed that "among them is considerable enterprise, frugality and wealth." The branch's depositors held economic aspirations that they hoped the bank and its administrators would help them realize. They prioritized buying land, starting businesses, and embarking on the new period of freedom with access to financial resources. Yet, for the depositors, a glaring problem persisted: lack of access to loans. In fact, Barnard recognized that the bank's limitations on lending to Black depositors in St. Louis stymied the branch's growth. The problem was that the cashier could not make loans to the depositors. Black people in St. Louis needed not only a savings bank but a financial institution that would lend them money to help them buy land and invest in the wealth of their communities. According to Barnard, when the depositors realized that the only legal lending that occurred happened through the bank's principal office in Washington, not at their branch, they reconsidered their patronage. "But when needing money and finding that the Bank where they deposited could not loan they had to withdraw their business," Barnard detailed.[81]

What's more, some of the depositors had become skeptical about the trustees' and administrators' underlying dedication to the bank's fundamental mission of serving freed people. They had come to believe that the bank was a "Drag-Net," and that the bank had been "accumulating and sending off funds much needed at home."[82] Barnard acknowledged and even seemed to sympathize with the depositors' concerns. The reality was that tens of thousands of Black depositors could not use their financial relationship with local bank branches to apply for and receive loans. This practice hurt the bank's business as much as it hampered economic growth in Black communities across the nation. Barnard recognized, "Any legislation which would authorize the investment of deposits here would at once largely increase business."[83] The Black depositors of the St. Louis branch demonstrated that they were not the bank's major problem. They had been using the bank for its intended purpose. They even desired more from the bank and its administrators. But as Barnard's notes suggested, Black depositors were seeing the bank for what it had become—a reservoir of capital for white borrowers in Washington, DC. And the supply was drying up.

The bank examiners' reports showed an ineluctable fact, that the bank's administrators needed to correct course. Meigs and the other examiners revealed in their reports that between February 1873 and February 1874, the bank was unable to pay its debts.[84] The trustees could not

collect the collateral on many of the loans.[85] The collapse of Jay Cooke
& Company combined with the ensuing financial crisis depressed the
price of many of the bank's most valuable assets, properties, and securities. And, most important, the trustees and cashiers ignored the recommendations that the examiners previously proposed.

⁊

BANK DEPOSITORS LISTENED to and absorbed the messages
about financial instability in the American market. They understood
what the panic meant. Runs on the bank communicated a dire message
to depositors. They understood that their money was no longer safe. The
examinations of 1873 and early 1874, combined with the bankruptcy of
Jay Cooke & Company and the Panic of 1873, caused depositors to withdraw $1.8 million in the eighteen months after the first examination.[86]

Moreover, during and after the bank's second examination, the
board of trustees was in turmoil. The resignations of Cooke and Huntington in early 1872, the revelation that bank administrators misman-
aged freed people's money, the bad press because of unflattering bank
examinations, and the national economy being in a depression led to a
series of trustees resigning their positions with the board in January 1874.

Yet one of the most consequential resignations came on March 14,
1874. This time, it was Freedman's Bank president John Alvord who
resolved not to resign completely but to instead "retire" from the presidency. He did not completely step away from his affiliation with the
bank. He remained on the board, serving on the agency committee.[87]
For some trustees, Alvord's retirement was a godsend. They were ready
to install another, more prominent, voice during this tumultuous time.

In Alvord's stead, the board tapped one of the most influential
Black men in America to usher the bank out of this dark period. They
proposed the candidacy of the most visible and prominent orator in
the United States. Gaining a nearly unanimous vote of confidence,
the trustees selected Frederick Douglass to be the next president of the
Freedman's Savings and Trust Company.

CHAPTER SEVEN

The Bank's Last President, 1874

Some one has said that "experience is the best teacher."
Unfortunately the wisdom acquired in one experience seems
not to serve for another and new one; at any rate, my first lesson
at the national capital, bought rather dearly as it was, did not
preclude the necessity of a second whetstone to sharpen my
wits in this, my new home and new surroundings. It is not
altogether without a feeling of humiliation that I must narrate my
connection with the "Freedmen's Savings and Trust Company."

—FREDERICK DOUGLASS, *THE LIFE AND
TIMES OF FREDERICK DOUGLASS*[1]

**Balance due Freedman's Bank depositors, as of
March 1874: $3,229,201.00 ($89.1 million today)**

ON SATURDAY, APRIL 19, 1873, LESS THAN A YEAR before he accepted the position as the president of the Freedman's Bank in March 1874, Frederick Douglass arrived at a train depot in Louisville, Kentucky. Greeted by music and throngs of admirers, he stepped off the train onto the platform as the guest of honor at a Fifteenth Amendment celebration organized by the city's African American community. Douglass had a packed schedule, filled with meetings and parties. He planned on visiting prominent supporters in the city to preach the gospel of civil and voting rights legislation. His trip to Louisville included receiving a faction of whites. Indeed, "[h]e was visited by a great many of our leading white citizens, who seemed to vie with each other in honoring the man."[2]

He also agreed to attend several church services as the day's featured speaker. Sunday morning, one stop on Douglass's agenda was the Ninth Street Church, to address the children who attended Sunday school. However, news of his speech attracted an unusually large crowd for a Sunday morning. As he entered the church building, the audience welcomed him by breaking into song. "My country 'tis of thee, Sweet land of liberty" echoed as the crowd's enthusiasm rose in anticipation of witnessing the morning's esteemed guest. The noise, the music, and the spectators swelled to such a point that Douglass "declined in addressing the children," to the disappointment of those who had traveled to catch a glimpse of the famous orator. "The sight, and the music too, were grand," one observer revealed.[3] Despite the congregation's excitement, Douglass continued his church tour of Louisville. The next day, he gave two speeches at the city's Exposition Hall. These events attracted a biracial set of spectators, including the mayor, a judge, and a former Confederate army general.

Douglass's final stop, however, garnered the most public attention. On the evening of Tuesday, April 22, 1873, he spoke at Judah Hall, the

church of an infamous Presbyterian minister who, during the antebellum era, was prone to "defending slavery as a divine institution." It
was likely not lost on Douglass that he, a formerly enslaved man, was
invited to give a lecture in a site founded by an ardent defender of slavery. The topic of his address reflected the perspective of a man who had
dedicated his adult years to refashioning himself and his image, from a
bondman to an orator who was arguably the most recognizable person
in nineteenth-century America. That evening, Douglass delivered one
of his most famous speeches—"Self-Made Men."[4]

In this speech, Douglass articulated his ideas of political and economic self-making. He expressed his vision for African American
self-sufficiency, as the almost four million formerly enslaved people continued their ascendance as freed people in the United States. Within the
first few minutes of his speech, he made a proclamation that he hoped
the Black audience would absorb. "Properly speaking," he declared,
"there are in the world no such men as self-made men." Then he posed
a series of questions. "Who are self-made men?" and "What is the true
theory of their success?" he queried.[5]

Douglass's questions, and his answers, reflected his own evolution
as a person, as a man, and as a citizen. More directly, he was expressing
his evolving economic philosophy.[6] "It is not luck, nor is it great men-
tal endowments," he preached, "but it is well directed, honest toil."[7]
During Douglass's time as a traveling orator, he had been conveying
in his public-facing messages to Black people the benefits of diligence,
hard work, and moral fortitude. This was particularly true throughout
the 1860s as African Americans were forging paths for themselves amid
the unpredictability of emancipation. He argued for Black people to
embrace the reality of success through hard work.

"Self-Made Men" reflected Douglass's growth as a public figure. He
had been crafting his image as a man shaped by the violence of slavery,
the courage to seek his own emancipation, and the triumph of overcom-
ing insurmountable odds. To this audience, he continued his mission of
encouraging Black people to work, earn, and save to provide for themselves and their families. He connected economic success with morality.
Stopping short of advocating the trope of Black people pulling them-

selves up by their bootstraps, Douglass encouraged those in the audience to approach the diligence of work as the key to inclusion in the body politic.[8]

But his speech was not just about hard work. He also argued for a Black self-sufficiency free from the white gaze. Speaking to the white members of the audience, "Give the Negro fair play and let him alone" was the phrase that he deployed. Douglass articulated this idea twice in his speech to reinforce the notion that "fair play" from whites and Black autonomy would help African Americans enjoy their newly endowed constitutional rights. It was a message of Black people's political success realized through economic self-determination. Though he did not mention the Freedman's Savings and Trust Company by name, the language that he used, that of thrift, diligence, and self-sufficiency, mirrored the rhetoric that bank administrators employed to attract Black depositors across the South.

Douglass had been giving versions of his "Self-Made Men" speech since 1859. On this day, however, he may have been wondering about the viability of self-making and the challenges to Black self-sufficiency when Black people faced the continued threat of white violence. The Panic of 1873 exacerbated white fear of Black autonomy and political power, especially in states such as Louisiana. Perhaps, during his speech, Douglass's thoughts drifted to the recent outbreak of racial violence seven hundred miles southwest of Louisville. On April 13, 1873, in Colfax, Louisiana, 150 to 200 African Americans were murdered by a mob of whites outside of the Grant Parish courthouse. A local election was the precipitating event. As African American men had begun exercising their voting rights, often voting for Republican candidates, whites were resisting, frequently using violence to quell Black people's demonstration of their enfranchisement.[9] The massacre at Colfax would be one of the single most violent events of the Reconstruction era. News reports circulated quickly, and it is likely that Douglass became aware of the violence in Colfax during his travels to Louisville. Perhaps the African Americans murdered in Colfax gave new meaning to ideas he expressed in his speech on Black self-sufficiency.

Douglass gave "Self-Made Men" frequently between his first unveiling in 1859 and the celebration in Louisville on April 22, 1873. In this speech, he offered his own meditations on the economic promise of capitalism and democracy for African Americans. According to Douglass, freed people required *both* economic and political rights. As he accepted the position as the Freedman's Bank president a year after his Louisville visit, he tried to put these ideas into practice. But he faced a difficult question: Could he fix an institution that had become such a source of pride for the nation's freed people?

Douglass, for a short time, believed that he possessed the necessary skills and knowledge to bring Black people's trust back to the Freedman's Savings and Trust Company. And the messages that he conveyed in "Self-Made Men," the moral and social benefits of hard, meaningful work, guided his decision to make this new professional move. Yet his economic vision for African Americans, and his advocacy for Black economic self-making, would be put to the test as he transitioned into the next phase of his career. He went from orator and publisher to bank president. It was a transition for which, even by his own admission, he was completely unprepared.

✦

BY THE TIME HE BECAME the fourth president of the Freedman's Savings and Trust Company, Frederick Douglass was arguably the most recognizable Black person in America. Indeed, by the end of the nineteenth century, he would also become the most photographed American, exceeding Lincoln and Grant.[10] Douglass's reputation as an abolitionist, writer, and orator encouraged bank trustees to approach him with a proposition to become more involved in the bank's business. His messages about economic self-reliance surely encouraged the trustees to advocate for his candidacy.

Douglass's acceptance of the role as the Freedman's Bank president manifested a much longer relationship with the institution. Before he accepted the position in March 1874, he had been a vocal supporter of the bank, its mission, and the depositors. He used his role as publisher of the *New National Era* to report on the bank. In the first edition of the newspaper under his tutelage, he ran a favorable article about the bank.

The article was a summary of a November 1869 Colored Convention in Washington, DC, in which a committee of five Black men outlined their support of the institution. They also urged the bank to open branches in "all the principal cities of the South" so that "colored people should unite in establishing these Savings Banks."[11] Douglass decided to include this bit of information to go along with other pertinent announcements. This article was the first of many to run in his newspaper. Beginning on January 13, 1870, which marked the beginning of his tenure as the newspaper's publisher, there was an article about the Freedman's Bank in every issue of the *New National Era*.[12] Included in the bank's announcements was information about which branches were opening and how much in deposits the individual branches were drawing from Black depositors. There was always a positive message included with the financial information, meant to encourage more deposits and depositors. In the January 20, 1870, edition of the *New National Era*, for example, Douglass stated, "The exhibit reveals a remarkable vitality in the management, and a wonderful appreciation of the benefits and the safety of the bank."[13]

In addition to covering the bank for his newspaper, Douglass slowly became involved with the board of trustees. "I could and did occasionally attend the meetings of the Board of Trustees," he explained, "and had the pleasure of listening to the rapid reports of the condition of the institution, which were generally of a most encouraging character." He opened an account in 1871, eventually depositing $12,000, both by necessity and as a show of support.[14]

Douglass decided to involve himself more with the bank, beyond being a depositor and sometime board meeting attendee, in January 1871, when he was officially nominated to the board of trustees.[15] According to his own perspective on his time with the bank, he was an eager advocate but grudging participant in the life of the bank prior to his presidency. He supported the bank out of a broader interest in freed people's economic uplift. He believed, "It seemed fitting to me to cast in my lot with my brother freedmen and to help build up an institution which represented their thrift and economy to so striking advantage." His faith in the Freedman's Bank emerged from his goal of African Americans attaining political rights through economic empowerment. For Douglass, the political and the economic were intertwined. "For the more millions accumulated there," he reasoned, "the more consideration and respect would be shown to the colored people of the whole country."[16] While he did publicly support the bank, advocate for its expansion, and patronize it as a depositor, between 1871 and 1874 he remained on the periphery, electing not to get too involved in the bank's business.

Despite his hesitancy, when Douglass became a board member in 1871, he joined a growing list of Black trustees. Dr. Charles Purvis continued to work as a trustee, even transitioning into the position of the bank's vice president in March 1873, first serving alongside Alvord, then serving with Douglass in 1874.[17] Before Douglass's addition, Purvis began recruiting more Black men to be involved in spreading positive news about the bank. He did this by tapping into the growing network of educated and well-connected African Americans in Washington, DC. Purvis succeeded in convincing John Mercer Langston to join in February 1872.[18]

John Mercer Langston was born in 1829, in Louisa, Virginia. The free-born son of an emancipated Black mother and her white enslaver, Langston spent his formative childhood and teenage years in Virginia and then in Ohio after his parents' death. One of the first Black students to matriculate at Oberlin College, he studied law after graduating from one of the first colleges to admit African American students. He also had the distinguished honor of being the first African American person to pass the bar exam in Ohio, in 1854.[19] In addition to practicing law in Ohio, he worked as an abolitionist, supporting the political endeavors of the American Anti-Slavery Society and helping establish the National Equal Rights League alongside Frederick Douglass in 1864. During the Civil War, Langston helped to recruit Black soldiers to fight for the Union cause, perhaps witnessing the benefits of economic as well as political rights for Black people willing to fight for the Union and for their freedom.[20]

During the first years of Reconstruction, Langston worked for the Freedmen's Bureau as an inspector of schools in Virginia. By 1870, however, a new challenge confronted him. He took his legal education to Washington, DC, to serve as a law professor. He assumed the role of

Professor John Mercer Langston, Howard University, between 1868 and 1875; the first Black congressman from Virginia, elected in 1890

the first dean of the law faculty at Howard University. With him at its helm, the law school was in the vanguard of not only higher education but legal education in America. Under his tutelage, the law faculty did not discriminate "on account of sex or color."[21]

It was at this time that Langston heeded Purvis's call to become more involved and engaged in the Freedman's Bank. He decided to accept Purvis's invitation by agreeing not only to serve on the board but to take a position on the bank's finance committee in 1872, joining in the wake of Cooke's resignation. In this position, Langston became the finance committee's first Black member. He would take this responsibility seriously, using his place on the committee to inquire into the underlying rationale behind the bank's liberal lending policies for white borrowers.

Between 1872 and 1874, Purvis and Langston exercised more influence than the Black men who had joined the board in the 1860s. Together, they started to openly criticize the finance committee, joining the chorus of trustees, including Stewart and Ketchum, who wanted to see the board comport more closely with the regulations outlined by Congress and in the best interests of the depositors. Importantly, the Black trustees were at the forefront of removing Alvord from his position as the bank's president. They believed that if the bank was going to survive the rampant malfeasance, which started at the top with the trustees, then they needed "to get rid of an element which was believed to be the cause of our disasters." According to Purvis, "All the colored trustees, I may say, discussed the matter and determined to change the president." He even stated that if a new president could not change the bank's culture, they would seek to oust Stickney, admitting that "the actuary was to be changed" as well. By late 1873 Purvis and Langston had begun to blame Alvord for the bank's problems. They recognized, though, that they would face an uphill battle to fire him because of his strong ties to influential members of the board. Purvis noted, "We looked upon Mr. Alvord as old and incompetent; but he had strong friends who stuck to him."[22]

Purvis and Langston, likely picking up on the murmuring within Black communities, especially in Washington, started to become more openly critical of the bank for its lending practices. And they had given more scrutiny to the bank's lending activities than the previous Black trustees. Instead of simply attending board and committee meetings and allowing the white trustees to use their names to show that the bank embraced Black men's inclusion, Langston and Purvis began attempting to shape how the board of trustees operated, especially in relation to Black depositors' financial interests. But they could only do so much. Therefore, they devised a plan. "[W]e colored men put into the bank Mr. Douglass," Purvis admitted proudly.[23]

Langston and Purvis pushed for Douglass to be the bank's next president. According to Douglass, "I was solicited by some of its trustees to allow them to use my name in the board as a candidate for its presidency."[24] At first, Douglass took a more passive stance on his affiliation with the bank. He was slow to express enthusiasm for the position. From his perspective, he acquiesced to the requests made by Purvis and Langston to consider his nomination to replace Alvord.

Before Alvord resigned in March 1874, Douglass had met with him and with Stickney to discuss the bank's finances. Perhaps they

were priming him to take Alvord's place or maybe they were gaug-
ing how eager he was about the prospect of taking a more active and
public-facing role with the bank. Whatever their motivations, Douglass wrote of his surprise at the proposal to be the bank's next president, recounting the moment when he found out in early 1874 about
not just his candidacy but his election. "So I waked up one morning
to find myself seated in a comfortable arm chair, with gold spectacles
on my nose and to hear myself addressed as President of the Freedmen's Bank," he revealed.[25] Though he may have been writing with a
bit of dramatic flair, his candidacy as the next Freedman's Bank president was surely a politically astute one, for both the trustees and
Douglass himself.

The bank presidency was Douglass's opportunity to make an entrée
into politics. He had been turning down pleas from "many of my
respected fellow-citizens, both colored and white, and from all sections
of the country" to relocate to a region of the South with a large African American population in order to win a seat in Congress, even in
the Senate. Though he admitted, "Upon the whole I have never regretted that I did not enter the arena of Congressional honors to which I
was invited," Douglass did not entirely abandon the idea of becoming
involved in political life. Likely, he saw the Freedman's Bank presidency
as a vehicle to fulfill his interest in public office without entering the
world of electoral politics.[26]

In the bank's early years, Douglass's attention was elsewhere.
Between 1865 and 1870, he was not concerned directly with the bank.
His time, energy, and finances went toward politicking with members
of Congress and of the Johnson administration who would support his
push for what would be the Fourteenth and Fifteenth Amendments to
the Constitution. He was trying to convince politicians in Washington to support political rights for Black men and citizenship rights for
African Americans more broadly. For him, voting rights needed to be
secured for freed people to take full advantage of the economic privileges. However, as he became more involved in politics, he felt pulled
toward institutions that he believed could provide real benefits to Black
people, especially the recently emancipated.

When Douglass was elected to and accepted the role of the bank's president, he represented the pinnacle of Black men's influence on the bank's board of trustees. Nine years in the making, the ascendance of Douglass, Purvis, and Langston was meant to signal to Black depositors that the board was taking their concerns and economic prosperity seriously.

Douglass entered the position in March 1874 with the best of intentions. He intended to use his position as president to build on his esteemed career as an orator, political activist, and publisher of both the *North Star* and the *New National Era*. As he saw it, he was positioned to help freed people in a new way. He had been accustomed to using his skills as a speaker to spread the gospel of abolition. He deployed his talents as a writer to unveil the horrors of slavery. Douglass had been channeling his political energies toward citizenship and voting rights. His next challenge would be to champion economic uplift through African Americans' continued patronage of the Freedman's Bank.

As for the trustees, they were aware that the bank was in desperate need of good press. They hoped that Douglass would restore Black people's trust in the Freedman's Savings and Trust Company.

❦

"I WAS ELECTED TO that position, about the middle of March, 1874, but hesitated about taking the office until about the first of April," Douglass revealed.[27] His hesitation was well founded. He recognized that his first step would be to figure out "the real condition of the bank and its numerous branches." And, he realized, "[t]his was no easy task."[28] As soon as he became president, he quickly noticed inconsistencies between the information he was receiving about the state of the bank's finances and what he observed in the books.

Douglass inherited a bank in a downward spiral. And unfortunately, he was unprepared for the tumultuousness that he found. Though he had established and run two major publications, he was neither a financier nor a banker. He even admitted that he knew little of bank finance. Despite this lack of formal financial knowledge, the trustees understood his background. Their actions suggest that they wanted an African American man at the helm of the bank as they attempted to steer it through this unpredictable moment. Ultimately, the trustees had misaligned intentions regarding Douglass's candidacy. Men such as Langston and Purvis wanted him to usher in a new era for the bank and for the depositors. They wanted to put the depositors' needs at the forefront of the bank's mission. However, not all of the trustees proceeded with the same goals.

The white trustees' decision to move forward with Douglass as bank president ensured that African Americans would bear the brunt of public criticism of the bank's ultimate demise. The narrative would be that Black administrators mishandled the bank and Black depositors were unable to handle the economic responsibility of freedom.

Though Douglass entered the position with the best of intentions, he quickly discerned the abysmal state of the bank's finances.[29] The finance committee and cashiers at branches around the country were making loans without requiring collateral. The board of trustees had approved buying buildings to house branches that the bank could not financially support. Untrained cashiers were not keeping accurate track of depositors' money. Moreover, branch cashiers continued to send deposits to the central office in Washington. When depositors wanted to withdraw money, in September 1873 for example, local branches did not have enough money on hand to fulfill the depositors' demands. The depositors became increasingly concerned about the bank's stability, causing them to make runs on their local branches. Despite the problematic state of the bank, the trustees assured Douglass that all was not lost. Though, as Douglass detailed, "its assets amounted to three millions of dollars . . . its liabilities were about equal to its assets."[30] However, he was not immediately deterred. He believed that by closing unprofitable branches and cutting unnecessary expenses he could help bring the bank "safely through the financial distress then upon the country."[31]

Douglass's enthusiasm was short-lived. Within his first few weeks, Stickney approached him with an unusual proposition. Speaking as the bank's actuary, Stickney "stated that we must have ten thousand dollars that day, or the bank would have to close."[32] While considering this proposal, Douglass, in a state of shock, pulled together as many trustees as he could on short notice to a meeting at the central office. He polled the bank's leadership on next steps to avoiding insolvency and panic. Bank administrators seconded Stickney's claim that the bank needed $10,000 immediately.

As the trustees in attendance admitted that they could not—and would not—loan the bank that amount of money, Alvord offered a solution. He turned to Douglass and said, "Mr. Douglass, you have ten thousand dollars here that might be used for this purpose in United States bonds, and if we could have these for a few days it would help us push through, and it will all be right in a few days."[33]

Though Douglass was not a wealthy man, he had been making a living from his myriad speaking engagements, in addition to his years in newspaper publishing.[34] The positions he held and the experience he gained helped him develop as a businessman and, in some ways, an entrepreneur. But the amount of money that Alvord, the trustees, and bank administrators were relying on Douglass to offer was staggering. In a room of predominantly white men, men who were titans of industry, business owners, and were directly involved in the political life of a nation, a Black man born into slavery was being asked to financially rescue the bank.

Douglass acquiesced. It was then, in April, when he realized that the bank was in an extremely tenuous position. "I naturally enough began to doubt the soundness of the bank," he revealed, as this spurred him to delve more deeply into its finances.[35] In fact, he was the only member of the bank's board of trustees who had deposited money into the bank. Perhaps it was because the request was for $10,000 in bonds and not in paper money, but he put up the money. "The money, though it was repaid, was not done so as promptly as, under the supposed circumstances, I thought it should be," he admitted.[36] He began examining the bank's accounting, and what he found would upend the next several months of his life.

Douglass's fears about the potential insolvency were confirmed by a report released by the Office of the Comptroller of the Currency a mere four days before he took office, on March 10. Charles Meigs finalized and submitted the report of his second examination of the Freedman's Bank to his boss, John Jay Knox. The findings in the report revealed myriad problems that stemmed from the trustees and the cashiers. The problems had to do with lending. The examination uncovered that from June 1870 to January 1874, the finance committee had $1,473,226.55 in outstanding loans on its books. And the reality was that the data that Meigs and his examiners accumulated was an undercounting. It did not account for the totality of the lending that occurred within the board of trustees *and* loans that the actuary and the finance committee had been making off the books.[37]

In addition to the trustees making risky loans in Washington, DC, the cashiers there and in Beaufort, Jacksonville, and Vicksburg had been engaged in the type of lending for which Meigs had previously criticized the finance committee. For example, not only had the Jacksonville branch been making illegal loans, but by March 1874, all of its loans were overdue.[38] The same type of lending had been occurring at the Montgomery and Atlanta branches. In fact, the loans at the Atlanta branch were so egregious that the branch cashier, Phillip D. Carrie, was officially under investigation for embezzling an estimated $10,000.[39]

Douglass observed this news with dread. When he entered the role as the bank's president, he wanted to inspire confidence in the bank among the Black depositors. Importantly, he needed to assure African Americans that the bank was safe. He and the trustees had no choice but to confront the damning report. The results of Meigs's second examination were presented to Congress in April 1874—a few weeks after Douglass took office. Though Meigs couched his findings in language that suggested he still had faith in the trustees and the institution as a whole, the data in his report could only lead to a specific set of conclusions. The trustees had not cleaned up the mess they made in the aftermath of Henry Cooke's resignation and the Panic of 1873. Black depositors' money was not secure. Ultimately, there was one unavoidable conclusion: there was very little that the trustees, the comptroller, or Congress could do to save the bank.

Despite the reality of the bank's status, Douglass needed to display confidence about the bank—and not merely because his new role required it. The board, the Black trustees in particular, hoped that Douglass could do some damage control. They needed him to change the public's perception that the bank was a failing institution and that the trustees had ruined its once-stellar reputation, especially among African Americans. By April 1874, he was front and center in the trustees' campaign to rehabilitate the bank's image.

It was clear to Douglass that he needed to make a more official public pronouncement. One of his first decisions, in addition to meeting with the board and getting a clearer sense of the bank's finances, was to issue a formal public message, called a *circular*, to broadcast to depositors reassurances of the bank's stability. A response to the Meigs examination in a newspaper was one way to convey his message. Therefore, he issued the first circular shortly thereafter.

In an official message, "To the Depositors of the Freedman's Savings and Trust Company," Douglass addressed the unflattering Meigs report, in which he found that the bank was close to being insolvent. The report revealed that there were continued problems with lending, both at the central office and at bank branches, despite pressure from Congress and the comptroller of the currency for cashiers to discontinue the practice. Meigs's report showed that the bank's "liabilities exceeded our assets to the extent of $217,000," and since the report was completed, the trustees had not made concerted strides "to materially diminish the space between assets and liabilities."[40]

Moreover, many of the loans that the bank's administrators made were "of a character that should not appear on the records of a savings-bank."[41] Douglass conveyed to depositors that the bank was sound, that they should not withdraw their money, and that the trustees had recognized their mistake and were moving forward to rectify past missteps.[42] He admitted that the trustees had become too eager to compete with older and more established savings banks and, in doing so, had put profit over the safety of deposits. Moving forward, Douglass declared, the trustees would be making important changes in the way that they approached financial responsibility. "They have also given up their wild and visionary schemes of banking, and have abandoned the policy of establishing branches in remote corners of the country," he stated.[43]

Douglass affirmed his belief that if depositors continued to maintain their faith in the bank and in the bank's administrators, the institution would "flourish despite the machinations of its enemies."[44]

Understanding that this message would shape how the depositors and the public viewed him, Douglass approached his remarks with a frankness that he hoped would reignite depositors' confidence in the bank. He also hoped that his words would inspire depositors to trust in him as president. He believed that if he confronted the bank's financial woes head-on, and attempted to chart a path forward, he could quiet depositors' fundamental concerns about the bank's stability.

Douglass's message did not shore up depositors' trust. The negative press spread quickly. In April 1874, depositors from around the country began withdrawing their deposits. On April 28, for example, depositors at the Charleston branch caused a "heavy run." At first, the cashier could fulfill all the requests, but it did not take long for the cashier to make a decision to pay "only 20 per cent of their deposits and required sixty days notice for the balance."[45]

In a frenzy, trying to stem the leakage of bad press and depositors' loss of confidence, Douglass called a meeting of the board on May 7. The trustees realized that they needed to call in all the bank's overdue loans, both at the central office and at branches throughout the country. Therefore, Douglass led the board "to press all loans now overdue to payment and to take such measures as were necessary to collect."[46]

Despite the unflattering news circulating about the bank, Douglass persisted in trying to shift the public narrative. He attempted to clarify in circulars, in reports to the press, and to the other trustees that he was confident in the message that he conveyed to depositors.

Some of the trustees did not agree. In fact, they did not share his confidence. They argued that he was not emphatic enough in communicating to depositors his faith in the bank's soundness. They blamed him for the fact that depositors had lost faith in the bank, arguing that he had not been convincing enough. "I expressed myself in some parts of these circulars so doubtfully," Douglass divulged, "that I was charged before the trustees with having destroyed the credit of the bank by these very circulars."[47] In response, he contended that he did believe in the "solvency" of the bank. After all, he was assured by Stickney and Sperry that the institution was on solid financial ground—and that the depositors' money was safe. Douglass explained, "I had confidence also in several other gentlemen connected with the bank, and I got from them assurances of the same sort and it was upon assurances of that kind that I signed those circulars."[48]

By May, the press was ambivalent about Douglass's ability to redeem the bank. In an editorial published in the *New York Herald*, and republished in the *New National Era*, the newspaper partially owned by Douglass and run by his sons, he was the focus of pointed critique. "Mr. Douglass has, therefore, a peculiar responsibility," the editorial surmised. "He must rescue the bank from the embarrassments which surround it."[49] The next article, directly from the *New National Era*, offered a more confident perspective on Douglass's position at the bank's helm. "It is impossible to read the report of Bank examiner Meigs on the condition of the Freedman's Savings Bank and not be thankful that Frederick Douglass is placed at its head," the writer declared.[50]

※

WHILE DOUGLASS WAS trying to control the public narrative about the Meigs report and the bank's future, members of Congress had decided to intervene. H.R. 3265, "An Act to Amend the Charter of the Freedman's Savings and Trust Company," was introduced in Congress in April 1874. The Committee on Banking and Currency wanted to begin another official inquiry into the "management and condition of the National Freedman's Savings and Trust Company . . . to best protect the interests of the class for whom the bank was chartered."[51] Its timing coincided with depositors steadily making runs on their local bank branches.

At the end of April, branches across the country were signaling to depositors that the bank was having cash-flow problems. News reports were circulating on April 27 and 28 that the bank's trustees were looking to close a slew of unprofitable branches. The *Chicago Daily Tribune* even reported that people had heard murmurings that the "Freedman's Savings and Trust Company had closed its doors" but that these reports "were unfounded."[32]

The press's coverage was not entirely untrue. At branches across the country, cashiers had been forced to impose guidelines on depositors, preventing them from walking up to their local branches and withdrawing money. The New York branch, for example, required that depositors give cashiers a sixty-day notice before withdrawing more than five dollars from their accounts. Such information caused depositors to lose trust, which spurred them to withdraw money as quickly as possible.

Depositors had become suspicious of the Washington branch as well. On April 27, news leaked that the House Banking and Currency Committee was considering the proposal of a bill that would force the bank's trustees to close the entire bank and "wind up the affairs of the whole concern."[33] This information nearly caused a run on the Washington branch, as depositors "called at the bank with their checkbooks for the purpose of closing their accounts." The trustees, "fearing a run on the institution," instituted a strategy deployed by administrators at the New York branch—that depositors give "sixty days' notice previous to the withdrawal of deposits." While the Washington branch staved off some of the depositors and avoided a bank run, the cashiers did acquiesce to the requests of certain customers. Specifically, they fulfilled the requests of "depositors requiring money for current business purposes."[34] This move—to accommodate depositors who needed money for "business" reasons—illuminates who the bank's cashiers prioritized. The cashiers believed that the Black depositors who needed quick access to their savings accounts were less important than the white depositors who held business accounts. It did not matter that the OCC and the bank's examiner had recently chastised the trustees and administrators for privileging white depositors and their business interests over the financial stability of African American patrons. The decisions of the Washington branch directors, guided by the trustees, perfectly exemplifies the hurdles that Douglass needed to overcome as bank president.

Douglass again attempted to counter the narrative and ease depositors' concerns. He argued on April 28 that "depositors need give themselves no uneasiness" about the bank's perceived instability. The bank's administrators assured him that "if the depositors will be patient for a very short time the bank and its branches will be able to pay dollar for dollar."[35] Less than two months into Douglass's tenure, his job was less about managing the bank's finances and more about helping reinforce depositors' faith in the institution. But as he shifted into crisis mode, to allay public concerns with the spate of bad press, he became more fully aware of the reality of his and the bank's situation. By this point, the Freedman's Savings and Trust Company's future was in Congress's hands.

As Douglass and the trustees confronted the damaging report from the Office of the Comptroller of the Currency, they also had to contend with increased scrutiny from Democrats in Congress. On May 14, Congressman F. G. Bromberg of Alabama took the opportunity to call attention to what he believed was a concerted effort to suppress the comptroller's second examination of the bank. He chaired the House committee responsible for the congressional investigation of the Freedman's Bank in the spring of 1874. In this May 14 speech before his fellow congressmen, Bromberg compelled Knox, as the comptroller, to make Charles Meigs's second examination more public. Knox submitted Meigs's report to Congress on March 10, 1874, and Bromberg questioned why neither the comptroller nor any member of Congress wanted to discuss, in an official way, Meigs's findings. Moreover, Bromberg used his political capital not only to question Meigs as an examiner but also to expose Meigs's findings.

Congressman Bromberg was not an apolitical actor in the partisan drama that revolved around the bank. An early supporter of the bank, specifically the Mobile, Alabama, branch, Bromberg served on Mobile's advisory board, generating local support for the bank's mission. And in July 1867, he invested in the bank even more, opening an account and becoming a depositor.[56] At the time of his affiliation, he served as Mobile County treasurer. He argued that when Congress amended the bank's charter, two years before he was elected to Congress, he did not believe that the amendment put depositors' money in danger. "I continued my countenance to the bank," he admitted, "giving it all the assistance in my power."[57] Bromberg's feelings about the bank changed, however, during the Panic of 1873.

He witnessed the cashiers and administrators of the Mobile branch suspending payments to depositors who were seeking to withdraw their funds. One disgruntled depositor "resorted to legal proceedings, obtained an attachment, put the sheriff in possession of the branch at Mobile, and locked it up for more than one day." Though Bromberg did not detail how this event devolved from a run on the bank to a local sheriff's locking up of the branch, he positioned himself as a steadfast supporter of the bank and of the Black depositors, even amid the chaos. "I was one of the two sureties to procure its release from the hands of the officers of the law that it might go forward in its work," he confessed, "and did my best to stay the panic among the colored people." Bromberg deployed this piece of information to offer a show of support for the bank. "I think that after this record," he declared, "no man can stand upon this floor and charge me with being unfriendly to the institution."[58]

Bromberg's praise for the bank stopped there. He used his position in Congress to generate more interest in the status of the Freedman's Bank, especially after the financial downturn. He was ready to put Meigs, Knox, Douglass, and the trustees on trial. He charged them with willfully mismanaging freed people's funds—and doing so for their own benefit. More important, he argued, there was no mechanism to make public the bank's business. There were no checks and balances. Bromberg claimed, "That committee has deliberately nullified the purpose of the resolution, and smothered the evidence which it was the object of the resolution to elicit."[59] He then accused Meigs of downplaying that there was "gross carelessness in the keeping of the ledgers."[60] For this reason, and perhaps to gain political points with Democrats, Bromberg pushed for more widely publicizing Meigs's second examination.

He asked the congressional clerk to read, word for word, Meigs's report to the entire House of Representatives. Though motivated by the desire to score political points, Bromberg was on a mission to expose the behavior of the bank's trustees, cashiers, and administrators, to prove that they had not worked diligently enough to protect freed people's money. Before the clerk began his reading, Bromberg asserted, "It is an important document, and, carefully studied, shows that the bank is absolutely insolvent."[61]

Meigs's report revealed that the bank was teetering on the brink of bankruptcy. The trustees and cashiers had continued flagrantly lending money while preventing Black depositors from gaining access to their accounts. For example, as depositors at some branches had to wait sixty days to withdraw money, white borrowers continued to seek and receive loans from the finance committee. One person who continued to exploit his relationships with the bank's trustees was J. V. W. Vandenburg. As of January 26, 1874, the bank had allowed him to borrow $180,068. And as of the Meigs examination, he still had $144,164 in outstanding loans.[62] Bromberg believed that these types of transactions needed to be highlighted for the American public, and for the bank's Black depositors.

Bromberg, however, did not merely introduce the idea of circulating Meigs's findings. At the end of his speech, he proposed that Congress consider closing the bank for good. He argued, "It is an edifice with crumbling walls and undermined foundations." He then invoked the Black depositors. "A prolongation of its existence is not kindness but cruelty to the present depositors and the colored people in general," he concluded. Bromberg put into words a reality that Republicans feared, Democrats anticipated, and freed people dreaded. The Freedman's Savings and Trust Company could not be redeemed as it stood.

On June 3, Congress intervened. Instead of mandating that the bank immediately shut down, members of Congress attempted to make a final push to reform the bank. The House of Representatives passed H.R. 3265, which required the comptroller of the currency to "appoint three competent men, to be styled and known as commissioners," who would be responsible for taking "possession of the books, assets, and records . . . of said corporation and subordinate branches." The comptroller and the commissioners would have, moving forward, the authority to "collect all debts due," "sell or compound all bad or doubtful debts," and sell any of the property owned by the bank.[63] Members of Congress were concerned, first and foremost, with liquidating the bank's assets and compelling borrowers to pay back their loans. But that was not all. They also expressed grave concerns about the bank's current trustees being unable to effectively change the way that they ran the bank without greater reform. For this reason, Congress made the bold step of amending the bank's charter.

On June 20, Congress voted on and approved a measure to fundamentally modify the charter. The amendment attempted to address the bank's lending practices and to outline how bank administrators would ensure that depositors received just compensation. First, Congress mandated that the trustees could not allow a single borrower to receive a loan over $10,000. In addition, the bank would be monitored more closely by the Treasury Department and the comptroller of the currency. The trustees would be responsible for nominating three commissioners who would act as outside fiduciary advisors. Congress, the Treasury secretary, the comptroller of the currency, and the trustees would empower the commissioners to conduct a series of audits across the branches. They would close unprofitable branches, ensure that branches did not lend to borrowers outside the region where the branch was located, and guarantee that the bank's trustees did not authorize more than a 5 percent yearly interest payment on deposits.[64] The June 20 amendment created the infrastructure to regulate the bank's administrators, cashiers, and trustees more effectively.

Congress forced the trustees, with the Black board members taking the lead, to respond. Douglass called a meeting of the board on the afternoon of June 24 at the bank's central office. The ten people in attendance likely felt a shared sense of somber anticipation. How would they address the drastic changes mandated by Congress? Douglass directed Stickney to start the meeting, by outlining to the rest of the trustees the list of assets and their respective values, including the buildings that the bank owned across the country and the collateral on unpaid loans. Then Langston spoke up in his capacity as a member of the finance committee. He proposed a resolution that the bank's executive officers approach the bank's management "for the time being" with the depositors in mind. He wanted the trustees to figure out a way to ensure that the depositors would be paid the entirety of the money the bank held in their accounts.[65]

At the same time, Douglass was preparing what would be his final circular. He broke the news of the bank's status to depositors in a June 25 announcement in the *New National Era*.[66] He first addressed the bank's deficit, $217,000, and argued that Meigs's report gave a false reporting of the bank's finances. In fact, Douglass declared that the bad loans that appeared in Meigs's report "have turned out to be good loans." He also recognized that the bank's directors "endeavored to make the Freedman's Bank compete with older and better-established institutions of the kind." This meant that they had been in the habit of "attracting and securing a large amount of deposits by holding out the inducement of a larger per centage of interest than was warranted by the earnings of the bank." Douglass admitted that the bank's administrators had been moving away from its original mission, to serve freed people, and instead had attempted to lure in the deposits of wealthier white individuals who would deposit larger amounts of money into their accounts. Douglass then addressed the bank runs, which drained the bank of necessary capital, and, importantly, the efforts by congressional Democrats and whites in the South to destroy an institution that had come to represent so much for freed people. Deploying his gift of prose, he maintained that the bank represented "the idea of progress, and elevation of a people who are just now emerging from the ignorance, degradation, and destitution entailed upon them by more than two centuries of slavery."[67]

Douglass affirmed a desire for the bank's remaking. He hoped that the recent disturbances would usher in a new era, that the "Freedman's Savings and Trust bank may be made not only a success in itself, but a grand means of success to the colored people of the South, to whom it has already taught important lessons of industry, economy, and saving." And in a statement that Douglass would later regret, he assured depositors of the bank's stability. "In respect to the future of the Bank," he wrote, "some of the main sources of danger and ruin have been entirely removed."[68]

Though Douglass tried to reestablish depositors' faith in him and in the trustees, he glossed over the realities of the bank's status. He would offer a fuller explanation in the years to come. By the end of June, there was little that he or any of the other trustees could do to avoid the inevitable. Four days after Douglass issued his message, the trustees agreed to close the bank.

On June 29, 1874, the board of trustees made the difficult and inescapable decision to suspend operations. Eleven trustees, including Douglass, Langston, Purvis, and Alvord, met at 3 p.m. at the bank's central office. They agreed that it was "impractical to continue the Company under its charter as amended" and "they hereby direct that the Bank be closed up" according to procedures outlined by Congress.[69]

The trustees' work, however, was not complete. They still needed to elect three trusted advisors who would act as bank commissioners. As the June 20 amendment from Congress outlined, the commissioners would be responsible for figuring out how to compensate the remaining depositors through liquidating the bank's assets. But before this process could begin, the trustees had to agree on who the three commissioners would be. This proved to be a hurdle for the remaining trustees. Douglass did not believe that the commissioners should be connected, in any way, to the bank or the trustees. He wanted to avoid the types of conflicts of interest that had led the bank down the path to insolvency. Ultimately, Douglass was overruled. On July 1, the trustees made their selection. The three commissioners would be Robert Leipold, an accountant with the Department of the Treasury, John A. J. Creswell, former postmaster general, and Robert Purvis, a Black abolitionist and father of bank trustee Dr. Charles Purvis.[70] Members of Congress believed that it would take the commissioners two years to complete a total assessment of the bank and its thirty-four branches. These three men would be responsible for selling the bank's assets, updating Congress, and compensating the 61,144 depositors who still held $2,993,790.68 in bank accounts. "It is thought that with proper management," news reports detailed, "ninety-three cents on the dollar will be realized."[71] Yet this valuation would prove to be an overly optimistic one. It would only temporarily soothe depositors' anxieties that they might not ever have access to their accounts.

ON JULY 2, 1874, the trustees wrote to the secretary of the Treasury, B. H. Bristow. They announced that it was "impractical in the present condition" for the bank "to continue its current business satisfactorily." In the end, they believed "it advisable to close up its entire business."[72] These words meant that depositors could not withdraw their money. These words also conveyed to depositors that the bank was shutting down operations for good.

In the immediate aftermath of the bank's closure, Douglass took the brunt of the public's ire. He was taking the fall—and the hit to his reputation. He would be known as the president of the Freedman's Bank as it plummeted into the financial abyss. He did not escape the criticism of African Americans. Though Douglass wrote and spoke of his disappointment over his affiliation with the bank in its final months after the bank closed, he received some of the harshest critiques from the African American press. A writer to the *Christian Recorder* exemplified this condemnation. "It will hardly console the people to tell them that he went into the Freedmen's Bank with his eyes shut," the writer charged. "That is worse than no excuse," the writer continued.[73]

Douglass would, however, gain clarity about the bank's failure and his role in it in the years to come. Though his tenure was short, he would continue to face criticism and questions about the bank—both from depositors and from members of Congress. Even though the bank closed in the summer of 1874, Douglass would be one of many people to be called before Congress to account for their role in its failure. Beginning in the fall of 1874, Congress would embark on a yearslong quest, through interrogating all those involved with the bank and its operations, to uncover the true culprits of the debacle. In the process, Douglass would endeavor to clear his name.

CHAPTER EIGHT

Fallout, 1874–1911

No event more unfortunate has recently occurred than
the suspension of the Freedman's Savings Bank.

—*THE WEEKLY CLARION*, JACKSON, MISSISSIPPI[1]

Despite my efforts to uphold the Freedman's Savings and Trust
Company it has fallen. It has been the Black man's cow, but the White
mans milk. Bad loans and bad management have been the death of
it. I was ignorant of its real condition till elected as its president.

—FREDERICK DOUGLASS TO GERRIT SMITH, JULY 3, 1874[2]

**Total business of the Freedman's Bank, as of
March 1, 1874: $57,000,000 ($1.5 billion today)**

IN JULY 1874, WAVES OF DEPOSITORS RUSHED TO THEIR local bank branches to find out if the news that they'd been hearing was true. The Freedman's Bank was closing—and they would not have immediate access to the money that the bank held in their accounts. After the previous fall's economic downturn, some depositors had decided to wait it out and see what would happen to the bank, and with their local branches. Unlike the thousands of other depositors who withdrew their money in a wave of bank runs at branches across the country, an estimated sixty-one thousand depositors decided to keep their accounts open, hoping that other bank patrons had simply overreacted. After all, the bank's president, Frederick Douglass, had urged calm. But when thousands of depositors arrived at the thirty-four bank branches across the nation in July 1874, they faced locked doors and cashiers who had to break the disappointing news that they could not withdraw their money. Depositors also faced a startling reality: the bank that had been promising for the past nine years to keep their money safe had failed to do just that. Depositors would soon find out that the bank held less than $400 in U.S. bonds and had less than $50,000 cash on hand. The Freedman's Savings and Trust Company was bankrupt.[3]

The bank's maxims about "saving the small sums" and the need for depositors to trust in the bank's administrators for their money to grow proved, in the end, to be lies. What's more, the administrators, who used the institution as their personal investment fund, benefited from the messages that they were sending to Black depositors, that opening accounts and placing their savings in the Freedman's Bank was the safest way to augment their wealth. Having the backing of the federal government, advertisements argued, meant that depositors' money was safe and secure. The depositors did not realize that the threats to their financial well-being came not only from external factors, such as lack of economic opportunities and the specter of white racial violence, but also from the bank administrators' greed.

By July 1874, the three commissioners were put to the task of grappling with thirty-four branches, as far north as New York City and as scattered as Jacksonville and Tallahassee, Florida; New Orleans, Louisiana; Little Rock, Arkansas; and St. Louis, Missouri. Creswell, Purvis, and Leipold began their investigation with a set of objectives. They would start by collecting as much cash as possible from the various branches, pursue borrowers with outstanding loans, then deposit the money that they gathered with the Treasury Department. Then they planned to evaluate the amount that the bank held in governmental securities and liquidate those holdings to "meet the demands of the depositors."[4]

To reduce expenses, the three commissioners believed that they needed to begin "discharging all employes [*sic*] that could be dispensed with, and closing up several branches at the earliest practicable moment." Ultimately, the commissioners realized that they needed to get a full accounting of the financial state of the bank, while eliminating expenses paid to maintaining bank branches and paying employees. They had to conduct a complete audit, an excavation into the volumes of financial records to "ascertain as speedily as possible the true condition of the liabilities and assets of the company."[5] The implied intention moving forward, for the commissioners and for the bank's trustees, was to rebuild the Freedman's Bank, for the benefit of the 61,144 depositors who still held accounts.

But as the commissioners' examination proceeded through the late summer and early fall of 1874, it became clear that the bank was beyond redemption. The people who would suffer the most were the depositors who had placed their faith and trust not only in the bank but also in the financial promises that administrators had been making since 1865. The suspension of the bank's operations was the unfortunate end to one chapter for depositors. Its closing, however, also marked the beginning of another. The summer of 1874 began a nightmare for depositors that would continue for decades.

THE BANK SUSPENDED OPERATIONS with a staggering amount of money in loans on its books. Importantly, the commissioners also needed to evaluate the bank's expenses. For example, over the bank's nine years of operation, trustees had begun approving the purchases, not rentals, of office space in cities around the South. In Nashville, the bank owned and maintained a building to house the bank branch and rented office spaces to tenants. While the renters brought in a valuable stream of income, the bank was responsible for paying for the costs of the building and basic maintenance. These expenses increased the bank's operating costs over the years—a cost that bank administrators willingly passed on to depositors. Meanwhile, depositors continued to appeal to their local cashiers, pleading for information about how to recoup the money the bank held hostage in their accounts. As commissioners, Purvis, Leipold, and Creswell had to decide the best course of action. Their task was to implement a multipronged approach to resolving such a multifaceted problem.

Part of the congressionally approved restructuring process required that the commissioners urge depositors to go to their local branches and submit their passbooks for updating, with the goal of the cashiers and depositors having a record of how much each depositor had in his or her account. The commissioners advertised in newspapers in cities with bank branches to let depositors know that they needed to keep their passbooks to qualify for reimbursement.[6] Depositors had to trust the accounting skills of their local cashiers, in hopes that they would receive their just compensation.

Though the trustees closed the bank on June 28, with Congress mandating four days later that they suspend operations, a small group of trustees continued to engage in business as usual. They took advantage of the chaos that surrounded the bank's closure to continue lending out depositors' money—what was left of it. The primary perpetrator was George Stickney. He used the commotion around the bank's suspension to sneak in a few extra loans, specifically to his business partners. Arguably the most egregious example occurred on June 29. Stickney loaned a staggering $33,366.66 to his friend and bank agent Juan Boyle, split into two separate payments.[7] The loans were not approved by the trust-

NOTICE.

OFFICE OF THE COMMISSIONERS OF THE ⎫
Freedman's Savings and Trust Company, ⎬
Washington, D. C., July 29, 1874. ⎭

Notice is hereby given to all persons, other than
depositors, who may have claims against the
FREEDMAN'S SAVINGS AND TRUST COMPANY
or any of its branches that they are called upon to
present the same and to make legal proof thereof
to the Commissioners of said company, at their
office, No. 1507 Pennsylvania avenue, Washington,
District of Columbia. Pass books, when properly
adjusted, will be deemed sufficient proof of the
balances shown to be due thereon. Depositors
will therefore present their pass books to the respective branches by which they were issued as
soon as possible, that they may be properly veri-
fied and balanced,   JOHN A. J. CRESWELL,
                              ROBERT PURVIS,
                              R. H. T. LEIPOLD,
au4 tfe24   Commissioners.

New Orleans Republican, *November 26, 1874*

ees or the finance committee. To make matters worse, Stickney did not require Boyle to offer any form of collateral or security. And this transaction was not Boyle's first loan from the bank. Between July 1870 and June 1874, he received nine loan installments, on the books, from the finance committee for a total of $44,270.04. Eaton, and then Stickney, recorded the loans and committed them to the official record. As Boyle became even more indebted to the bank, he continued forging stronger ties to the institution through working directly with Alvord and Stickney. Boyle agreed to sell the bank's bonds to buyers in Baltimore during the bank runs of September and October 1873. In the process of evaluating the bank's accounting, the commissioners discovered that Boyle had been skimming money from his transactions, in the amount of approximately $21,000. And as of 1880, the bank, and therefore the depositors, had lost an estimated $31,000 on Boyle's loans, which included the principal and interest payments.[8] Instead of pursuing criminal charges against him, Stickney "cover[ed] up the transaction," likely because to do otherwise would undermine Stickney's credibility as the bank's actuary when the institution collapsed.

Boyle's loan was not the only one that Stickney approved after operations were suspended on July 2. Six people received bank loans from him after July 2, which suggests that he continued to exploit his position to enrich select people in his professional network. Even Union general O. O. Howard borrowed $400 on July 14, using a $1,000 bond from the First Congregational Church. He ultimately paid back the loan on October 14, but he received the loan interest-free.[9] The final crop of loans served as an example to the commissioners, to members of Congress, and to depositors that redemption for this once-esteemed institution would be impossible.

As the trustees, including a beleaguered Frederick Douglass, grappled with the commissioners' intervention, the bank continued to advertise its services. These advertisements to Black depositors continued in Black publications, namely the *Christian Recorder.* Despite the news that circulated around the country of the bank's closure, cashiers and local administrators at branches across the South sustained their appeals for Black depositors to resume their patronage. The cashier of the Philadelphia branch, William Whipper, urged the trustees to keep the bank open. "The sale of the effects of 60,000 person [*sic*], whose value reach three millions of dollars, without a *necessary cause,*" he argued, "finds no parallel in the slave marts of the world."[10] Perhaps Whipper's consistent appeals throughout the fall of 1874 reflected his belief in the promise of economic uplift for Philadelphia's Black population. His message underscored the reality that the depositors were not to blame for the bank's closure. They were being punished for the trustees' mismanagement—and Congress's failure to properly regulate the institution.

One depositor who kept his account open and held out hope for the bank's recovery was Frederick Douglass. After the bank's closure in the summer of 1874, and during the subsequent series of investigations and examinations, he decided to not seek compensation. Instead, he wrote, "I determined to take my chances with the other depositors, and left my money, to the amount of two thousand dollars, to be divided with the assets among the creditors of the bank."[11] He wanted to demonstrate to depositors his trust in the process and in the investigators who were attempting to shed light on the bank's wrongdoing. Douglass wrote on

October 24, 1874, of his belief that "a large percentage, of the deposits of the *Freedman's Saving* and *Trust Company* will yet be paid." He also made a sobering admission. "I do not believe this result will be reached in less than two years from this time."[12] The commissioners decided that the best option for offering the depositors liquidity as of fall 1874 was to find a willing buyer of the bank's illustrious Washington, DC, building. The selling of the bank's central office signaled that the commissioners had to unload the bank's most visible asset to satisfy the depositors' financial needs.

The attempted sale of the central office was just one step in the arduous process of closing the Freedman's Bank for good. By the fall of 1874, the three commissioners went to work examining the bank's branches and the trustees' records to craft as extensive an assessment of the bank's finances as possible. On December 15, 1874, Creswell, Leipold, and Purvis presented their findings in a 119-page report to the comptroller of the currency, who then passed it along to the House Committee on Banking and Currency.

The report yielded the most complete financial picture of the bank's nine-year run. It was even more incriminating than previous accounts. The commissioners' report revealed that the problem had not been the depositors. As some critics of the bank surmised, the problems stemmed from not only the practice of lending but the flagrant nature of the finance committee's approach to lending, even after the removal of Cooke and Huntington. According to the report, "Most of the loans held by the company are overdue, and on many of them interest had been allowed to accumulate for two and in some cases three years."[13]

The problem extended from the central office to the branches. Though Meigs and his team of examiners had illuminated the widespread lending that had been occurring at bank branches, with cashiers at branches in Jacksonville, Beaufort, and even Washington making small loans without requiring applicants to show collateral, the commissioners offered a more comprehensive look. "The same may substantially be said of the branch loans," the commissioners charged. "[A]s a class, these appear to be the worst in possession of the company, and we doubt," they argued, "whether even fifty per cent of their amount will

ever be collected."[14] The commissioners' report showed just how rampant the practice had become.

The data that Purvis, Creswell, and Leipold accumulated reflected
an astounding deficit. Their report echoed the warning that Meigs made
in his 1873 examination, that "the institution was subject to a constant
outlay, far beyond the immediate profits on the deposits."[15] Congress and
the bank's administrators, even Douglass, came to terms with the fact
that that the bank had been operating in the red. For the bank's entire
existence—as depositors were putting tens of millions of dollars collectively into savings accounts—trustees, cashiers, and administrators were
not being faithful financial stewards. Since 1867, when Eaton took out
the first bank loan, the bank log counted 1,108 unique borrowers. The
total amount that the finance committee lent to borrowers amounted
to approximately $3.5 million.[16] The average value of the loans that had
not been repaid was $2,024. Moreover, 75 percent of the bank's loans
were made between 1870 and 1872. For the loans that reached their date
of maturity, meaning when borrowers agreed to pay back the loans with
interest, which was 83 percent of the loans that the bank made, 95 percent were in default and remained unpaid.[17]

After submitting a forty-page list of outstanding loans, the commissioners came to a startling conclusion. They could not recommend that
depositors receive compensation just yet. "The present condition of the
books and accounts of the company, too, is such that even if we have the
necessary funds, now, to declare a dividend, it would not only be impru-
dent," they declared, "but unsafe to do so."[18] They could not tell Congress or depositors when it would be "safe" for depositors to receive their
money; the commissioners were recommending that depositors continue waiting. The commissioners then asked Congress to allow them
to resume the work of selling bank properties, and recouping loans, to
find a strategic way of reimbursing the depositors.

The commissioners' show of faith convinced members of Congress
to allow them to continue their work over the next two years. They used
the time to excavate the bank's books and sell the bank's assets. As the
months, then years, passed, the expected return that depositors hoped
to receive diminished. By November 1875, the commissioners offered

depositors a 20 percent dividend payment. This meant that the depositors who still held money in their accounts could receive only 20 percent of their money.[19]

Democratic members of Congress and state legislators around the country used the Freedman's Bank suspension, and the dwindling hope of depositors, to hurl political attacks at bank officials, at Republicans, and even at depositors. One member of the North Carolina Senate, Democrat Charles M. Busbee, argued, "[O]f all the swindles ever perpetuated upon an innocent people, the radical Freedman's Bank swindle is the most infamous."[20] It did not matter that the victims of the swindle were freed people. Groups of Democrats looking to score political points cared little for the plight of African Americans. All that mattered to them was that the bank, founded and run by radical Republicans, had failed spectacularly. Some writers even blamed freed people for misplacing their trust. "Radical carpetbaggers whom the negroes follow in elections are unable to enlighten them," was one attack that appeared in a December 1874 issue of the *Memphis Appeal*.[21] Politicians eagerly used the bank as ammunition to undermine the political and social work of Reconstruction throughout the South.

༄

IN JANUARY 1876, the Democratic majority of the House of Representatives decided to make a political move against Republicans and their Reconstruction policies. They ordered an official investigation of the bank. Members of Congress mandated the formation of the Select Committee on the Freedman's Bank, which would consist of nine congressmen, to investigate the bank's failure. Congressional Democrats, seeking to reorient the political conversation about Reconstruction and its failures, led the charge to publicize Republicans' missteps with propping up the bank. One by one, the committee called bank administrators, such as John Alvord and other members of the board of trustees, to account for their crimes.

The congressional examinations were not unpartisan. Indeed, congressional Democrats were eager to use the flagrant mismanagement of the bank to lob political charges against the dwindling Republican influence in Congress. The examination was led by Virginia congressman B. B. Douglas, who served as the chairman of the Select Committee on the Freedman's Bank. A Democrat first elected in 1874, Douglas served as a lieutenant and then major with the Confederate army during the Civil War. So it came as no surprise that his initial comments in the January 1876 congressional report were tinged with hatred for the Republicans and the Freedmen's Bank. He took pleasure in berating bank administrators and spoke with a false concern for the plight of the depositors. Democrats such as Douglas sought to discredit not only the bank's administrators but northern bankers and the industry writ large.

He had taken it as his personal duty to expose the effects of Republican legislation on the status of the Freedman's Bank and freed people across the South. A Democrat by political affiliation, Douglas understood his role as the chairman of the Joint Select Committee on the Freedman's Bank. But unlike his Republican colleagues, he had no intention of painting a positive portrait of the bank. Instead, he wanted to use the bank failure as an example of Republican mismanagement and the failure of freed people to properly understand the realities of political and economic freedom.[22]

Douglas represented a cohort of Democrats welcomed back into American political life after the radical push for the legislative actions that characterized Reconstruction for African Americans. The Democrats increased their attacks. In a June 1874 congressional debate on the bank, E. D. Sandiford, a Democratic congressman from Kentucky, attacked the Republicans who he argued had spent years enabling the bank's trustees and protecting their political allies. They did so, Sandiford argued, at the expense of the South's economic stability. "The South is and has been suffering from a lack of currency, and this has been one of the drains which has helped to deplete it in that respect." But his critiques were not merely about the structure of the bank's operations. Instead, he used the bank, and freed people's economic uplift through their patronage of the bank, to argue against governmental intervention in the South. He contended, "The principle upon which the bank was organized was wrong." He continued by conveying a message to freed people. "This experiment in banking will be a valuable lesson that will teach the colored people to look to their home institutions for the safety of their surplus cash," he argued, "and to not depend upon the Government for everything."[23] In an argument that underscored Democrats' rejection of governmental policies that Republicans had enacted to support freed people's transition from slavery to freedom, Sandiford equated federal legislative intervention with unnecessary welfare policies for the formerly enslaved. Douglas's series of 1876 inquiries put Sandiford's critiques on public display. He would use the testimonies of bank officials, and bank depositors, to discredit and destroy congressional Republicans.

The testimonies began in January 1876. Douglas used his position as the committee chairman to criticize governmental officials for enabling Henry Cooke, Republicans for failing to properly regulate the bank, and the Treasury Department and Office of the Comptroller of the Currency for allowing the bank to devolve into financial ruin. Once the hearings began, Douglas and his Democratic colleagues worked until May 1876 to expose the perpetrators of the bank fraud. One by one, bank administrators were carted out before members of Congress, called to account for their crimes.

One of the first people to testify was bank commissioner John Creswell. On January 10, 1876, Creswell sat before eight congressmen, ready to answer their questions about his investigation into the bank's failure. In his short testimony, he confirmed the fact that by the time Congress brought in the three commissioners, "[t]he bank was largely insolvent."[24]

The committee heard testimonies from people such as J. V. W. Vandenburg and George Stickney, each of whom attempted to frame his involvement with the bank in positive terms. But the committee's most controversial witness was John Alvord. Weary from years of travel and financial hardship, Alvord sat before the committee on February 8, 1876, to answer their questions, and to try to absolve himself from purposeful wrongdoing against the bank's depositors.[25] Douglas harbored a special enmity toward Alvord. In his initial statements that framed the committee's charge, Douglas singled him out. He contended, "It was not until Alvord became president and the bank in fact brought to Washington, where it was subjected to all manner of malign influences, polit-

ical and speculative, sole and corporate, that the 'irregularities' of which
the management was guilty, became so frequent and portentous as to
attract attention, and call forth the animadversions of such newspapers
as were not subsidized to conceal or paliate [*sic*] the abuses."[26] Douglas's
antipathy toward Alvord seeped through his inquiries.

In the committee's questioning of Alvord, very little focused on
the work of the bank's first two presidents. And while this might make
sense considering that Alvord was the president when the bank moved
to Washington and when the charter was amended, it is worth questioning why Douglas did not inquire about the bank's executive committee
before he called Alvord to testify. Instead, he focused his attention on
Alvord's mismanagement.

The committee asked Alvord about his leadership of the bank's
trustees, specifically his signing off on the millions of dollars of loans
that continued to go unpaid during his presidency. Douglas had decided
to deploy a politically deft strategy in questioning Alvord. For example,
he did not officially blame Alvord for his mismanagement of the bank.
Instead, he and other Democratic congressmen alluded to Alvord's
absence from Washington and inability to control the finance committee's actions, especially once he became president in 1868. And surely
Alvord deserved some of the blame. Despite his initial, and some would
argue continued, enthusiasm about the bank and its mission, he did not
pay enough attention to how the trustees and administrators were handling the bank's investments—the freed people's deposits.

Though Alvord's presence before the committee took up most
of its time on February 8, the committee members were not satisfied
with his first testimony. They called him again on February 10 and 15
to clarify his statements. In one of the longest exchanges, Douglas led
the committee in asking Alvord about his post-bank professional life.
Shortly after the bank ceased operations, Alvord became the president
of the Seneca Sandstone Company—the company, owned in part by
Henry D. Cooke, that had received tens of thousands of dollars in
loans from the bank.[27] Of course, the committee asked Alvord if he
had been involved with the company while he held positions with the
Freedman's Bank. He said that he had not. He kept these two posi-

tions separate, to prevent conflicts of interest. But the committee was not satisfied. Its members wanted to know about how and why Alvord was such a stalwart supporter of the bank as he became aware of the rampant malfeasance.

Alvord stated that as he traveled around the South, especially between 1868 and 1874, inspiring Black people to open accounts and deposit money, he heralded the claim that the bank was still a fully functioning institution. In fact, Alvord stated that he was ignorant of the bank's irregularities for most of the time that he was affiliated with it. But he had inklings of the finance committee's mishandling of the deposits. Though he sat in on meetings, he indicated, he did not have voting power in the committee. But considering that he was president between 1868 and 1874, it is striking that Alvord did not hold himself accountable for the loans that the finance committee, Cooke and Eaton specifically, was making. Instead, he shifted responsibility. "The reckless men (I mean the enterprising men)," Alvord declared, "were always reckless."[28] The men to whom Alvord referred were Cooke, Clephane, and Huntington, "Mr. Huntington, especially," Alvord revealed. But illegal loans, such as the Seneca Sandstone loan, which were not recorded officially or voted on officially by the finance committee, were enacted under his stewardship of the bank. Alvord called it an "out-of-door arrangement, entirely unknown at the time to the finance committee, and which never went on record."[29] His testimony served only to highlight Douglas's rationale for dedicating time and resources to the hearings.

In a pointed exchange, Douglas asked Alvord if he regretted recruiting Black depositors to a financial institution he knew was engaged in illicit pursuits.

CONGRESSMAN DOUGLAS: While you were making your tours in the southern country, persuading the freedmen to deposit their money in the bank known as the Freedman's Savings and Trust Company, did you ever think of telling them that their funds were being squandered by the payment of overdrafts, by loans on bad or insufficient security, and otherwise endangered by the illegal proceedings of its managers in Washington?

ALVORD: I should have done it, if I had known it; but when I was
in my work of establishing branches we invested in Government
bonds only.[30]

Douglas's goal was to humiliate Alvord, to show that he was an inept
president whose primary concern was not the economic well-being of
freed people and the safety of their deposits. Instead, Douglas wanted to
prove, Alvord was naïve at best, cunning and scheming at worst.

One of the most controversial testimonials came from Dr. Charles
Purvis, who testified on February 19, 1876. In his questioning, he illuminated that when more Black men joined the board of trustees, first in
1873, then with Douglass in 1874, they attempted to wield control of the
bank. This was particularly true for the finance committee. Because the
trustees met only once a month, they were not regularly being apprised
of who was receiving loans from the bank and how much in loan volume
the bank was making. "As the thing was, we, trustees—meeting but
once a month, and then only hearing statements—could really know
nothing about the affairs of the bank," Purvis detailed.[31]

Moreover, Purvis had personal reasons for supporting Douglass's
candidacy, and for being so outspoken since the bank's failure in 1874.
"I have been called a pimp and a black leg . . . by the Star and other
papers," Purvis argued. "We found that we were losing our control
among the colored people, and we had hopes to get it back again,
and to control the bank as well."[32] For that reason, the Black trustees pushed strongly for Douglass's presidency. And though Purvis did
not regret advocating for Douglass or his time with the bank, he did
believe that the bank attracted some trustees interested in exploiting
freed people's new status.

Very little of the congressional hearing was dedicated to the experiences of the freed people who deposited approximately $57 million into
the bank. The hearings focused almost exclusively on the trustees and
the mishandling of the deposits by the bank's administration. So when
Sander L. Howell, a Black minister from the Nineteenth Street Colored
Church in Washington, DC, testified before the committee on March
18, 1876, he was the exception. Howell had the opportunity to put on

the record his experience with the bank—and his disappointment in the institution's failure. Born in Charlotte, Virginia, in 1835, Howell spent the years immediately after the Civil War as a theology student and as a missionary.[33] He opened a Freedman's Bank account on February 20, 1873, in the bank's Washington, DC, branch.[34]

At first, he was enthusiastic about depositing his earnings into, and investing in, the Freedman's Bank because he believed in the bank's righteous mission. Howell assumed that his deposits would be safe because, he argued before the committee, he believed that the government would guarantee his money.[35] When the bank failed in June 1874, he had about $760 in his account. He was one of the few depositors who received payment in the years after the bank's closure. But he could not recoup the entirety of his money. He received $153.92, a mere 20 percent of the amount he had in his account at the time of the bank's closing.[36]

Howell then relayed a conversation he had with one of the commissioners, Leipold, after the bank closed. Specifically, he wanted Leipold to answer for why the bank would not pay depositors the full amount that they had in their accounts at the time of the bank's failure. Instead, Howell argued, reports circulated that the bank would pay only ninety-five cents, then seventy-five cents, on the dollar. These figures confused and, importantly, angered Howell. He questioned Leipold about "how we came to be so misled as to the value of the bank," as the depositors were told that "the Government was bound for the money deposited in the bank." According to Howell, Leipold told him that the government had not backed the bank or the deposits. Leipold also told him that freed people were "foolish to put our money in there." He then criticized the Republicans for supporting a bank for freedmen, suggesting that the entire enterprise was a foolish endeavor.[37]

Howell finished his testimony by stating that he moved to Washington from Virginia in search of a new life and new opportunities. He wanted to make "something to try to start on." But, he divulged, "I lost all I had in the bank." Howell's experience with the bank likely mirrored that of the other tens of thousands of freed people who put their hopes in the institution.[38]

The testimonies that filled the Douglas committee hearings in 1876 illuminated the factors that precipitated the bank's downfall. With the testimonies of bank personnel, borrowers, and even, with Samuel Howell, a depositor, the Douglas committee used the bank's collapse to cast the trustees as villains. In the end, the committee recommended that John Alvord, Henry Cooke, Lewis Clephane, Hallett Kilbourn, John O. Evans, and Jay Cooke be indicted for fraud. The charges would never come. Despite the scale of their crimes, the defrauding of freed people, these men experienced only a temporary tarnishing of their reputations and their wealth. In the meantime, freed people continued to advocate for Congress to compel the bank commissioners to pay them. As the years wore on, depositors would have one more opportunity to get more information out of the bank's personnel. This time, the person leading the charge would not be a white Democrat but a Black Republican senator representing Mississippi: Blanche K. Bruce.

SENATOR BLANCHE K. BRUCE understood what hung in the balance, as he attempted to do what he could for the thousands of depositors who continued to advocate for their money. Not only did Bruce want to draw out an explanation for the bank's demise from bank administrators, but he also wanted to seek justice for the depositors because he understood their plight. Born enslaved in Virginia in 1841, Bruce grew up having witnessed both the degradation of slavery and the joyful promise of freedom.[39] Having learned to read and write as a child, he escaped to Kansas during the Civil War. After the war, he relocated to Mississippi, where he launched his political career. The only U.S. senator to have been formerly enslaved and the first Black senator to serve a full term, Bruce made his run for Congress from Mississippi, where the majority of Black voters used their voting power to send him to the Senate to represent their interests in 1875.[40]

During his term as senator, one of Bruce's main legislative priorities was justice and recompense for the Freedman's Bank depositors. Though he could do little to force the federal government, specifically the Office of the Comptroller of the Currency, to compel the bank to

Senator Blanche K. Bruce

compensate depositors, he could help commit the bank's failure to the official record. He could preserve the bank's memory through a second congressional inquiry.

Bruce noted, before the inquiry of 1879 officially began, that if the trustees had been "men of great discretion, great integrity, and entire devotion to the purpose of the enterprise under their control," there was no reason why the bank should have succumbed to the vagaries of the Panic of 1873.[41] Bruce's responsibility, therefore, was to delve into the trustees' actions that led to the bank's untimely failure. In this capacity, he stepped up to be chairman of the Senate Select Committee on the Freedman's Savings and Trust Company.

Senator Bruce's investigation revealed more information than did the Douglas hearings of 1876. The nation's political backdrop had shifted as well. The bank's failure in the summer of 1874 occurred as Democrats successfully gained an advantage in Congress.[42] Bruce wanted to use what he would soon come to realize was the last opportunity for a Black man to wield his position as a U.S. senator to illuminate, for the tens of thousands of depositors, why they remained unable to recoup the contents of their accounts with the bank. (Bruce would not be reelected. He left office in 1881, after having served a full term in the Senate.) Though his inquiries and those of Douglas were steeped in partisanship, both men had similar goals: to highlight how the bank trustees mishandled Black people's deposits and how they pilfered millions of dollars in the process, especially after 1867.

The initial congressional inquiries that took place after the bank's closure were not unbiased examinations. Instead, they were used by Democrats to take the reins of Congress for their own political ends. It was in this rare moment during Reconstruction when the political interests of Democrats, on the rise in Congress, aligned with those of the Black Republicans in Congress. Both groups, whose political alignments rarely intersected, worked together to forge common ground. They argued that they wanted bank officials to be held accountable for their misdeeds. Congressional Democrats, with Douglas leading the charge, wanted revenge for what he believed were renegade policies of the radical Republicans. Black Republicans wanted governmental authorities to compel bank officials to pay for their crimes against freed people. Not only were they seeking compensation, they wanted proof that their fight for freedom during the Civil War had not been in vain. If the government could not enforce the rule of law for economic crimes, then what hope would they have that the federal government would hold white Americans to account for committing public acts of racial violence and intimidation against newly enfranchised Black Americans? Bruce was likely motivated by a myriad of factors. Yet the continued economic violence that the bank's depositors faced in advocating for themselves and their economic interests perhaps shaped his perspective on the hearings. The question of economic violence was front and center in the minds of people such as Robert Smalls.

Though Smalls was not called to testify, he did offer his perspective to Bruce on the bank's collapse early in the senator's preparation for the hearings. Smalls wrote a letter to him, which was then included in the committee's official report. On July 31, 1879, writing from his home in Beaufort, South Carolina, Smalls decided to address his heartbreak at the bank's closure, and the extent of the Beaufort cashier Scovel's wrong-doing, for the official record.[43] As a depositor at the Beaufort branch, and a prominent member of the South Carolina General Assembly, Smalls witnessed how Scovel ran the branch and was perhaps privy to conversations among the Black depositors about the loans that Scovel was making—and about his lavish lifestyle. Smalls's letter to Bruce revealed the extent to which the bank administrators' mishandling of depositors' money affected the daily lives of Black people living in communities around the South.

Bruce had a similar list of witnesses to Douglas's. And one of the most important witnesses was John Alvord. On May 27, 1879, Alvord sat before Bruce and three other members of the Senate select committee, ready, but perhaps tentative, about opening up again about this time in his professional life. In a departure from his testimony three years earlier, Alvord was confused, misremembering dates and stumbling over recollecting major events of the bank's nine-year operation. His testimony was short. They asked him to state the years of his presidency, whether he had any involvement in the bank since its closure, and whether he had examined any of the commissioners' report. Then the committee dismissed him from what turned out to be a staid testimony that offered no new information. Alvord admitted that he was traveling to Colorado to visit his children and stated that he would not be available if they requested his presence at a later date. He confessed that he was more than happy to answer their questions, but the committee did not question him, perhaps believing that they could get the information that they wanted from other, more reliable, witnesses.[44]

Bruce spent the summer and fall of 1879 questioning witnesses such as Creswell and Leipold about the loans that they discovered and even about their own appointment as commissioners. However, of the witnesses called to testify, perhaps the most anticipated one was Henry Cooke. Finally, Bruce did what Douglas did not do: call Cooke to appear before the Senate. As a person whose name popped up frequently in the hearings, his participation was important. He appeared before Bruce and the committee on January 15, 1880, to finally testify about his involvement in the Freedman's Savings and Trust Company.

As a witness, Cooke equivocated and hedged about his involvement with the bank and his service on the finance committee. For having played such an important role, that of the finance committee chairman, Cooke made sure to not incriminate himself, Huntington, or Eaton.[45] Instead, he argued that the loans that he received as a stockholder of the Seneca Sandstone Company and the Maryland Freestone Mining and Manufacturing Company were legal and that he did nothing to undermine the bank. In fact, he declared that he could not remember specific details of his time with the bank. When a member of the Senate committee, Senator Withers, scolded Cooke, arguing, "These indefinite answers and hypothetical suggestions amount to nothing. We want you, Mr. Cooke, to examine and see whether these things occurred," Cooke, ever the cunning lobbyist, demurred, stating that the records were not well kept.[46] He frustrated the Republican members of the committee and after the questioning, he left the hearing, surely pleased at his performance.

When Bruce began questioning those involved with the bank during its demise, including Creswell, Leipold, and Cooke, he inevitably encountered the bank's last president: Frederick Douglass. On February 14, 1880, Frederick Douglass walked into the room designated for the Senate Committee on Manufactures, with the expectation that he would be called to answer the questions of the five-person committee, which that day included Republican Angus Cameron of Wisconsin, Democrat John B. Gordon of Georgia, Democrat Robert E. Withers of Virginia, and Democrat A. H. Garland of Arkansas.[47]

The committee reflected the political shifts that had been occurring in Congress since the election of 1876. Democrats and Republicans in Congress had reached a compromise over the election of Republican Rutherford B. Hayes to the presidency in the fall of 1876. In exchange for his agreeing to withdraw federal troops from the South and not enforcing civil rights legislation, Democrats would certify Hayes as president. It would mark the official end of the government's Reconstruction policies in 1877. Hayes's election, and the subsequent political decisions, also known as the Compromise of 1877, ended the government's dedication to the plight of freed people. It was under this political cloud that Bruce conducted his investigation into the bank. Moreover, other than Bruce and Cameron, who were Republicans, Douglass faced Democrats such as Gordon, the senator from Georgia. In Gordon, Douglass confronted a former member of the Confederacy and the leader of Georgia's Ku Klux Klan.[48]

Douglass was likely prepared for his testimony. Bruce's committee had been conducting interviews since April 1879, so it was only a matter of time before Douglass would be called to account for his actions. As he sat before the five senators, he was more than ready to answer the committee's questions, and to clear his name. In his testimony, Douglass took advantage of the opportunity to explain his involvement with the bank, to exculpate himself on the record. He detailed that he was convinced by friends and political allies in Washington to support the bank by accepting the trustees' nomination for the bank's presidency in February 1874. He was given two to three weeks to accept. According to Douglass, the outgoing president, John Alvord, had been forced out of the role—though he continued to maintain a position on the bank's board. The trustees had become unsure about his ability to properly steward the bank, especially after the release of a critical report from the Office of the Comptroller of the Currency in February 1874. Skeptical of the offer, but interested in moving more formally into politics, Douglass begrudgingly accepted.[49]

Douglass revealed that when he assumed the position of president, he realized there were myriad problems with the bank. Stickney sent him reports in which he provided updates he was receiving from the various bank agents throughout the country. To obscure the correspondences, Stickney and the agents wrote in code, "usually in cipher," as Douglass remembered. He believed that the shadowy nature of the correspondences meant that there were aspects of the bank's business about which Stickney did not want him to know. Douglass was frustrated. He stated that the obscurity of the bank's accounting "increased my suspicion of the unsoundness of things about that bank."[50]

Douglass told the committee he learned that between 1867 and 1872, Cooke and Huntington had been concealing their communications about the bank and about their other business dealings by writing in code. They deployed this strategy in their business correspondences

with Cooke's brother, Jay, during the 1860s. By coding their communications, and decoding their letters using a key, Cooke and Huntington shrouded their borrowing from the Freedman's Bank from prying
eyes—even from the gaze of fellow finance committee members.[51] They
carried this strategy into the communications about the Freedman's
Bank and their borrowing habits from the bank.[52] This meant that
years of the bank's financial information were obscured so that only the
people with the key could decipher the letters. Douglass believed that
there was an asymmetry of information and that he, as president, was
not fully apprised of all the information he needed to properly lead the
bank. He believed that he was set up to fail.

Douglass had a final complaint about his time with the bank. He
noticed days after taking the position of president that he was the only
trustee who had deposited any money into the bank. This meant that he
was the only person on the board of trustees who had a financial obligation to ensure the bank's success. This fact underscored his discomfort with his decision to be the bank's final president, especially the one
during the bank's ultimate demise.

After Douglass's testimony, the committee called forward its next
set of witnesses. The bank's former inspector and former paymaster of
the Freedmen's Bureau, Anson M. Sperry, took his turn in front of the
committee. Senator Garland jumped into the questioning and asked
Sperry about a topic that Douglass had introduced: the bank's shadowy
communication methods, that is, the ciphers. Sperry responded, "With
reference to the cipher used by the bank, I will say that I prepared that
myself."[53] He then explained the rationale behind his use of ciphers in
bank communications. He argued that bank personnel had to protect
the banking information that they were transmitting, in terms of information that cashiers from bank branches were sending to the central
office in Washington. According to him, bank administrators had to
safeguard their information and the cipher helped them accomplish this
goal. "The sole object of this cipher," Sperry maintained, "was to protect
the bank from the leakages in the telegraphic companies' offices in the
South."[54] They did it "for self-protection," and he contended, "[I]t is no
more than any other moneyed institution does."[55]

Sperry then rebutted Douglass's contention that he was not privy
to the cipher or the information contained in the coded correspondences. "There was no concealment and no intention of concealment
of the cipher, or of the key to it, that I am aware of, from anybody who
had any business to know it," Sperry justified. He even went as far as to
state that there was no plan to keep Douglass from obtaining a copy of
the cipher. But Sperry did not absolve himself. In the next sentence, he
stated, "It was simply to protect ourselves from outsiders."[36] His mention
of "outsiders" in a conversation about ciphers, codes, and Douglass not
having had the necessary information to fully understand the state of
the bank's business was telling. This comment underscored Douglass's
testimony and brief experience as the bank president. The bank's white
administrators kept him from being an effective chief executive, even in
what would become the bank's final months.

The rounds of testimony, from Douglass and others, suggest that
the bank's trustees and administrators brought Douglass in and elected
him as president for a specific reason. They wanted him to take the fall
for the bank's inevitable collapse. Douglass came to this stark realization when he penned his third autobiography in 1881. He wrote, "The
fact is, and all investigation shows it, that I was married to a corpse."
Despite the central office's beautiful facade, tasteful construction, and
sophisticated decor, by the time Douglass became the bank's president,
it was rotten from the inside out. Douglass recognized, "[T]he LIFE,
which was the money, was gone, and I found that I had been placed
there with the hope that by 'some drugs, some charms, some conjura-
tion, or some mighty magic,' I would bring it back."[37]

But not all the Black trustees were ready to blame the bank's failure on all the members of its board. Charles Purvis announced in
his testimony, when Bruce asked him about the cause of the bank's
collapse, "The bank failed, in my opinion, from natural causes."[38] He,
however, offered a caveat. Purvis wanted to separate the pre- and
post-Cooke periods, arguing that the finance committee of the post-
Cooke time was composed of "men who attempted, and no doubt
desired, to serve the interests of the bank."[39] He did not address
whether the plunder was a natural byproduct of lax regulation and

greedy bank administrators. Perhaps he wanted to show that he and the other Black trustees attempted to act as responsibly as possible. In fact, it was Purvis who had decided to fully explore the involvement of Henry Cooke in the bank's eventual downfall.

Purvis put the extent of Cooke's borrowing on public display for the committee—and ultimately for the depositors. Though at the time of his borrowing, mostly in 1871, the loan to Jay Cooke & Company of $50,000 appeared to be one of the larger amounts loaned, Charles Purvis attempted to set the record straight. He revealed to the committee that Cooke had, in fact, borrowed upwards of $600,000, a number far in excess of the documented loans in the 1874 examination and the 1876 Douglas report. Purvis's testimony put the bank's demise on the shoulders of the finance committee. Without the meddling of Cooke, Huntington, and Eaton, according to Purvis, the bank could have survived to continue operating in service of the nation's freed people.[60]

Senator Bruce concluded his investigation in 1880. Though he led the Republican charge to resolve the issues around the availability of information, so that the public and the depositors could better understand what caused the bank's failure, the hearings did little to quell depositors' fears that they would never get their money back.

※

IN OCTOBER 1883, the National Colored Men's Convention addressed the continued problem of depositor compensation. The convention's attendees adopted the issue as one of their eleven goals. In the sixth goal, they made a pointed critique of the bank. Their statement read:

> The failure of the Freedman's Savings Bank and Trust Company is a marvel of our time. It was established to receive the earnings of persons heretofore held in bondage and the descendants of such persons. It was established by the government and thought to be solvent. In changing its charter the trustees transcended their authority and thereby made themselves liable. The government, in appointing special machinery to close the insolvent institution,

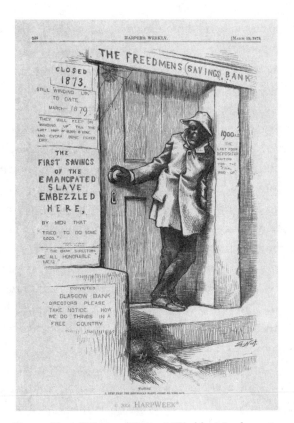

Thomas Nast, "Waiting," Harper's Weekly, March 29, 1879

violated the United States Statutes on bankruptcy, and should, therefore, reimburse the creditors of the bank.[61]

African Americans fought to have their claims recognized by members of Congress. But as the rise in racial violence shifted political conversations about Black people away from the economics of freedom toward survival, the plight of the Freedman's Bank depositors evolved. The commissioners released their last dividend in 1883. Depositors who could prove that they had money in the bank at the time of its closing could receive a meager 7 percent of the money that they held in their accounts.[62] In the end, the depositors had to forgo approximately $330,000, paid to the commissioners, examiners, and investigators who uncovered the reasons for the bank's demise. But the depositors cared less about the reasons, and more about the actual crime. They continued to seek recompense.[63]

A few members of Congress maintained the fight to reimburse the depositors. White Democratic congressmen from the South introduced bills in 1875, 1879, 1881, and again in 1910.[64] Yet some of these efforts were geared more toward winning political points than working on behalf of African Americans. In an April 4, 1888, hearing, for example, senators discussed "a bill to reimburse the depositors of the Freedman's Savings and Trust Company for losses incurred by the failure of said company."[65] The *Christian Recorder* reported on the bill's movement through Congress. "The Senate has justly passed a bill appropriating $1,000,000 to reimburse the depositors of that rotten concern, which was known as the *Freedman's Saving and Trust Company*," it read. "A large number of our people lost their *savings* with the failure of this bank, and it is to be hoped that the House, although with its democratic majority, will see fit to pass this bill."[66] But as in the previous attempts for depositors to receive just compensation, none of the bills were signed into law.

Into the early twentieth century, depositors put pressure on Congress and governmental officials to compensate them. These calls came from Black business and civil rights organizations, who continued to see the effects of the bank's demise in Black communities across the South. Demands for compensation also came from an unexpected place: former paymaster and inspector Anson M. Sperry. Throughout the 1880s and 1890s, and into the early twentieth century, Sperry was a consistent advocate for the depositors, writing to lawmakers and administrators with the Department of the Treasury, and to the subsequent comptrollers of the currency, to convince them to seriously consider a strategy to reimburse the remaining depositors and their families.

Ultimately, Sperry argued that he wanted the bank to succeed, and he wanted freed people to thrive economically within the tumultuousness of freedom. When the bank failed, he was devastated. Upon finding a long-lost 1870 bank document, Sperry noted in 1906, "I must have found it in the Washington files and took it as a keepsake. It is my sole memorial of 8 years hard work that I still believe in."[67] In the memorandum, Sperry reflected on his many years of dedication to the institution and to the people it served. He called the bank "the darling of my heart, the foundation of my real life."[68]

Sperry believed strongly in the bank's good work, and he decided that he would continue to advocate on the depositors' behalf. In fact, his most sustained correspondence in the early 1900s was with Minnesota congressman W. S. Hammond. Sperry wrote to him as late as 1909 and 1910. Hammond responded to him in 1910 that "82% of the amount due depositors in the Freedman's Savings and Trust Company have been paid" and that the work of the Committee on Banking and Currency proved that Congress could not do much else for the depositors. He even declared that "there is no legal obligation resting upon the Government to make good the losses of depositors."[69]

In a statement that Hammond surely penned to end Sperry's inquiries, he wrote that he did not believe that the federal government had a "moral obligation" to pursue justice for the depositors.[70] In fact, bank administrators like Sperry and the depositors themselves were at fault for the bank's demise. According to Hammond, the bank's mismanagement by the administrators was the price that depositors paid for their blind faith in the soundness of the institution. What Hammond could not fully appreciate were the streams of propaganda that the depositors absorbed about the Freedman's Bank. Of all the lofty messages that depositors received about the bank, the most important one was that it was backed by the federal government.

Hammond made a claim that many Democrats began to make in the late nineteenth and early twentieth centuries to sidestep the Freedman's Bank issue. "You were an inspector of the company until the bank failed," he charged, "and before that time had intimate knowledge of the manner in which the depositors were received." And he was not done lobbing charges. He asked, "Were representations made to the negroes to the effect that the Government was behind the institution?"[71] This question, about the purported relationship between the federal government and the Freedman's Bank that bank administrators advertised throughout the bank's operation, would be the loophole that Hammond and other Democrats used to evade responsibility for the economic harm done to the bank's depositors. Sperry could not deny Hammond's indictment. Bank trustees, administrators, and cashiers repeatedly touted governmental officials' support for the bank's estimable work.

Sperry, though, did respond. One might wonder why he continued to be a supporter of depositors' rights. He may have been a true believer in the bank's original mission. After all, Sperry was in a unique position. Having worked for the Union army as a paymaster during the Civil War and with the Freedman's Bank since September 1865, he was a grassroots member of the bank's administrative team. He collected deposits from depositors who did not have direct access to a bank branch. He had the privilege of interacting directly with thousands of freed people throughout the South, serving as a witness to the promise of freedom and the violence that faced African Americans as well. He, perhaps more than any other white person in the bank's central office or on the board of trustees, understood what the bank meant to the tens of thousands of freed people. Sperry was one of thousands of people who mounted sustained appeals to members of Congress and public servants in their quest for recompense.

The final bill was introduced in Congress on April 13, 1911, by Republican Ernest W. Roberts of Massachusetts. But the bill to reimburse the depositors of the Freedman's Savings and Trust Company had little congressional support.[72] The comptroller of the currency made the final report about bank disbursements nine years later, on December 1, 1920. John Skelton Williams, the then comptroller, closed the issue for good. He stated to Congress, "[T]his may be considered a final report as all funds in hand have been disbursed, and there are no further assets to be collected."[73] Williams's declaration, that there would be no continued governmental effort into reimbursing the depositors, did not convince African Americans who held accounts to stop their petitions. In the 1920s and 1930s, they sent letters of appeal by the thousands to secretaries of the Treasury, the attorney general, and the comptroller of the currency. They hoped that someone with political influence would hear their calls for reimbursement.

African Americans even appealed to U.S. presidents. In July 1937, Mrs. Catherine A. Johnson wrote to President Roosevelt asking for his help. She was seventy-six years old, in poor health, and a Freedman's Bank depositor. She had received her final dividend payment of twelve dollars in 1900. She wanted Roosevelt to extend her and her sister "some consideration," especially given that "he had done so much good for the poor."[74] There is no record of a response to Johnson from President Roosevelt, but depositors kept up their campaign to recoup their money into the twentieth century. Unfortunately, it was a campaign that did not yield more dividends for the depositors or their families.

CONCLUSION

The Problem of Finance
in the Age of Emancipation

"This is our bank," said they; and to this institution the
intelligent and the ignorant, the soldier fresh from the field of
battle, the farmer, the day laborer, and the poor washerwoman,
all alike brought their earnings and deposited them in
the Freedman's Bank. This place of safety for their scanty
store seemed to be the hope of the race for the future.

—WILLIAM WELLS BROWN, 1880[1]

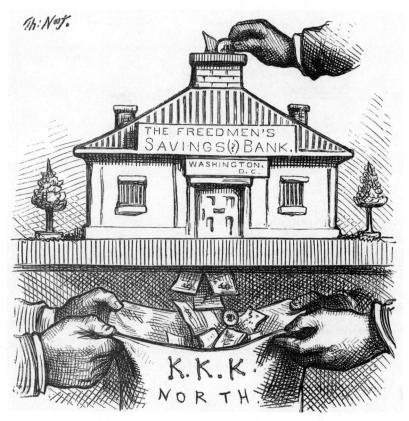

Thomas Nast, "Blood Money," January 1, 1900

IN 1880, MARY SUSAN HARRIS WAS NO LONGER THE eleven-year-old girl who strode into the Richmond branch of the Freedman's Bank with her mother, father, and younger brother to open her own bank account. Six years after the bank failed, she was a twenty-one-year-old washerwoman, living in Richmond with her family. When the bank failed, she had $25.87 in her account.[2] Though she never recovered all her money, she did take advantage of the opportunity to reclaim what little she could. Harris was among the two thousand depositors of the Richmond branch who appealed to the bank's commissioners to recoup her deposits during the first call in 1875. In total, she received $13.45, 63 percent of the total money in her account, paid out between 1875 and her final dividend payment in 1883. While the amount that she received was small in comparison to the almost $3 million that remained in the bank when it closed, the money surely could have helped Harris weather the challenges of life as a young Black woman in the late nineteenth-century American South.

It is unclear whether or not the full contents of her account could have helped extend her life. Mary Susan Harris died on September 3, 1886, in Richmond, at the age of twenty-six, just three years after her final payment. The cause of death was listed as an "ovarian tumor."[3] While the historical record does not reveal much more about her short life, we do know that she, with her family's help, embraced from a young age the adage of saving "the small sums" and investing in her future. But she misplaced her hope and trust in the promise of the bank's message. The financial potential of depositors such as Mary Susan Harris are lost to history. We will never know the full scope of African Americans' economic possibilities had the bank succeeded and not succumbed to both the unpredictability of the global capital market and the greed of white capitalists.

We do, however, have a better understanding of the bank administrators' financial misconduct. When the bank collapsed in 1874, it had approximately $3.5 million in outstanding loans, across 1,797 loans and 1,108 individual borrowers.[4] In addition, for the loans that reached their date of maturity, when borrowers had to repay, which was 83 percent of the loans by July 1874, 95 percent of the loan amounts were left unpaid. This suggests that borrowers, the vast majority of whom were white, who lived in Washington, and who had personal and professional ties to bank trustees, decided *not* to repay the money that they borrowed from the bank—and from Black depositors. Even after understanding that their loans were funded by freed people, and that the bank was closing because of insolvency, white borrowers made the strategic decision *not* to fulfill their financial obligations to the bank and to its African American patrons.[5]

Therefore, the failure of the Freedman's Bank represented many things to many people. For freed people, it represented the failure of the federal government, elected officials, white capitalists, and even African Americans with economic and political influence to protect their economic interests. The bank's failure, during the end of Reconstruction, represented the economic violence and terrorism that came to characterize the challenges that African Americans faced when they put political freedom into action. As the historian Aaron Carico contends, African Americans continued to be bound by the economic structures that shaped their lives during the period of slavery.[6] They confronted white racial violence. They faced economic and labor exploitation. They felt abandoned by federal authorities—and by the nation that they fought to build and protect during the Civil War.

The bank's collapse was seared into African Americans' collective memory into the twentieth and twenty-first centuries, encoded in the interactions between African Americans and Wall Street.[7] When, in the 1930s, interviewers from the Works Progress Administration interviewed the last living generation of African Americans to have experienced slavery, African Americans talked quite candidly about money. They told interviewers about the strategies that they used to save money, where they stored it, and how they approached ideas of personal finance. But there were no references to the Freedman's Bank. No one talked about their parents or grandparents investing in the bank as depositors or their perspectives on banking in Black communities. Instead, they revealed that they placed money under mattresses or with a trusted white person who they hoped would keep their money safe. These traditions are among the vestiges of the bank's failure. The bank's collapse was encrypted in African Americans' approach to engagement with banks and other white-owned financial institutions.

꒰꒱

IN THE END, the Freedman's Bank was not designed to succeed. Instead, the administrators allowed the bank to fail, letting depositors' money and their faith in the banking industry go up in flames. The bank's directors knew the risk, but behaved in ways that put Black people's money, and their hopes for a strong financial future, in jeopardy. Perhaps Frederick Douglass's words put it best: "To the freedmen was given the machinery of liberty, but there was denied to them the steam to put it in motion. . . . [T]hey were called citizens, but left subjects; they were called free, but left almost slaves."[8] Douglass's comment is an accurate one, when used to examine African Americans' economic climb out of slavery during the era of Reconstruction—and beyond.

Unfortunately, the fraud continued long after the bank closed, long after Congress stopped holding hearings, and long after the political will of politicians, bankers, and the federal government receded. As the bank faded from public memory, the descendants of the depositors attempted to keep the bank's existence, and its demise, alive. But they faced politicians who cared little for their pleas, and a banking industry that did not see the benefit of rehashing old stories about the failure of a bank created to serve African Americans. The Freedman's Savings and Trust Company represented the promise of African American economic uplift during a period of dramatic social and cultural change. At the same time, the bank also epitomized the reality of capitalism—and capitalists—left unchecked. Ultimately, the people who could least afford to be deprived of the benefits of wealth generation were on the losing end of capitalists' greed for more wealth. The depositors of the Freedman's Bank learned that they would have to think twice about putting their economic *trust* and *faith* in white financial institutions. This was a message that African Americans learned during the pivotal era of Reconstruction and that has shaped Black communities across the nation since the bank's collapse in 1874. This lesson about distrust of the broader financial marketplace influences the fraught relationship between African Americans and the financial services industry today.

The failure of the Freedman's bank continues to govern the very nature of Black economic life in America. According to a 2023 report released by the Federal Reserve, "The typical White family had about six times as much wealth as the typical Black family, and five times as much as the typical Hispanic family."[9] Based on the Survey of Consumer Finances, the median wealth of Black families in 2022 was $44,900, while the median wealth of white families was $285,000. This meant that the typical Black family held about 15 percent of the wealth of the typical white family. Relatedly, according to a 2021 report by the FDIC that examined unbanked and underbanked households in the United States, Black households were more likely than white households to be underbanked, meaning to not have a sustained relationship with a financial institution. Among households with between $30,000 and $50,000 of yearly income, for example, 8 percent of Black households were unbanked compared to 1.7 percent of white households.[10] It is difficult to read this data and not draw connections between the economic state of Black America today and the ways in which African Americans have been at times both ignored and exploited by the financial services industry.

THE FREEDMAN'S BANK was supposed to be a shining beacon of economic empowerment to help usher African Americans into a new era of political freedom. Though the bank was founded by Republicans eager to guide freed people economically out of slavery, its priorities shifted as the makeup of the bank's administrators and trustees changed. At the same time, the principles that guided the bank's founders, the idea that freed people could achieve economic uplift through saving and building wealth, ceased to be part of the administration's main priorities. It took only two years after the bank's founding for this ideolog-ical change to occur. The administrators—men such as Henry Cooke, William Huntington, D. L. Eaton, and George Stickney—were not dedicated to freed people's financial success. Even John Alvord, whose primary motivations appeared to have been altruistic, failed to protect African American depositors' economic interests. Instead, Alvord and the bank's trustees stole freed people's money to fund their own specu-lative ventures. By 1870, many of the trustees exploited their affiliation with the bank and with freed people to find new ways to enrich them-selves. And they continued to find ways to convince Black depositors to trust them. They expanded the bank's advertising campaign. They even added more Black cashiers and administrators. For example, by the time of the bank's closing, the trustees had appointed seventeen Black men as cashiers. In total, twenty-one Black men worked in local branches.[11] In the end, Black peoples' trust in the promise of the institution, and in those who worked for it, went unreciprocated. The very people who vowed to ensure the safety and growth of Black people's money were the ones who embezzled millions of dollars of it. In this way, African Amer-icans learned that the financial services industry would not serve them and would not fulfill their economic needs.

The federal government cannot escape blame. The failure of gov-ernmental authorities to properly regulate the bank destroyed African American wealth after the Civil War. Elected officials such as Congress-man W. S. Hammond used their political power to strategically deny recompense to the descendants of depositors who lost their money when the bank failed in 1874. At the same time, the failure of the Freedman's Bank caused a transfer of wealth from recently emancipated African Americans to whites that would not be repeated until the early twenty-first century. The fact that the bank's collapse occurred in the immedi-ate aftermath of slavery's violent end is telling. It suggests that federal authorities and members of Congress were protecting bankers instead of the very people whose labor helped build America's wealth and fought on the side of the Union during the Civil War. Weak governance by elected officials marked the downfall of Reconstruction. But the lack of political will along with the rise of congressional Democrats from the

South also had dire effects for African Americans, many of whom were seeking to forge economic safeguards for themselves in the aftermath of slavery.

Intellectual and writer W. E. B. DuBois spent the early part of his career researching the effects of economic divestment that African Americans experienced at the hands of white Americans during and after Reconstruction. In "The Negro Landholder in Georgia," DuBois argued, "One of the greatest problems of emancipation in the United States was the relation of the freedman to the land."[12] And land was what most freed people during the era of Reconstruction desired. They understood that property rights were intimately connected to economic and political rights. For this reason, the bank's failure proved to be particularly devastating. In 1901, DuBois wrote in the *Atlantic Monthly* about the economic challenges that African Americans faced during Reconstruction. He identified the implosion of the Freedman's Bank as a pivotal and destructive moment. He argued, "Not even ten additional years of slavery could have done as much to throttle the thrift of the freedmen as the mismanagement and bankruptcy of the savings bank chartered by the nation for their especial aid."[13] DuBois's arguments about the bank's failure foreshadowed the economic challenges that African Americans continued to face in the late nineteenth and early twentieth centuries. One could even say that DuBois's words are particularly poignant given the persistence of the financial industry's predation and the expansion of the racial wealth gap.

"The sin of capitalism is secrecy," DuBois wrote in 1947. He explained that for capitalism to function, it required "the deliberate concealing of the character, methods, and result of efforts to satisfy human wants."[14] Such secrecy, bound up in the trustees' acceptance of financial and political corruption, was what destroyed the Freedman's Bank, and the immediate economic prospects of African Americans. With the bank's collapse, African Americans learned a hard lesson in distrust: a distrust of the intentions of the federal government, a distrust of the promise of democracy, and a distrust of capitalism free from regulation. Freed people had been sold a message about saving, banking, and the privileges of landownership. By saving money in Freedman's

Bank accounts, depositors necessarily bought into the bank's messaging about the benefits of saving money with a formal financial institution. They initially believed that the bank, and the administrators who shaped its mission, would help them secure their status as landowners, and therefore as citizens, who deserved all the privileges that wealth and status were supposed to bestow. Instead, when the bank ultimately imploded, freed people gained clarity about the relationship between the ideals of democracy and the reality of capitalism. African Americans would have to turn inward to fulfill their own economic needs. Unfortunately, depositors recognized the ruse too late. Once the bank ceased operations, all they asked for was the money that they and their ancestors had put into their bank accounts, not more or less. They were not requesting reparations; they wanted what they and members of their family had worked hard to earn and save. Instead, African Americans would have to reformulate Frederick Douglass's message in "Self-Made Men"—Black communities across the nation would have to sustain and support themselves.

⟜

THE BANK'S FAILURE has many lessons. One of the biggest concerns America's racial wealth gap. Too often, the racial wealth gap has been explained as a product of African Americans' deficiencies, their historical inabilities to adjust to the demands of life in a democratic society guided by capitalist ideals. The Freedman's Bank offers a different story. Collectively, we have taken for granted that white wealth was built from Black work and Black ingenuity. Consider the fact that formerly enslaved people deposited approximately $57 million ($1.5 billion today) into the Freedman's Bank. They worked and saved to secure assets that they could transfer to their families and descendants. African Americans, especially the formerly enslaved, hoped that with slavery's end they could fully benefit from the profits of their own labor. The Freedman's Bank was supposed to aid them in this goal.

The history of the Freedman's Bank reveals the story of a people who put their faith, their money, and their trust in a financial institution that represented the promise of freedom after slavery's violent end. For a short period of time, the Freedman's Bank was a pillar of the American banking industry. It was a manifestation of freed people's dedication to the ideals of democracy and freedom. It embodied the promise of free labor, as slavery as an economic and social institution ended. Importantly, the Freedman's Savings and Trust Company represented economic freedom. Indeed, it was African Americans' public expression of their dedication to the principles of democracy and capitalism that drove their involvement with the bank.

Ultimately, the relentlessness of capitalism, the plunder by white capitalists, and the federal government's complicity are the story of the Freedman's Bank and the African Americans who hitched their financial future to the institution. The bank is a piece of American history that many would like to leave behind. But to understand where we as a nation and society are now, we must examine the past. And issues such as the racial wealth gap and economic inequality are not without a history. In many ways, the bank offers a lens through which to understand the economic and political issues that shape America as it is today. The history of the Freedman's Bank is more relevant today than perhaps ever before.

Acknowledgments

THOUGH THE AUTHOR'S NAME IS ON THE BOOK'S COVER, I've found that writing a book is always a collaborative process. I am blessed to be surrounded by people who have supported me and championed my ambitions during the research and writing process. I am extremely grateful to my family, friends, and colleagues who have encouraged me during the grueling task of finishing this book.

First, my students and research assistants. I have had the privilege to work with a dynamic, brilliant, and outstanding group of research assistants on this project. Alisia Simmons was the first student who agreed to join me on this adventure. She helped me figure out what the archive looked like for the Freedman's Bank. Alisia was eager to help me construct my own archive of primary and secondary sources to understand the direction in which this book would go. As a USOAR student during her first year at UVA, she proved to be diligent and highly analytical, with seemingly boundless amounts of energy. She even continued to do research and transcription work during her semester abroad in Paris. I'm eager to see what her future holds. Charlotte Gimlin worked with me on this project during her final semesters at UVA. I had the pleasure of having her in one of my undergraduate seminars and she has been an amazing assistant on this project. We even went on a research adventure together at the National Archives in College Park. I appreciated her patience and attention as she helped me with the final weeks of archival research. Though I have not had the pleasure of meeting Savannah Salazar in person, she helped me find valuable records at the Huntington Library in San Marino, California. Toward the end of the revision process, I had the opportunity to work with undergraduate students Margaret Zirwas and Jiawen Davis, who did the tedious work of proofreading chapters, chasing down the odd footnote, and building the book's graphs. Chloe Porche, Bethany Bell, and Crystalina Peterson helped me complete research and transcriptions as I was finishing the first draft of this book.

I feel very fortunate to be a faculty member at the University of Virginia, where we have a brilliant group of graduate students who are eager to delve into the history of the Civil War era and Reconstruction. The Nau Center for Civil War History has become my intellectual home. I'm not sure I could have written this book in the same way without this community of scholars.

Claudrena Harold, Elizabeth Varon, Caroline Janney, Calvin Schermerhorn, Dave Thomson, Cynthia Nicoletti, and Nadine Zimmerli offered extensive comments on the manuscript at a crucial point in the editing process. They descended onto Charlottesville, and some engaged through Zoom, for a rewarding conversation about the first full draft. Each brought their unique perspective on how I could improve the book, from Dave's knowledge of the Cooke brothers to Claudrena's insights into how the bank's economic success reflected Black people's economic power. It was an amazing experience, one for which I am extremely appreciative. My graduate students Jake Calhoun and Carrington OBrion were gracious enough to take time away from their dissertation research and comprehensive exam prep to help me in my manuscript workshop. I give a special thanks to them. Laurent DuBois, Jessica Kimpell Johnson, Vivian Feggans, and the staff at UVA's Karsh Institute of Democracy hosted this invaluable manuscript workshop and awarded me a summer grant that helped me finish the book.

I received generous financial support from the Carnegie Corporation of New York and the Mellon Foundation. Having the Carnegie Fellowship and the Mellon New Directions Fellowship provided me with an unprecedented two-year sabbatical to transform, as best I could, into a writer. At UVA, I have been supported by the Corcoran Department of History and the School of Arts and Sciences, which approved my extended sabbatical.

I had the opportunity to engage with a variety of scholars as I was writing this book. Pamela Laird, Gideon French, Claire Célérier, Purnoor Tak, Sam Bisno, and Ellora Derenoncourt offered ideas about how to make the book more impactful. I was invited to present and receive feedback on various chapters of the book at the University of Georgia, the University of Iowa Law School, the Iberia African American History Society, and Princeton University.

I first met my editor, Jon Durbin, in 2017. I received an email from him before the Southern Historical Association conference that year, asking if I'd like to meet to discuss my work. I was blown away because I knew the caliber of scholarship that W. W. Norton produced. Even though my first book did not go to Norton, I knew that I wanted to work with Jon and with Norton on my second book. Jon has advocated for this project, and I could not have asked for a better editor. I look forward to working on more books together in the future.

My agent, Tanya McKinnon, is a force. After I finished my first book and prepared to find out whether I would receive tenure, I knew that my second book would be on the Freedman's Bank. I also recognized that I wanted to write the book for a broader audience. I reached out to colleagues, and one person's name kept coming up: Tanya McKinnon. I sent a query email, praying that the project would resonate with her. She responded with an enthusiasm about the project that matched my own. As I was revising the book, she pushed me to be braver and bolder. Thank you, Tanya, and your team at McKinnon Literary, for your belief in me and in my ability to write this book.

My friends Audrey Dorélien, Creston Higgins, Jennifer D. Jones, Ava Purkiss, Sarah Milov, Corinne Field, Valeria López Fadul, and Amanda Gibson have provided me with support, laughs, gossip, and fun. I could not ask for a better community of friends. Brenda Doremus-Daniel has helped me understand why this work continues to be important to me. One of my best friends, Neferterneken Francis, was brilliant, beautiful, and fearless. She passed away after a yearslong battle with cancer as I was putting this book to bed. She had a luminous spirit and I hold her memory in my heart.

My daughter, Kenadie, has a level of patience with me that far exceeds her teenage years. She has willingly let me bounce ideas off her, been patient as my head was buried for months at a time in archival records, and has understood my early-morning and late-night writing sessions. Most impressive of all, she was my first proofreader. I knew that if my brilliant sixteen-year-old could engage with this book, and ask incisive questions, then I was on the right track. I am so proud of her and could not love her more.

My family has been the greatest source of love and inspiration. I hope I have made Stephanie Bryan, Ernest Stewart, Lorenzo Hill (and his new family), Theda Edwards-LaBome, Ashley Hill, Allan Hill, Terence Bryan, Kim Bowden, and my Bryan and extended Plunkett families proud. My mother, Deborah Bryan, has always been, and continues to be, my biggest cheerleader and supporter. She believes that I can achieve anything that I set my mind to. When I talked to her about the work that I was doing on this book, she would always respond with questions and comments, always stressing the importance of my work. I would not be where I am today without her unconditional support and love. This book is for her.

My husband, Kenneth, has seen this project from start to finish. In fact, he encouraged me to write this book. He would tell me that this story needed to be told, and that I needed to be the one to do it. At his urging, I decided to write a more audacious and a more ambitious book. I am lucky to be married to someone who is perhaps more dedicated to understanding the economic plight of Black America and the historical lineages of the racial wealth gap than I am. Thank you for your love, encouragement, and inspiration. I love you.

Appendix

BANK BRANCH OPENINGS

Norfolk	June 1865
Washington, DC	August 1865
Lynchburg	September 1865
Richmond	October 1865
Natchez	October 1865
Vicksburg	December 1865
Huntsville	December 1865
Memphis	December 1865
Savannah	January 1866
Mobile	January 1866
New Bern, North Carolina	January 1866
New Orleans	January 1866
Charleston	January 1866
Augusta	March 1866
Baltimore	March 1866
Jacksonville	March 1866
New York	July 1866
Tallahassee	August 1866
Beaufort	October 1866
Raleigh	January 1868
Shreveport	June 1868
Macon	October 1868
Wilmington	October 1868

Chattanooga	March 1869
Philadelphia	January 1870
Atlanta	January 1870
Columbia, Tennessee	January 1870
Nashville	March 1870
Little Rock	June 1870
Montgomery	June 1870
Columbia, Mississippi	August 1870
Louisville	October 1870
St. Louis	November 1870
Lexington	November 1870

BUSINESS OF THE FREEDMAN'S
SAVINGS AND TRUST COMPANY

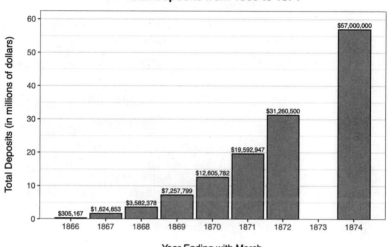

Total Deposits from 1866 to 1874

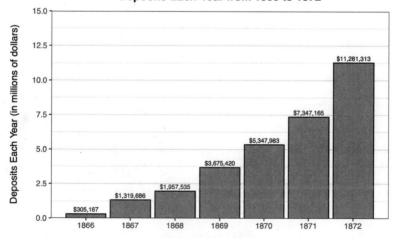

Deposits Each Year from 1866 to 1872

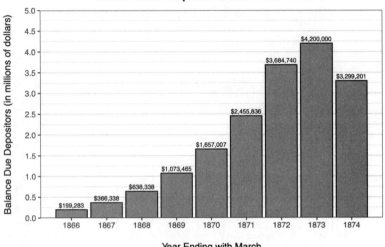

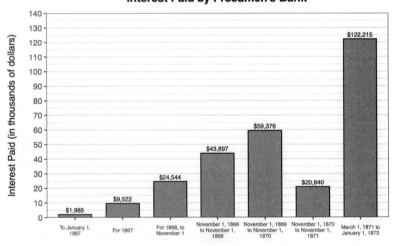

FREEDMAN'S BANK BRANCH LOCATIONS

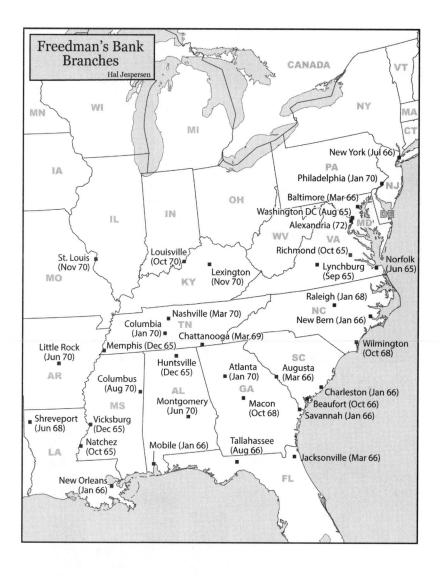

Freedman's Bank Branches
Hal Jespersen

Notes

PREFACE

1   The Treasury Annex was renamed the "Freedman's Bank Building" in January 2016. See Julie Zauzmer, "Treasury Department Renames Building for Post-Civil War Black Bank," *Washington Post*, January 7, 2016.

INTRODUCTION

1   For a summary of the history of slavery and Alabama and the literature on the topic, see Kelly Kennington, "Slavery in Alabama: A Call to Action," *Alabama Review* 73, no. 1 (Jan. 2020): 3–27.

2   US Census, *1870, Ward 7, Mobile, AL*, roll *M593_31*, p. *227B*.

3   C. A. Woodward, *Savings Banks: Their Origin, Progress and Utility, with a History of the National Savings Bank for Colored People* (Cleveland: Fairbanks, Benedict & Co., 1869), 56.

4   *Registers of Signatures of Depositors in Branches of the Freedman's Savings and Trust Company, 1865–1874*, RG *101: Records of the Office of the Comptroller of the Currency, 1863–2006*, ARC identifier *566522*, National Archives Catalog.

5   Woodward, *Savings Banks*, 58.

6   Samuel H. Williamson, "Seven Ways to Compute the Relative Value of a U.S. Dollar Amount, 1790 to Present," MeasuringWorth, accessed December 1, 2023.

7   *Freedman's Record*, October 1, 1868; "United States, Freedman's Bank Records, 1865–1874," database with images, FamilySearch.org, Enon T Wright, Mobile, Alabama, United States, NARA microfilm publication M816, National Archives and Records Administration, Washington, DC, 1970, FHL microfilm 928,572.

8   *Registers of Signatures of Depositors*.

9   For the scholarship on the Freedman's Bank, see Mehrsa Baradaran, *The Color of Money: Black Banks and the Racial Wealth Gap* (Cambridge: Harvard University Press, 2017), 10–39; Claire Célérier and Purnoor Tak, "Finance, Advertising and Fraud: The Rise and Fall of the Freedman's Savings Bank," *Proceedings of the EUROFIDAI-ESSEC Paris December Finance Meeting 2022* (June 17, 2022), http://www.paris-december.eu/; John Martin Davis Jr., "Bankless in Beaufort: A Reexamination of the 1873 Failure of the Freedmans Savings Branch at Beaufort, South Carolina," *South Carolina Historical Magazine* 104, no.1 (2003):

25–55; Walter L. Fleming, *The Freedmen's Savings Bank: A Chapter in the Economic History of the Negro Race* (Chapel Hill: University of North Carolina Press, 1927); Eric Foner, *Reconstruction: America's Unfinished Revolution, 1863–1877* (New York: Harper Perennial Modern Classics, 2014), 531–32; D. C. Giedeman, "Fannie Mae, Freddie Mac, and the Freedman's Savings Bank," *Review of Black Political Economy* 38, no. 3 (2011): 205–26; Abby L. Gilbert, "The Comptroller of the Currency and the Freedman's Savings Bank," *Journal of Negro History* 57, no. 2 (1972): 125–43; Barbara P. Josiah, "Providing for the Future: The World of the African American Depositors of Washington, DC's Freedmen's Savings Bank, 1865–1874," *Journal of African American History* 89, no. 1 (2004): 1–16; Jonathan Levy, *Freaks of Fortune: The Emerging World of Capitalism and Risk in America* (Cambridge: Harvard University Press, 2014), 104–49; Carl Osthaus, *Freedmen, Philanthropy, and Fraud: A History of the Freedman's Savings Bank* (Urbana: University of Illinois Press, 1976); Nicholas Osborne, "Little Capitalists: The Social Economy of Saving in the United States, 1816–1914," (PhD diss., Columbia University, 2014); Luke Stein and Constantine Yannelis, "Financial Inclusion, Human Capital, and Wealth Accumulation: Evidence from the Freedman's Savings Bank," *Review of Financial Studies* 33, no. 11 (November 2020): 5333–77; Virginia Traweek and Malcolm Wardlaw, "Freedman's Savings and Trust Bank Passbook and Dividend Repayment Records," *Journal of Slavery and Data Preservation* 3, no. 1 (2022); Karin Zipf, "Money in the Bank: African American Women, Finance, and Freedom in New Bern, North Carolina, 1868–1874," in *New Voyages to Carolina: Reinterpreting North Carolina History*, ed. Larry E. Tise and Jeffrey J. Crow (Chapel Hill: University of North Carolina Press, 2017), 166–93.

10 *Southern Workman* 1, no. 1 (January 1, 1872).

11 Williamson, "Seven Ways to Compute."

12 For innovative analyses of the slow end of slavery and incarceration as a new regime of forced labor, see Michelle Alexander, *The New Jim Crow: Mass Incarceration in the Age of Colorblindness* (New York: New Press, 2020); Douglas A. Blackmon, *Slavery by Another Name: The Re-Enslavement of Black Americans from the Civil War to World War Two* (London: Icon Books, 2012); Sarah Haley, *No Mercy Here: Gender, Punishment, and the Making of Jim Crow Modernity* (Chapel Hill: University of North Carolina Press, 2016); Talitha L. LeFlouria, *Chained in Silence: Black Women and Convict Labor in the New South* (Chapel Hill: University of North Carolina Press, 2015).

13 Fleming, *Freedmen's Savings Bank*, 124.

14 See for example, William A. Blair, *The Record of Murders and Outrages: Racial Violence and the Fight over Truth at the Dawn of Reconstruction* (Chapel Hill: University of North Carolina Press, 2021); Kidada E. Williams, *I Saw Death Coming: A History of Terror and Survival in the War against Reconstruction* (New York: Bloomsbury, 2023).

15 Célérier and Tak, "Finance, Advertising and Fraud," 6.

16 Célérier and Tak, 34.

17 Célérier and Tak, 30–31.

18 DuBois to W. L. Freeman, September 20, 1927, W. E. B. Du Bois Papers (MS 312), Special Collections and University Archives, University of Massachusetts Amherst Libraries. For Black business organizations and their advocacy for compensation for bank depositors, see Ronny Regev, "The National Negro Business League and the Economic Life of Black Entrepreneurs," *Past & Present* 262, no. 1 (May 2023).

19 "Letter from Our Readers, Letter from Frederick Douglass," Frederick Douglass Papers, Yale University Beinecke Library.

20 See Christy Ford Chapin, "'Going Behind with That Fifteen Cent Policy': Black-Owned Insurance Companies and the State," *Journal of Policy History* 24, no. 4 (2012): 644–74; Shennette Garrett-Scott, *Banking on Freedom: Black Women in U.S. Finance before the New Deal* (New York: Columbia University Press, 2019); Robert E. Weems and Jason Chambers, eds., *Building the Black Metropolis: African American Entrepreneurship in Chicago* (Urbana: University of Illinois Press, 2017). For an analysis of the historical evolution of racial economic inequality in America, see William A. Darity Jr. and A. Kirsten Mullen, *From Here to Equality: Reparations for Black Americans in the Twenty-First Century* (Chapel Hill: University of North Carolina Press, 2020).

21 James Storum, *Banking* ([Washington, DC?], 1897), James Storum and Daniel Murray Pamphlet Collection, p. 14, https://www.loc.gov/resource/lcrbmrp.t0a15/?st=pdf.

22 Stephen Mihm, *A Nation of Counterfeiters: Capitalists, Con Men, and the Making of the United States* (Cambridge: Harvard University Press, 2009), 11.

23 Richard Rothstein, *The Color of Law: A Forgotten History of How Our Government Segregated America* (New York: Liveright, 2017); Keeanga-Yamahtta Taylor, *Race for Profit: How Banks and the Real Estate Industry Undermined Black Homeownership* (Chapel Hill: University of North Carolina Press, 2019).

24 Eric Foner, *The Second Founding: How the Civil War and Reconstruction Remade the Constitution* (New York: W. W. Norton, 2019). For a history of Reconstruction, one that stretches to 1920 with the passage of the Nineteenth Amendment, see Manisha Sinha, *The Rise and Fall of the Second American Republic: Reconstruction, 1860–1920* (New York: Liveright, 2024).

CHAPTER ONE: THE BANK'S FOUNDING, 1864–65

1 "Hugh McCulloch, the First Comptroller," OCC.gov, accessed January 14, 2019.

2 Davis, "Bankless in Beaufort," 30.

3 *Free South* (Beaufort, SC), October 1, 1864, Chronicling America. See also Davis, "Bankless in Beaufort," 30–31.

4 *New South* (Port Royal, SC), September 3, 1864, Chronicling America.

5 *New York Herald* (New York, NY), September 17, 1864, Chronicling America.

6 Dan Wadhwani argues that commercial banks in the nineteenth century did not serve "individuals of modest means." Savings banks filled this gap. R. Daniel Wadhwani, "Protecting Small Savers: The Political Economy of Economic Security," *Journal of Policy History* 18, no. 1 (2006): 126–45. For a history of banking, including the creation of mutual savings banks, in the early United States, see Bray Hammond, *Banks and Politics in America, From the Revolution to the Civil War* (Princeton: Princeton University Press, 1957).

7 George Alter, Claudia Goldin, and Elyce Rotella, "The Savings of Ordinary Americans: The Philadelphia Saving Fund Society in the Mid-Nineteenth Century," *Journal of Economic History* 5, no. 4 (1994): 735–767; Alan L. Olmstead, "Investment Constraints and New York City Mutual Savings Bank Financing of Antebellum Development," *Journal of Economic History* 32, no. 4 (December 1972): 811–40; Robert Wright, "Origins of Commercial Banking in the United States, 1781–1830," EH.Net Encyclopedia, ed. Robert Whaples, March 26, 2008.

8 Wadhwani, "Protecting Small Savers," 128.

9 *New South*, September 3, 1864.

10 *New South*, September 3, 1864.

11 *Freedman's Record*, August 1, 1865.

12 *The Memoirs of General W. T. Sherman, Complete* (New York, 1889; Project Gutenberg, 2006). For a description of Green's house in Savannah, see the National Register of Historic Places Inventory for the Green-Meldrim House.

13 "Newspaper Account of a Meeting between Black Religious Leaders and Union Military Authorities," *New-York Daily Tribune*, February 13, 1865, Freedmen and Southern Society Project. Self-emancipation during the era of slavery, especially in the antebellum era, was rare but not unheard of. See Julia Bernier, "'Never Be Free without Trustin' Some Person': Networking and Buying Freedom in the Nineteenth-Century United States," *Slavery & Abolition* 40, no. 2: 341–60.

14 Jacqueline Glass Campbell, *When Sherman Marched North from the Sea: Resistance on the Confederate Home Front* (Chapel Hill: University of North Carolina Press, 2003); Burke Davis, *Sherman's March* (New York: Random House, 1980); Jeff Dickey, *Rising in Flames: Sherman's March and the Fight for a New Nation* (New York: Pegasus Books, 2018).

15 *Memoirs of General W. T. Sherman.*

16 Emancipation Proclamation, January 1, 1863, RG 11: Presidential Proclamations, 1791–1991, General Records of the United States Government, National Archives. For a brilliant analysis of the experiences of enslaved people in Union refugee camps, see Amy Murrell Taylor, *Embattled Freedom: Journeys through the Civil War's Slave Refugee Camps* (Chapel Hill: University of North Carolina Press, 2020). See also Anne Sarah Rubin, *Through the Heart of Dixie: Sherman's March and American Memory* (Chapel Hill: University of North Carolina Press, 2014).

17 "Newspaper Account of a Meeting."

18 "Newspaper Account of a Meeting."

19 "Newspaper Account of a Meeting."

20 "Newspaper Account of a Meeting."

21 "Gen. Butler and the Blacks," *New York Times*, December 12, 1863.

22 "Gen. Butler and the Blacks."

23 Eric Foner, *Free Soil, Free Labor, Free Men: The Ideology of the Republican Party before the Civil War* (Oxford: Oxford University Press, 1970); Heather Cox Richardson, *To Make Men Free: A History of the Republican Party* (New York: Basic Books, 2014).

24 Special Field Order No. 15, Freedman and Southern Society Project, accessed January 14, 2023; Carole Emberton, *Beyond Redemption: Race, Violence, and the American South after the Civil War* (Chicago: University of Chicago Press, 2013), 73–76; Leon Litwack, *Been in the Storm So Long: The Aftermath of Slavery* (New York: Vintage Books, 1979), 400–408.

25 *Memoirs of General W. T. Sherman.* See also Bennett Parten, "'Somewhere toward Freedom': Sherman's March and Georgia's Refugee Slaves," *Georgia Historical Quarterly* 101, no. 2 (2017): 116–46. For a brilliant analysis of the experiences of enslaved people in Union refugee camps, see Taylor, *Embattled Freedom*. It is difficult to determine the exact number of freed people who followed Sherman and stayed with the Union army in Savannah.

26 "Order by the Commander of the Military Division of the Mississippi," January 16, 1865, Freedmen and Southern Society Project, accessed December 19, 2023.

27 *Memoirs of General W. T. Sherman.*

28 There was recent precedent for this policy. In 1862 and 1863, Black residents of the South Carolina Low Country had negotiated with the Union military officials to temporarily take possession of approximately two thousand acres of coastal land that had been abandoned by

white plantation owners in the throes of war. Secretary of War Stanton had been communicating with Union generals in South Carolina about their efforts to administer a program called the Port Royal Experiment. Northern capitalists and abolitionists then paid freed people to cultivate cotton. The experiment ended in 1865 with President Johnson retreating from Lincoln's Reconstruction policies. See Kevin Dougherty, *The Port Royal Experiment: A Case Study in Development* (Jackson: University Press of Mississippi, 2014); Akiko Ochiai, "The Port Royal Experiment Revisited: Northern Visions of Reconstruction and the Land Question," *New England Quarterly* 74, no. 1 (2001): 94–117; Willie Lee Rose, *Rehearsal for Reconstruction: The Port Royal Experiment* (New York: Oxford University Press, 1964).

29   For an analysis of the origins of the Homestead Act, see Keri Leigh Merritt, *Masterless Men: Poor Whites and Slavery in the Antebellum South* (New York: Cambridge University Press, 2017).

30   Rose, *Rehearsal for Reconstruction*, 330. On African Americans and land redistribution in 1865, see Steven Hahn, *A Nation under Our Feet: Black Political Struggles in the Rural South from Slavery to the Great Migration* (Cambridge: Harvard University Press, 2005), 135–46.

31   Parten, "Somewhere toward Freedom," 116–46; Elizabeth Varon, *Armies of Deliverance: A New History of the Civil War* (New York: Oxford University Press, 2019), 381.

32   Nicholas Guyatt, "'An Impossible Idea?': The Curious Career of Internal Colonization," *Journal of the Civil War Era* 4, no. 2 (June 2014): 234–63.

33   For an analysis of colonization during the Civil War era, see Sebastian Page, *Black Resettlement and the American Civil War* (Cambridge: Cambridge University Press, 2021).

34   *Collected Works of Abraham Lincoln*, ed. Roy P. Bassler and the Abraham Lincoln Association, vol. 5 (New Brunswick, NJ: Rutgers University Press, 1953), 373.

35   Frederick Douglass, "The President and His Speeches," *Douglass Monthly*, September 1862.

36   Paul A. Cimbala, "The Freedmen's Bureau, the Freedmen, and Sherman's Grant in Reconstruction Georgia, 1865–1867," *Journal of Southern History* 55, no. 4 (1989): 598.

37   According to section 11 of the Confiscation Act of 1862, "[T]he President of the United States is authorized to employ as many persons of African descent as he may deem necessary and proper for the suppression of this rebellion, and for this purpose he may organize and use them in such manner as he may judge best for the public welfare."

38   "The Militia Act of 1862," Freedmen and Southern Society Project, accessed March 22, 2024.

39   For analyses on the experiences of Black soldiers during the Civil War, see Douglas R. Egerton, *Thunder at the Gates: The Black Civil War Regiments That Redeemed America* (New York: Basic Books, 2016); James G. Hollandsworth, *The Louisiana Native Guards: The Black Military Experience During the Civil War* (Baton Rouge: Louisiana State University Press, 1995); Holly A. Pinheiro Jr., *The Families' Civil War: Black Soldiers and the Fight for Racial Justice* (Athens: University of Georgia Press, 2022).

40   "54th Massachusetts Regiment (U.S. National Park Service)," National Park Service, accessed December 19, 2023.

41   "Massachusetts Black Corporal to the President," September 28, 1863, Freedmen and Southern Society Project, accessed December 19, 2023.

42   "Law Equalizing the Pay of Black Soldiers," June 15, 1864, Freedmen and Southern Society Project, accessed December 19, 2023.

43   Walter L. Fleming, "The Freedmen's Savings Bank: A Paper," *Yale Review* (1906): 40; Garrett-Scott, *Banking on Freedom*, 19–24; Levy, *Freaks of Fortune*, 111.

44   *Richmond Palladium* (Richmond, IN), March 23, 1864, Chronicling America.

45 *Muscatine Weekly Journal* (Muscatine, IA), December 23, 1864, Chronicling America. See also Fleming, *Freedmen's Savings Bank*, 19–22; Garrett-Scott, *Banking on Freedom*, 22.

46 J. W. Alvord to Myrtilla Mead Alvord, Letters of Rev. John W. Alvord, FromthePage, accessed January 18, 2023, https://fromthepage.com/uvalibrary/letters-of-rev-john-w-alvord/1864–01–07-letter-a-alvord-to-mydear/display/25196862.

47 J. W. Alvord to Editor Independent, Letters of Rev. John W. Alvord, FromthePage, accessed January 18, 2023, https://fromthepage.com/uvalibrary/letters-of-rev-john-w-alvord/1865–01–07-letter-a-alvord-to-editorofindependent/display/25198171.

48 As quoted in Woodward, *Savings Banks*, 49.

49 Davis, "Bankless in Beaufort," 34.

50 S. Doc. No. 88, Report of the Comptroller of the Currency upon the Condition of the Savings Banks of the District of Columbia, 1873, 6 (hereafter cited as Meigs Report, 1873); Levy, *Freaks of Fortune*, 115.

51 Levy, 122.

52 Martin B. Duberman, *The Antislavery Vanguard: New Essays on the Abolitionists* (Princeton: Princeton University Press, 2015), 194.

53 For the economic and political influence of New York's elite, see Sven Beckert, *The Monied Metropolis: New York City and the Consolidation of the American Bourgeoisie, 1850–1896* (New York: Cambridge University Press, 2001).

54 Rev. John W. Alvord to General O. O. Howard, February 5, 1865, Oliver Otis Howard Papers, George J. Mitchell Department of Special Collections & Archives, Bowdoin College Library, Brunswick, Maine, accessed January 18, 2023, https://library.bowdoin.edu/arch/mss/ooh-pdf/M91b03f005_transcripts.pdf (hereafter cited as Howard Papers).

55 Journal of the Board of Trustees: January 27, 1865–July 9, 1874, RG 101: Records of the Office of the Comptroller of the Currency, Series: Minutes and Journals of the Freedman's Savings and Trust Company, National Archives Catalog, accessed January 18, 2023, https://catalog.archives.gov/id/231945579?objectPage=2 (hereafter cited as Journal of the Board of Trustees).

56 Journal of the Board of Trustees, 3.

57 For the literature on the enslaved economy, see Ira Berlin and Philip Morgan, eds., *The Slaves' Economy: Independent Production by Slaves in the Americas* (London: Routledge, 1991); Justene Hill Edwards, *Unfree Markets: The Slaves' Economy and the Rise of Capitalism in South Carolina* (New York: Columbia University Press, 2021); Jeff Forret, *Race Relations at the Margins: Slaves and Poor Whites in the Antebellum Countryside* (Baton Rouge: LSU Press, 2006); Jeff Forret, *Slave Against Slave: Plantation Violence in the Old South* (Baton Rouge: LSU Press, 2016); Kathleen M. Hilliard, *Masters, Slaves, and Exchange: Power's Purchase in the Old South* (New York: Cambridge University Press, 2013); Roderick McDonald, *The Economy and Material Culture of Slaves: Goods and Chattels on the Sugar Plantations of Jamaica and Louisiana* (Baton Rouge: LSU Press, 1993); Dylan C. Penningroth, *The Claims of Kinfolk: African American Property and Community in the Nineteenth-Century South* (Chapel Hill: University of North Carolina Press, 2003).

58 William Craft and S. Schoff, *Running a Thousand Miles for Freedom: or, the Escape of William and Ellen Craft from Slavery* (London, 1860), 10–11. For a dramatic retelling of the Crafts' escape narrative, see Ilyon Woo, *Master Slave Husband Wife: An Epic Journey from Slavery to Freedom* (New York: Simon & Schuster, 2023). There has been a recent effort by historians to understand and grapple with the financial knowledge that enslaved people cultivated

through their experiences of being bought, sold, valued, and traded, especially in the first half of the nineteenth century, as the domestic slave trade expanded. See Justene Hill Edwards, "'This Slavery Business Is a Horrible Thing': The Economy of American Slavery in the Lives of the Enslaved," *Business History Review* 97, no. 2 (2023): 307–34.

59   Journal of the Board of Trustees, 3.

60   Oliver Otis Howard, *The Autobiography of General Oliver Otis Howard, Major General United States Army*, vol. 2 (New York: Baker & Taylor, 1907), 201–3.

61   Rev. J. W. Alvord to O. O. Howard, February 3, 1865, Howard Papers.

62   Alvord to Howard, February 5, 1865.

63   Osthaus, *Freedmen, Philanthropy, and Fraud*, 4.

64   Journal of the Board of Trustees, 5.

65   Alvord to Howard, February 5, 1865.

66   Davis, "Bankless in Beaufort," 36.

67   Joe Martin Richardson, *Christian Reconstruction: The American Missionary Association and Southern Blacks, 1861–1890* (Tuscaloosa: University of Alabama Press, 2008), 280.

68   Journal of the Board of Trustees, 5.

69   For a discussion of the varieties of paper money in the early national era, see Joshua R. Greenberg, *Bank Notes and Shinplasters: The Rage for Paper Money in the Early Republic* (Philadelphia: University of Pennsylvania Press, 2020).

70   National Bank Act of 1863, 12 Stat. 665, 37th Cong., 3rd Sess., Ch. 58 (1863). Also, Michael T. Cairnes, "The Greenback Union: The Politics and Law of American Money in the Civil War Era," (PhD diss., University of Virginia, 2014); Matthew Jaremski, "State Banks and the National Banking Acts: Measuring the Response to Increased Financial Regulation, 1860–1870," *Journal of Money, Credit and Banking* 45, no. 2/3 (2013): 379–99; Eugene Nelson White, "The Political Economy of Banking Regulation, 1864–1933," *Journal of Economic History* 42, no. 1 (1982): 33–40.

71   Journal of the Board of Trustees, 5.

72   "Letters of Rev John W Alvord," FromThePage, accessed December 19, 2023.

73   *Cong. Globe*, 38th Cong., 2nd Sess. 776 (1865); *Cleveland Morning Leader* (Cleveland, OH), February 14, 1865, Chronicling America; Fleming, *Freedmen's Savings Bank*, 41.

74   *Cong. Globe*, 38th Cong., 2nd Sess. 1311.

75   *Cong. Globe*, 38th Cong., 2nd Sess. 1311.

76   *Cong. Globe*, 38th Cong., 2nd Sess. 1311.

77   William Horatio Barnes, *History of the Thirty-Ninth Congress of the United States* (New York: Harper & Brothers, 1868), 277.

78   *Cong. Globe*, 38th Cong., 2nd Sess. 1311.

79   *Cong. Globe*, 38th Cong., 2nd Sess. 1311.

80   For his 1863 speech in the Senate on the National Banking Act of 1863, see Marion Mills Miller, *Great Debates in American History*, vol. 13 (New York: Current Literature, 1913), 213–14.

81   *Cong. Globe*, 38th Cong., 2nd Sess. 1311.

82   Osthaus, *Freedmen, Philanthropy, and Fraud*, 4.

83   "An Act to Establish a Bureau for the Relief of Freedmen and Refugees," *U.S. Statutes at Large, Treaties, and Proclamations of the United States of America*, vol. 13 (Boston, 1866), 507–9, Freedmen and Southern Society Project.

84   For a discussion of the Civil War's final campaign, see Earl J. Hess, *In the Trenches at*

Petersburg: Field Fortifications and Confederate Defeat (Chapel Hill: University of North Carolina Press, 2009).

85   *Freedman's Savings and Trust Company . . . [Charter and By-laws]* (New York: Wm. C. Bryant & Co., Printers, 1865), African American Pamphlet Collection, Library of Congress, https://www.loc.gov/item/06031793/ (hereafter cited as *Charter and By-laws*).

86   *Charter and By-laws*, 8–9.

87   *Charter and By-laws*, 8–9.

88   Claire Célérier and Purnoor Tak, "Exploiting Minorities through Advertising: Evidence from the Freedman's Savings Bank," Bocconi University, October 17, 2022.

89   Osborne, "Little Capitalists," 138.

90   *Charter and By-laws*, 9.

91   *Charter and By-laws*, 9.

CHAPTER TWO: GROWING PAINS, 1865–66

1   *Colored Tennessean* (Nashville, TN), March 24, 1866, Chronicling America.

2   Woodward, *Savings Banks*, 56.

3   "Brooklyn Correspondence," *Christian Recorder*, March 25, 1865. For a fascinating discussion of the ways in which African Americans have shaped American democracy and American political traditions, see Melvin L. Rogers, *The Darkened Light of Faith: Race, Democracy, and Freedom in African American Political Thought* (Princeton: Princeton University Press, 2023).

4   "Brooklyn Correspondence."

5   "Brooklyn Correspondence." For an analysis of Morel and his life in Weeksville, New York, in the nineteenth century, see Judith Wellman, *Brooklyn's Promised Land: The Free Black Community of Weeksville, New York* (New York: New York University Press, 2014).

6   Joseph Willson and Julie Winch, *The Elite of Our People: Joseph Willson's Sketches of Black Upper-Class Life in Antebellum Philadelphia* (University Park: Pennsylvania State University Press, 2000), 135n49.

7   "Brooklyn Correspondence."

8   Journal of the Board of Trustees, 9.

9   Osthaus, *Freedmen, Philanthropy, and Fraud*, 10.

10   *The War of Rebellion: A Compilation of the Official Records of the Union and Confederate Armies, Series I—Volume XLVII—In Three Parts, Part II, Correspondence. Etc.* (Washington, DC: U.S. Government Printing Office, 1895), 711.

11   *Charter and By-laws*, 15.

12   *Charter and By-laws*, 15.

13   Osthaus, *Freedmen, Philanthropy, and Fraud*, 12. Osthaus called Booth "window dressing" and argued that Griffith "seems to have been given no official function."

14   According to historian Brian Luskey, Webster was "opposed to slavery" and even garnered the moniker the "Black Republican" for his avowedly antislavery beliefs. Brian Luskey, *Men Is Cheap: Exposing the Frauds of Free Labor in Civil War America* (Chapel Hill: University of North Carolina Press, 2020), 11–13.

15   Journal of the Board of Trustees, 9.

16   "Children's Aid Society," *New York Times*, February 26, 1865; Osthaus, *Freedmen, Philanthropy, and Fraud*, 12. It is worth noting that Alvord was the secretary of the American Tract

Society and probably used his connection with Booth to encourage him to assume a position on the bank's board.

17   Rev. John W. Alvord to Myrtilla Mead Alvord, June 7, 1865, Letters of Rev. John W. Alvord, FromthePage, accessed April 1, 2024, https://fromthepage.com/uvalibrary/letters-of-rev -john-w-alvord/1865–06–07-letter-a-alvord-to-mydearwife/display/25198211.

18   See, for example, Rev. John W. Alvord to Myrtilla Mead Alvord, June 9, 1865, Letters of Rev. John W. Alvord, FromthePage, accessed April 1, 2024, https://fromthepage.com/uvalibrary /letters-of-rev-john-w-alvord/1865–06–09-letter-a-alvord-to-mydearwife.

19   For a discussion of the surrender of Lee to Grant, see Caroline E. Janney, *Ends of War: The Unfinished Fight of Lee's Army after Appomattox* (Chapel Hill: University of North Carolina Press, 2021).

20   Leslie Harris, *In the Shadow of Slavery: African Americans in New York City, 1626–1863* (Chicago: University of Chicago Press, 2003). Historians and archaeologists believe that people of African descent in New York during the 1860s lived in the neighborhoods known as Seneca Village and Little Africa, modern-day Central Park and Greenwich Village, respectively.

21   For a discussion of the hostility of Democrats in New York toward Black New Yorkers and runaway slaves during the antebellum era, see Jonathan Daniel Wells, *The Kidnapping Club: Wall Street, Slavery, and Resistance on the Eve of the Civil War* (New York: Bold Type Books, 2020).

22   Agency Committee minutes, Journal of the Board of Trustees, 1.

23   For a discussion of trust and banking in nineteenth-century America, see Mihm, *Nation of Counterfeiters.* Economist Benjamin Ho contends that trust is a crucial aspect of how economic actors are bound together. See Benjamin Ho, *Why Trust Matters: An Economist's Guide to the Ties That Bind Us* (New York: Columbia University Press, 2021).

24   Agency Committee minutes, 1.

25   Rev. John W. Alvord to Myrtilla Mead Alvord, June 7, 1865.

26   Rev. John W. Alvord to Myrtilla Mead Alvord, May 30, 1865, Letters of Rev. John W. Alvord, FromthePage, accessed April 1, 2024, https://fromthepage.com/uvalibrary/letters-of-rev -john-w-alvord/1865–05–30-letter-a-alvord-to-mydear/display/25198208.

27   Rev. John W. Alvord to Myrtilla Mead Alvord, May 30, 1865.

28   "An Interesting Item," *Christian Recorder*, June 24, 1865. Slave laws in states such as Virginia restricted enslaved people and even free people of color from congregating for fear that they were fomenting an insurrection. For an analysis of slave laws in the legal culture of the slaveholding South, see Sally Hadden, *Slave Patrols: Law and Violence in Virginia and the Carolinas* (Cambridge: Harvard University Press, 2001).

29   "Interesting Item."

30   "Interesting Item."

31   "Interesting Item."

32   "Interesting Item."

33   "Interesting Item."

34   "Interesting Item."

35   *Charter and By-laws*, 8–9.

36   "Interesting Item."

37   For a discussion of the American bond market during the Civil War, see David K. Thomson, *Bonds of War: How Civil War Financial Agents Sold the World on the Union* (Chapel Hill: University of North Carolina Press, 2022).

38   Agency Committee minutes, 3.

39   Agency Committee minutes, 2.

40   Agency Committee minutes, 5.

41   *Daily National Republican* (Washington, DC), September 12, 1865, Chronicling America. See also Osthaus, *Freedmen, Philanthropy, and Fraud*, 17.

42   Joshua Rothman, *The Ledger and the Chain: How Domestic Slave Traders Shaped America* (New York: Basic Books, 2021); Calvin Schermerhorn, *The Business of Slavery and the Rise of American Capitalism, 1815–1860* (New Haven: Yale University Press, 2015).

43   Robert S. Levine, *The Failed Promise: Reconstruction, Frederick Douglass, and the Impeachment of Andrew Johnson* (New York: W. W. Norton, 2021), 49–64.

44   Woodward, *Savings Banks*, 53.

45   Woodward, 54.

46   "Pres. Johnson's amnesty proclamation . . . Done at the city of Washington, the twenty-ninth day of May, in the year of our Lord one thousand eight hundred and sixty-five . . . Andrew Johnson" (Washington, 1865), LOC.gov. Johnson's amnesty plan was, on the surface, an extension of Lincoln's own plan for amnesty as of December 1863. But, in practice, he was far more lenient than Lincoln. See Varon, *Armies of Deliverance*, 424.

47   Legal historian Cynthia Nicoletti has argued that Johnson's lenience was reflected in his decision "not to seek retribution against the vast majority of ex-Confederates." Cynthia Nicoletti, "The American Civil War as a Trial by Battle," *Law and History Review* 28, no. 1 (2010): 81. Nicoletti also contends that Johnson's amnesty measures not only nullified Sherman's Special Field Order No. 15 but also directly undermined the concept of land distribution to freed people during Reconstruction. See Cynthia Nicoletti, "William Henry Trescot, Pardon Broker," *Journal of the Civil War Era* 11, no. 4 (2021): 478–506.

48   Frederick D. Hosen, ed., *Federal Laws of the Reconstruction: Principal Congressional Acts and Resolutions, Presidential Proclamations, Speeches and Orders, and Other Legislative and Military Documents, 1862–1875* (Jefferson, NC: McFarland, 2010), 160–62.

49   "Committee of Freedmen on Edisto Island, South Carolina, to the Freedmen's Bureau Commissioner, October 20 or 21, 1865; and the Latter's Reply, October 22, 1865," Freedmen and Southern Society Project.

50   "Committee of Freedmen on Edisto Island."

51   "Committee of Freedmen on Edisto Island."

52   "Committee of Freedmen on Edisto Island."

53   Though most Black people, both enslaved and free, did not have access to formal financial institutions during the period of legal slavery, communities of free Blacks in northern states, after 1780 with the proliferation of gradual emancipation laws, created mutual aid societies. These organizations, as the historian Juliet E. K. Walker has shown, pooled their money and deposited it into local banks in cities such as Philadelphia and New York. See Juliet E. K. Walker, *The History of Black Business in America: Capitalism, Race, Entrepreneurship* (Chapel Hill: University of North Carolina Press, 2009), 108–63.

54   Agency Committee minutes, 12.

55   William Pitt Fessenden and Thaddeus Stevens, *Report of the Joint Committee on Reconstruction, at the First Session, Thirty-Ninth Congress* (Washington, DC: U.S. Government Printing Office, 1866), 259.

56   Minutes of the Finance Committee: July 15, 1865–August 6, 1872, Journal of the Board of Trustees, 2.

57   *Christian Recorder*, May 12, 1866.

58   Fessenden and Stevens, *Report of the Joint Committee*, 260.

59   P. Gabrielle Foreman, "Black Organizing, Print Advocacy, and Collective Authorship: The Long History of the Colored Conventions Movement," in *The Colored Conventions Movement: Black Organizing in the Nineteenth Century*, ed. Sarah Lynn Patterson, Jim Casey, and P. Gabrielle Foreman (Chapel Hill: University of North Carolina Press, 2021), 24.

60   *Proceedings of the Council of the Georgia Equal Rights Association. Assembled at Augusta, Ga. April 4th, 1866. Containing the Address of the President, Captain J. E. Bryant, and Resolutions Adopted by the Council* (Augusta, 1866), Colored Conventions Project Digital Records.

61   *Proceedings of the Council.*

62   *Proceedings of the Council.*

63   Andrew Johnson, "Interview with a Colored Delegation Respecting Suffrage," February 7, 1866, The American Presidency Project, ed. Gerhard Peters and John T. Woolley.

64   Frederick Douglass, *The Life and Times of Frederick Douglass: Written by Himself* (Boston: De Wolf & Fisk Co., 1892), 421–24.

65   Douglass, *Life and Times*, 442.

66   Douglass, 442.

67   Johnson, "Interview with a Colored Delegation."

68   Levine, *Failed Promise*, 86.

69   Johnson, "Interview with a Colored Delegation."

70   Thomas C. Mackey, ed., *A Documentary History of the American Civil War Era*, vol. 1, *Legislative Achievements* (Knoxville: University of Tennessee Press, 2012), 151–58.

71   *Christian Recorder*, September 1, 1866.

72   Osthaus, *Freedmen, Philanthropy, and Fraud*, 16.

73   *Freedman's Record*, March 1, 1866.

74   *Camden Weekly Journal* (Camden, SC), July 20, 1866, Chronicling America.

CHAPTER THREE: THE TROUBLE WITH EXPANSION, 1866–67

1   Fleming, *Freedmen's Savings Bank*, 146.

2   For a discussion of Union and Confederate battles in New Orleans during the Civil War, see Gerald M. Capers, *Occupied City: New Orleans under the Federals 1862–1865* (Lexington: University Press of Kentucky, 1965).

3   For analyses on the multiethnic and multiracial demographic makeup of Louisiana, see Gwendolyn Midlo Hall, *Africans in Colonial Louisiana: The Development of Afro-Creole Culture in the Eighteenth Century* (Baton Rouge: LSU Press, 1992); Sophie White, *Voices of the Enslaved: Love, Labor, and Longing in French Louisiana* (Chapel Hill: Omohundro Institute and University of North Carolina Press, 2019).

4   See Alejandro de la Fuente and Ariela Gross, *Becoming Free, Becoming Black: Race, Freedom, and Law in Cuba, Virginia, and Louisiana* (Cambridge: Cambridge University Press, 2020).

5   Justin A. Nystrom, "New Orleans Free People of Color and the Dilemma of Emancipation," in *The Great Task Remaining before Us: Reconstruction as America's Continuing Civil War*, ed. Paul Cimbala and Randall M. Miller (New York: Fordham University Press, 2010), 130–31.

6   Hollandsworth, *Louisiana Native Guards*, 13–14; Justin A. Nystrom, *New Orleans after the Civil War: Race, Politics, and a New Birth of Freedom* (Baltimore: Johns Hopkins University

Press, 2010), 32–35.

7   *Colored Tennessean*, March 24, 1866.

8   Registers of Signatures of Depositors.

9   Registers of Signatures of Depositors; "U.S., Freedman's Bank Records, 1865–1874" (database online), Ancestry.com; "United States Census, 1870," FamilySearch.org, entry for Eugine Lubin and Ellen Lubin, 1870. For an examination of the experiences of enslaved people in New Orleans from the seventeenth to the early eighteenth century, see Rashauna Johnson, *Slavery's Metropolis: Unfree Labor in New Orleans during the Age of Revolutions* (New York: Cambridge University Press, 2016). For an interrogation of the lives of women of African descent in eighteenth-century New Orleans, see Jessica Marie Johnson, *Wicked Flesh: Black Women, Intimacy, and Freedom in the Atlantic World* (Philadelphia: University of Pennsylvania Press, 2020), 121–52.

10   Historian Karin Zipf offers a compelling analysis of Black women depositors in the New Bern, North Carolina, Freedman's Bank branch. She examines the ways in which we can look at freed women's engagement with the New Bern branch to better understand their ideas about finance and property. According to Zipf, at the New Bern branch, 29.5 percent of depositors were women. See Zipf, "Money in the Bank."

11   Traweek and Wardlaw, "Passbook and Dividend Repayment Records."

12   Black people in regions of the Deep South, in states such as Texas and Louisiana, experienced an avalanche of violence during Reconstruction. Historian William Blair contends that the lawlessness of violence in regions of the South during Reconstruction has been underestimated by historians. See Blair, *Record of Murders and Outrages*.

13   James K. Hogue, *Uncivil War: Five New Orleans Street Battles and the Rise and Fall of Radical Reconstruction* (Baton Rouge: LSU Press, 2011); James G. Hollandsworth Jr., *An Absolute Massacre: The New Orleans Race Riot of July 30, 1866* (Baton Rouge: LSU Press, 2001); Nystrom, *New Orleans after the Civil War*, 66; Donald E. Reynolds, "The New Orleans Riot of 1866, Reconsidered," *Louisiana History: The Journal of the Louisiana Historical Association* 5, no. 1 (1964): 13.

14   As quoted in Fleming, *Freedmen's Savings Bank*, 146.

15   *Christian Recorder*, May 12, 1866.

16   Thomson, *Bonds of War*.

17   *Christian Recorder*, October 20, 1866.

18   Journal of the Board of Trustees, 18.

19   Agency Committee minutes, 19.

20   Journal of the Board of Trustees, 12.

21   Rev. John W. Alvord to Myrtilla Mead Alvord, September 4, 1865, Letters of Rev. John W. Alvord, FromthePage, accessed December 19, 2023, https://fromthepage.com/uvalibrary/letters-of-rev-john-w-alvord/1865–09–04-letter-a-alvord-to-mydear/display/25201953.

22   Rev. John W. Alvord to Myrtilla Mead Alvord, September 4, 1865.

23   Agency Committee minutes, 24.

24   Fessenden and Stevens, *Report of the Joint Committee*, 259.

25   Fessenden and Stevens, 259.

26   Fessenden and Stevens, 259.

27   Fessenden and Stevens, 259.

28   Fessenden and Stevens, 259.

29   Journal of the Board of Trustees, 19.

30   Booth remained on the board until the summer of 1867 as a trustee. The argument about members of the bank's board not fully appreciating the work required to run a bank was one expressed by W. E. B. DuBois in *Black Reconstruction*. He contended that the trustees regarded the bank "as philanthropy and not worth the careful control and oversight of those who loaned their names to it." See W. E. B. DuBois, *Black Reconstruction in America, 1890–1880* (New York: The Free Press, 1998), 600.

31   Osthaus, *Freedmen, Philanthropy, and Fraud,* 139.

32   Journal of the Board of Trustees, 23.

33   Osthaus, *Freedmen, Philanthropy, and Fraud,* 140.

34   See, for example, Williams, *I Saw Death Coming,* 40–42.

35   For a record, though not complete, of the violence of Reconstruction, see the "Freedmen's Bureau Records relating to Murders and Outrages," https://www.freedmensbureau.com/outrages.htm.

36   "Freedmen's Bureau Records—Registered Reports of Murders and Outrages in Texas," https://www.freedmensbureau.com/texas/texasoutrages2.htm, accessed February 1, 2023. For a discussion of Reconstruction violence in Texas, see Blair, *Record of Murders and Outrages,* 106–28. W. E. B. DuBois also argued that the banks that struggled to receive national charters during Reconstruction strongly opposed the Freedman's Bank. See DuBois, *Black Reconstruction,* 600.

37   As quoted in Osthaus, *Freedmen, Philanthropy, and Fraud,* 140.

38   As quoted in Osthaus, 139.

39   Osthaus, 139.

40   *Registers of Signatures of Depositors.*

41   Part of the hurdle were the regular interest payments that the bank was required to give depositors. In January 1867, Hewitt stood firm in his decision that there would be no interest payments to depositors at the beginning of the year. The bank could not afford them, given the cost of maintaining the various branches.

42   Journal of the Board of Trustees, 25.

43   Edward D. Melillo, *Strangers on Familiar Soil: Rediscovering the Chile-California Connection* (New Haven: Yale University Press, 2015), 29.

44   Ellis Paxson Oberholtzer, *Jay Cooke, Financier of the Civil War* (Philadelphia: G. W. Jacobs, 1907), 91.

45   Oberholtzer, *Jay Cooke,* 92–93.

46   David K. Thomson, "Like a Cord through the Whole Country": Union Bonds and Financial Mobilization for Victory," *Journal of the Civil War Era,* 6 no. 3 (2016), 347–75.

47   Edward P. Moser, *The White House's Unruly Neighborhood: Crime, Scandal and Intrigue in the History of Lafayette Square* (Jefferson, NC: McFarland, 2019), 241.

48   Thomson, *Bonds of War,* 4.

49   For an analysis of the strategies that Lincoln and members of his administration used to raise money for the war effort, see Melinda Lawson, *Patriot Fires: Forging a New American Nationalism in the Civil War North* (Lawrence: University Press of Kansas, 2002), 40–64; Roger Lowenstein, *Ways and Means: Lincoln and His Cabinet and the Financing of the Civil War* (New York: Penguin Random House, 2022).

50   M. John Lubetkin, *Jay Cooke's Gamble: The Northern Pacific Railroad, the Sioux, and the Panic of 1873* (Norman: University of Oklahoma Press, 2014), 11.

51   *New York Herald*, January 4, 1872.

52   Benjamin Klebaner, *American Commercial Banking: A History* (Washington, DC: Beard Books, 2005), 65.

53   *The Commercial & Financial Chronicle, Bankers' Gazette, Commercial Times, Railway Monitor, and Insurance Journal* (New York: William B. Dana & Company, 1869), 252.

54   Journal of the Board of Trustees, 25.

55   Journal of the Board of Trustees, 26.

56   Journal of the Board of Trustees, 29.

57   *H.R. Report No. 502*, 44th Cong., 1st Sess. (1876), vi, Black Freedom Struggle in the United States, ProQuest (hereafter cited as Douglas Report).

58   Douglas Report, 107–8. See also Arthur Wentworth Hamilton Eaton, *The History of Kings County, Nova Scotia, Heart of the Acadian Land, Giving a Sketch of the French and Their Expulsion: And a History of the New England Planters Who Came in Their Stead, with Many Genealogies, 1604–1910* (Salem: Salem Press Company, 1910), 499; Howard, *Autobiography*, 30–43.

59   For a history of Howard University, specifically of its first century of existence, see Rayford Logan, *Howard University: The First Hundred Years 1867–1967* (New York: NYU Press, 1969), 3–17.

60   Osthaus, *Freedmen, Philanthropy, and Fraud*, 152; Paul Skeels Peirce, *The Freedmen's Bureau: A Chapter in the History of Reconstruction* (Iowa City: The University Press, 1900), 115–17.

61   Douglas Report, 55, 107–8. Henry R. Searle would also borrow $4,005.30 from the bank in 1871. Finance Committee minutes, 59, 76, 81. The investment of $12,000 proved that Alvord had used his various positions, with both the bank and the bureau, to secure his and his family's financial position. Just two years earlier, Alvord was expressing his concern about his finances. His investment in D. L. Eaton & Company demonstrates that he found ways, some dubious, to leverage his positions to earn more money.

62   Journal of the Board of Trustees, 30.

63   *H.R. Report No. 16*, 43rd Cong., 2nd Sess. (1874), 27, ProQuest (hereafter cited as Commissioners' Report); Célérier and Tak, "Finance, Advertising and Fraud."

64   Douglas Report, 99. This information was revealed by then cashier and future bank actuary George Stickney in 1876. Stickney was being questioned by the Douglas commission.

65   Journal of the Board of Trustees, 30.

66   *Christian Recorder*, September 1, 1866.

67   *Daily Dispatch* (Richmond, VA), August 30, 1867, Chronicling America.

68   Historians have considered the ways in which people of African descent in the United States have waged political battles over citizenship rights. The debates have often foregrounded the fight for political and economic rights as a major aspect of inclusion in the body politic. See Van Gosse, *The First Reconstruction: Black Politics in America from the Revolution to the Civil War* (Chapel Hill: University of North Carolina Press, 2021); Kate Masur, *Until Justice Be Done: America's First Civil Rights Movement, from the Revolution to Reconstruction* (New York: W. W. Norton, 2021).

69   Levy, *Freaks of Fortune*, 1–6; Sarah Quinn, *American Bonds: How Credit Markets Shaped a Nation* (Princeton: Princeton University Press, 2019), 22–47.

70   All African American newspapers published between 1865 and 1874 published at least one article about the Freedman's Bank. See Célérier and Tak, "Finance, Advertising and Fraud."

71   *New York Dispatch* (New York, NY), August 19, 1866, Chronicling America.

CHAPTER FOUR: A CHANGE IN PRIORITIES, 1868–70

1   *Tri-Weekly Standard* (Raleigh, NC), June 20, 1868, Chronicling America.

2   Richard Mattson, "The Evolution of Raleigh's African-American Neighborhoods in the 19th and 20th Centuries," Raleigh Historic Development Commission, November 1988, https://rhdc.org/sites/default/files/EvolRaleighAfricanAmericanNeigh.pdf.

3   *Christian Recorder*, February 8, 1868; *Tri-Weekly Standard*, May 16, 1868. See also Robert C. Kenzer, *Enterprising Southerners: Black Economic Success in North Carolina, 1865–1915* (Charlottesville: University Press of Virginia, 1997).

4   Ron Chernow, *Grant* (New York: Penguin, 2018); Ronald C. White, *American Ulysses: A Life of Ulysses S. Grant* (New York: Random House, 2017).

5   Osthaus, *Freedmen, Philanthropy, and Fraud*, 142.

6   Kate Masur, *An Example for All the Land: Emancipation and the Struggle over Equality in Washington, D.C.* (Chapel Hill: University of North Carolina Press, 2010); Tamika Y. Nunley, *At the Threshold of Liberty: Women, Slavery, and Shifting Identities in Washington, D.C.* (Chapel Hill: University of North Carolina Press, 2021).

7   Journal of the Board of Trustees, 27, 35.

8   Logan, *Howard University*, 65; Osthaus, *Freedmen, Philanthropy, and Fraud*, 142.

9   Margaret Hope Bacon, *But One Race: The Life of Robert Purvis* (Albany: State University of New York Press, 2012), 179; Logan, *Howard University*, 41–42; Osthaus, *Freedmen, Philanthropy, and Fraud*, 42; Julie Winch, *A Gentleman of Color: The Life of James Forten* (New York: Oxford University Press, 2002), 359.

10   Osthaus, *Freedmen, Philanthropy, and Fraud*, 144–45.

11   The Morrill Act of 1862, however, did not provide land or financial resources for people of color. Congress ratified the Second Morrill Act of 1890, a revised version that provided federal funds to create some of the country's first historically Black colleges and universities. For a discussion of the Morrill Act and the creation of land-grant colleges, see Nathan M. Sorber, *Land-Grant Colleges and Popular Revolt: The Origins of the Morrill Act and the Reform of Higher Education* (Ithaca: Cornell University Press, 2018).

12   Journal of the Board of Trustees, 43; Finance Committee minutes, 17.

13   Journal of the Board of Trustees, 42.

14   Journal of the Board of Trustees, 42; Finance Committee minutes, 17.

15   Finance Committee minutes, 18. Italics mine.

16   Finance Committee minutes, 19.

17   Finance Committee minutes, 19.

18   "An Act to Aid in the Construction of a Railroad and Telegraph Line from the Missouri River to the Pacific Ocean, and to Secure to the Government the Use of the Same for Postal, Military, and Other Purposes," July 1, 1862; Enrolled Acts and Resolutions of Congress, 1789–2011; General Records of the United States Government, RG 11; National Archives Building, Washington, DC, accessed March 28, 2024, https://www.archives.gov/milestone-documents/pacific-railway-act#transcript; Journal of the Board of Trustees, 37.

19   Journal of the Board of Trustees, 38.

20   Finance Committee minutes, 15.

21   The raising of funds to shift capital to companies that received government contracts to help

build intercontinental railroad lines through bond issuances began in 1861 with the Pacific Railway Act. By 1870, Jay Cooke was the exclusive bond agent of the Northern Pacific Railroad. See Charles R. Geisst, *Wall Street: A History* (Oxford: Oxford University Press, 2018), 56.

22 Finance Committee minutes, 15.

23 Fleming, *Freedman's Savings Bank*, 50.

24 *New National Era* (Washington, DC), January 12, 1870, Chronicling America.

25 Finance Committee minutes, 27.

26 Matthew Stewart, *An Emancipation of the Mind: Radical Philosophy, the War over Slavery, and the Refounding of America* (New York: W. W. Norton, 2024), 140.

27 Karl Marx, *Capital: A Critical Analysis of Capitalist Production* (London: Sonnenschein, 1889), 123–33. Marx published the original version of *Capital* in 1867. It was translated from German to English in 1889.

28 Journal of the Board of Trustees, 56.

29 Journal of the Board of Trustees, 63–64.

30 *New York Times*, October 18, 1869.

31 Journal of the Board of Trustees, 65.

32 Journal of the Board of Trustees, 69.

33 Freedman's Savings and Trust Company Bylaws, 11. Emphasis added.

34 Osthaus, *Freedmen, Philanthropy, and Fraud*, 146.

35 Journal of the Board of Trustees, 72.

36 U.S. House Journal, 41st Cong., 2nd Sess., March 21, 1870, 503.

37 *Cong. Globe*, 41st Cong., 2nd Sess. 2333.

38 *Cong. Globe*, 41st Cong., 2nd Sess. 2333.

39 *Cong. Globe*, 41st Cong., 2nd Sess. 2333.

40 *Cong. Globe*, 41st Cong., 2nd Sess. 2333.

41 *Cong. Globe*, 41st Cong., 2nd Sess. 2334.

42 *Cong. Globe*, 41st Cong., 2nd Sess. 2334.

43 *Cong. Globe*, 41st Cong., 2nd Sess. 2334.

44 *Cong. Globe*, 41st Cong., 2nd Sess. 2334.

45 *Cong. Globe*, 41st Cong., 2nd Sess. 2334.

46 *Cong. Globe*, 41st Cong., 2nd Sess. 2334.

47 *Cong. Globe*, 41st Cong., 2nd Sess. 2334.

48 Douglas Report, 37.

49 *Proceedings of the Colored National Labor Convention: Held in Washington, D.C., on December 6th, 7th, 8th, 9th and 10th, 1869* (Washington, DC: Printed at the Office of the New Era, 1870), Colored Conventions Project Digital Records, accessed May 12, 2023.

50 *Proceedings of the Colored National Labor Convention.*

51 *Proceedings of the Colored National Labor Convention.*

52 *Proceedings of the Colored National Labor Convention.*

53 *New National Era* (Washington, DC), December 28, 1871, Chronicling America.

54 *Proceedings of the Colored National Labor Convention.*

55 *Proceedings of the Colored National Labor Convention.*

56 *Proceedings of the Colored National Labor Convention.*

57 *Proceedings of the Colored National Labor Convention.* For a history of saving in African American communities, see Walker, *History of Black Business in America*, vol. 1.

58 Journal of the Board of Trustees, 65.

CHAPTER FIVE: A LENDING BONANZA, 1870–72

1   *New National Era*, October 24, 1872.

2   *Christian Recorder*, May 7, 1870; J. L. Brown, *Fifteenth Amendment Celebration! To Be Held May 4, '70 at Nashville* (Committee of Arrangements, 1870). Black women continued their fight for both voting rights and equal protection under the law, despite the passage of the Fourteenth and Fifteenth Amendments. For a discussion of African American women's political fights for equality in the nineteenth and twentieth centuries, see Martha S. Jones, *Vanguard: How Black Women Broke Barriers, Won the Vote, and Insisted on Equality for All* (New York: Basic Books, 2019).

3   David W. Blight, *Frederick Douglass: Prophet of Freedom* (New York: Simon & Schuster, 2018), 525–27.

4   *Registers of Signatures of Depositors.*

5   According to the 1880 census, Robert and Betsey Harris could neither read nor write. US Census, *1880, Richmond, Henrico County*, VA, enumeration district *095*, roll *1372*, p. *470B*. For an examination of literacy among enslaved and free Blacks in slavery and during Reconstruction, see Heather Andrea Williams, *Self-Taught: African American Education in Slavery and Freedom* (Chapel Hill: University of North Carolina Press, 2009).

6   Registers of Signatures of Depositors.

7   *New National Era*, March 17, 1870.

8   Though Congress charged accountants with digging into the bank's finances in the six years after the bank closed in 1874, the historical record suggests that the bank's trustees, administrators, and cashiers were not keeping an accurate accounting of deposits or lending activity. Therefore, it is possible that the documentary record, including the Board of Trustees minutes and the records of the Finance Committee, underreported the loan amounts and loan volume. Moreover, cashiers at individual branches were loaning money, against the bank's policies.

9   Kilbourn also served on a committee for "taking into consideration a plan for a change in the municipal government of this district" on January 12, 1870.

10   *Daily National Republican* (Washington City [DC]), December 21, 1867, Chronicling America. See also *Latta v. Kilbourn*, 150 U.S. 524 (1893).

11   Finance Committee minutes, 41.

12   *Evening Star* (Washington, DC), March 16, 1870, Chronicling America.

13   Journal of the Board of Trustees, 80.

14   Pamela Scott and Antoinette J. Lee, "Cooke's Row" [Washington, District of Columbia], in SAH Archipedia, ed. Gabrielle Esperdy and Karen Kingsley, Charlottesville: UVaP, 2012–, last accessed June 12, 2023.

15   Thomas M. Plowman receipt from H. D. Cooke, Henry David Cooke papers, Huntington Library, San Marino, California.

16   Journal of the Board of Trustees, 82; *Evening Star*, July 14, 1870. See also Building Committee minutes, April 28, 1871.

17   Report: To Accompany Bills S. 711 and S. 1581 (Washington, DC: U.S. Government Printing Office, 1880), 117; Garrett Peck, *The Smithsonian Castle and the Seneca Quarry* (Charleston: The History Press, 2013).

18   *Report of the Select Committee to Investigate the Freedman's Savings and Trust Company*

(Washington, DC: Government Printing Office, 1880), 117 (hereafter cited as Bruce Report).

19   Bruce Report, 117.

20   Finance Committee minutes, 41.

21   Bruce Report, 288.

22   *Evening Star,* January 15, 1870.

23   "An Act to Provide a Government for the District of Columbia," *Statutes at Large,* 41st Cong., 3rd Sess., 419–29.

24   Ulysses S. Grant Certificate to H. D. Cooke, Henry David Cooke papers, The Huntington Library, San Marino, California.

25   Ulysses S. Grant Certificate to H. D. Cooke.

26   Journal of the Board of Trustees, 75.

27   Journal of the Board of Trustees, 77.

28   Journal of the Board of Trustees, 77.

29   Journal of the Board of Trustees, 77.

30   Douglas Report, 74.

31   Journal of the Board of Trustees, 85.

32   Thomas Holt, *Black over White: Negro Political Leadership in South Carolina during Recon-struction* (Urbana: University of Illinois Press, 1979), 48; Cate Lineberry, *Be Free or Die: The Amazing Story of Robert Smalls' Escape from Slavery to Union Hero* (New York: St. Martin's Press, 2017); Edward A. Miller Jr., *Gullah Statesman: Robert Smalls from Slavery to Congress, 1839–1915* (Columbia: University of South Carolina Press, 1995).

33   Daniel C. Littlefield, "The Slave Trade to Colonial South Carolina: A Profile," *South Caro-lina Historical Magazine* 101, no. 2 (2000): 110–41; Peter C. Mancall, Joshua L. Rosenbloom, and Thomas Weiss, "Slave Prices and the South Carolina Economy, 1722–1809," *Journal of Economic History* 61, no. 3 (2001): 616–39.

34   Some historians believe that McKee could have been Smalls's father. See Lineberry, *Be Free or Die,* 38; Miller, *Gullah Statesman,* 7.

35   Lineberry, 45.

36   Eric Foner, *Freedom's Lawmakers: A Directory of Black Officeholders During Reconstruction* (New York: Oxford University Press, 1993), 198.

37   There is conflicting information about how much Smalls paid for the house on Prince Street. According to the National Park Service, he paid $605. Historian Edward A. Miller Jr. con-tends that he paid $600 and historian Andrew Billingsley cites $650. See Andrew Billingsley, *Yearning to Breathe Free: Robert Smalls of South Carolina and His Families* (Columbia: Uni-versity of South Carolina Press, 2007), 99; Miller, *Gullah Statesman,* 27; "The Robert Smalls House," National Park Service, accessed March 29, 2024, https://www.nps.gov/places/the-robert-smalls-house.htm. Robert Smalls was subsequently sued by William J. De Treville for his illegal procurement of the property. The case was tried before the US Supreme Court in 1878. The court ruled in favor of Smalls, contending that Smalls purchased the property because the De Trevilles had failed to pay property taxes during the war. See *De Treville v. Smalls,* 98 U.S. 517 (1878).

38   Commissioners' Report, 1874, 74; Fleming, *Freedmen's Savings Bank,* 63. Scovel's ambition would get him in trouble. In December 1872, A. M. Sperry discovered that Scovel had embez-zled over $10,000 in deposits. See Douglas Report, 5.

39   Osthaus, *Freedmen, Philanthropy, and Fraud,* 112–13.

40   *John Watson Alvord, Letters from the South, Relating to the Condition of Freedmen, Addressed*

to Major General O. O. Howard, Commissioner, Bureau R., F., and A. L. by J. W. Alvord, gen. sup't education, Bureau R., F., & A. (Washington, DC: Howard University Press, 1870), African American Pamphlet Collection, Library of Congress, LOC.gov.

41 Alvord to Howard, January 13, 1870, Howard Papers.

42 *Charleston Daily News* (Charleston, SC), March 26, 1870, Chronicling America.

43 *New National Era,* September 22, 1870.

44 US Census, *1860, Newton, Middlesex County, MA,* roll *M653_510,* p. *745,* Family History Library Film *803510;* US Census, *1870, East of Seventh Street, Washington, District of Columbia,* roll *M593_127,* p. *656A, RG 29: Records of the Bureau of the Census,* series *M653,* National Archives in Washington, DC.

45 *National Intelligencer,* March 10, 1869.

46 Journal of the Board of Trustees, 88.

47 Douglas Report, 1876, vii.

48 Douglas Report, 1876, 124.

49 Douglas Report, 1876, 124.

50 Journal of the Board of Trustees, 87, 42; Finance Committee minutes, 42, 61–62, 73. Alexander R. Shepherd was also the second territorial governor of Washington, appointed by Grant in 1873.

51 Douglas Report, 1876, 124.

52 Finance Committee minutes, 14, 15, 23, 35.

53 Bruce Report, viii.

54 Douglas Report, 1876, vii.

55 *Semi-Weekly Louisianian* (New Orleans, LA), May 18, 1871, Chronicling America.

56 Finance Committee minutes, 63.

57 Journal of the Board of Trustees, 103.

58 Finance Committee minutes, 80–81, 83.

59 Bruce Report, 119.

60 Finance Committee minutes, 76, 84–85; Bruce Report, 120.

61 Journal of the Board of Trustees, 105; Douglas Report, 31; Bruce Report, 120.

62 Howard was involved in the bank as a short-term trustee, informal advisor, and depositor. He held a personal account as well as power to access two other accounts, including a trust fund and the account of the Congregational church in Washington, DC. In the Bruce 1880 congressional inquiry, Howard revealed, "Money was frequently sent to me for disbursement, and I would deposit it in that way in the bank." See Bruce Report, 267–68.

63 George Whipple to John Alvord, February 12, 1874, Letters of Rev. John W. Alvord, FromthePage, accessed April 1, 2024, https://fromthepage.com/uvalibrary/letters-of-rev-john-w-alvord/1872–02–15-letter-a-whipple-to-alvord/display/25203185.

64 Commissioners' Report, 1874, 93. Pomeroy founded R. M. Pomeroy & Co., a boot and clothing company that had a contract with the federal government and the Union army to supply soldiers with boots during the Civil War. In terms of the loan that they received from the Freedman's Bank, Nichols and Pomeroy had difficulty paying it back. The finance committee, in September 1872, discussed having Stickney request that Nichols pay the balance due. This discussion was pushed off for several months and never resolved. See Finance Committee minutes, August 13, 1872–April 2, 1874, 12.

65 Finance Committee minutes, 82.

66 Douglas Report, 108.

67   Nina Mjagkij, *Light in The Darkness: African Americans and the YMCA, 1852–1946* (Lexington: University Press of Kentucky, 2021), 17.

68   Douglas Report, 99.

69   Douglas Report, 99.

70   Fleming, *Freedmen's Savings Bank*, 76.

71   Bruce Report, 288.

72   Bruce Report, 288.

73   Célérier and Tak, "Finance, Advertising and Fraud," 6.

74   Célérier and Tak, 60.

75   Finance Committee minutes, 55; Osthaus, *Freedmen, Philanthropy, and Fraud*, 120.

76   Osthaus, 120.

77   Osthaus, 120.

78   Osthaus, 120.

79   Bruce Report, 179.

80   Journal of the Board of Trustees, 119.

81   Blight, *Frederick Douglass*, 529.

82   *New National Era*, September 8, 1870; Célérier and Tak, "Finance, Advertising and Fraud," 4.

83   "United States, Freedman's Bank Records, 1865–1874," FamilySearch.org, entry for Frederick Douglass, 1871.

84   Douglass, *Life and Times*, 488.

85   Journal of the Board of Trustees, 92.

86   Journal of the Board of Trustees, 83–84.

87   Meigs Report, 1873, 2.

88   *New National Era*, December 14, 1871.

89   *New National Era*, December 14, 1871.

90   *New National Era*, December 14, 1871.

91   Douglass, *Life and Times*, 409.

92   Douglass, 409.

93   Douglass, 409–10.

94   Célérier and Tak, "Finance, Advertising and Fraud," 12; Fleming, *Freedmen's Savings Bank*, 50; Bruce Report, 248.

CHAPTER SIX: A BANK EXAMINATION AND A BANK FAILURE, 1871–73

1   *New National Era*, July 3, 1873.

2   Finance Committee minutes, 98.

3   Finance Committee minutes, 99.

4   Finance Committee minutes, 65.

5   Pamela Walker Laird, *Pull: Networking and Success since Benjamin Franklin* (Cambridge: Harvard University Press, 2006), 22.

6   Lawson, *Patriot Fires*, 57–58; Lubetkin, *Jay Cooke's Gamble*, 11.

7   "An Act to Aid in the Construction of a Railroad and Telegraph Line from the Missouri River to the Pacific Ocean, and to Secure to the Government the Use of the Same for Postal, Military, and Other Purposes," July 1, 1862, RG 11: General Records of the United States Government, Series: Enrolled Acts and Resolutions of Congress, National Archives.

8   Eugene Virgil Smalley, *History of the Northern Pacific Railroad* (New York: G. P. Putnam's Sons, 1883), 169–70.

9   Levy, *Freaks of Fortune*, 139; Richard White, *Railroaded: The Transcontinentals and the Making of Modern America* (New York: W. W. Norton, 2011), 56–87.

10   Oberholtzer, *Jay Cooke*, 157. Two important aspects of the building of the Northern Pacific Railroad were the land required to build the railroad and the labor that railroad companies used. Railroad investors wedged themselves into continued battles between Native American land rights and the federal government's policies vis-à-vis indigenous peoples' land divestment. See Manu Karuka, *Empire's Tracks: Indigenous Nations, Chinese Workers, and the Transcontinental Railroad* (Oakland: University of California Press, 2019). Approximately twenty thousand Chinese immigrants performed the backbreaking labor of constructing major parts of transcontinental railroads. For a discussion of Chinese immigration in the nineteenth and early twentieth centuries, see Gordon H. Chang, *Ghosts of Gold Mountain: The Epic Story of the Chinese Who Built the Transcontinental Railroad* (New York: Houghton Mifflin Harcourt, 2019); Beth Lew-Williams, *The Chinese Must Go: Violence, Exclusion, and the Making of the Alien in America* (Cambridge: Harvard University Press, 2018).

11   Journal of the Board of Trustees, 95.

12   Milo T. Bogard, *The Redemption of New York* (New York: P. F. McBreen & Sons, 1902), 287.

13   Bogard, *Redemption of New York*, 287.

14   Finance Committee minutes, 67.

15   Finance Committee minutes, 67.

16   Finance Committee minutes, 68.

17   Thomson, *Bonds of War*.

18   Osthaus, *Freedmen, Philanthropy, and Fraud*, 153. For a discussion of the ways in which political and financial corruption evolved in the Gilded Age, see Richard White, "Information, Markets, and Corruption: Transcontinental Railroads in the Gilded Age," *Journal of American History* 90, no.1 (June 2003): 19–43.

19   Finance Committee minutes, 68.

20   Finance Committee minutes, 69.

21   Finance Committee minutes, 69.

22   Finance Committee minutes, 69.

23   Journal of the Board of Trustees, 94; Finance Committee minutes, 69–70.

24   Finance Committee minutes, 69.

25   Lubetkin, *Jay Cooke's Gamble*, 65–79.

26   Journal of the Board of Trustees, 103.

27   In 1871, Ketchum began to intervene more directly in the discussions that the finance committee members were having about the loans that they were making. Specifically, he expressed that he had serious qualms about how the finance committee evaluated the riskiness of these loans. For example, in 1871, he was pushing the board to examine how much they were approving in salary increases to cashiers and members of the bank's executive committee. Ketchum's interrogation of Cooke and his borrowing habits represented an extension of his and Stewart's work to bring more accountability to the board—specifically to rein in Cooke, Huntington, and Eaton. See Finance Committee minutes, 78.

28   Lubetkin, *Jay Cooke's Gamble*, 75–79.

29   Finance Committee minutes, 99.

30   Journal of the Board of Trustees, 111.

31 Journal of the Board of Trustees, 111.
32 Journal of the Board of Trustees, 111.
33 Finance Committee minutes, 100.
34 Finance Committee minutes, 101.
35 Journal of the Board of Trustees, 112.
36 Osthaus, *Freedmen, Philanthropy, and Fraud*, 155.
37 Journal of the Board of Trustees, 121. See also Osthaus, 156–57.
38 Freedman's Savings and Trust Company Bylaws, 11.
39 Bruce Report, 288.
40 Inspector minutes, RG 101: Records of the Office of the Comptroller of the Currency, National Archives, 2–3.
41 M. T. Hewitt to A. M. Sperry, September 12, 1865, Anson M. Sperry Collection, 1865–1910, The Freedman's Bank, A. M. Sperry Collection, NARA, College Park, MD.
42 Journal of the Board of Trustees, 107; Osthaus, *Freedmen, Philanthropy, and Fraud*, 27–30.
43 Journal of the Board of Trustees, 124–25.
44 Journal of the Board of Trustees, 125.
45 Journal of the Board of Trustees, 125.
46 *Christian Recorder*, October 12, 1872.
47 *A Brief History of the National Banking System* (Washington, DC: Office of the Comptroller of the Currency, 1938), 16.
48 Gilbert, "Comptroller of the Currency," 128.
49 Gilbert, 128.
50 Meigs Report, 1873, 2.
51 Meigs Report, 1873, 2.
52 Meigs Report, 1873, 9
53 Meigs Report, 1873, 3
54 Meigs Report, 1873, 9.
55 Meigs Report, 1873, 9.
56 *Christian Recorder*, March 20, 1873.
57 *Christian Recorder*, March 20, 1873.
58 "Another Panic," *The New York Times*, September 19, 1873.
59 *Alexandria Gazette* (Alexandria, DC), September 18, 1873, Chronicling America.
60 *Wilmington Daily Commercial* (Wilmington, DE), September 18, 1873, Chronicling America.
61 *Alexandria Gazette*, September 18, 1873; *Evening Star*, September 18, 1873.
62 *Evening Star*, September 18, 1873.
63 *New York Herald*, September 14, 1873. Grant appointed A. R. Shepard to Cooke's position as governor after Cooke's resignation.
64 *Evening Star*, September 18, 1873.
65 *Evening Star*, September 18, 1873.
66 *San Francisco Evening Bulletin*, September 18, 1873.
67 *Wood County Reporter* (Grand Rapids [Wisconsin Rapids], WI), September 25, 1873, Chronicling America.
68 *Spirit of Democracy* (Woodsfield, OH), September 30, 1873, Chronicling America.
69 Nicolas Barreyre, "The Politics of Economic Crises: The Panic of 1873, the End of Reconstruction, and the Realignment of American Politics," *Journal of the Gilded Age and Progressive Era* 10, no. 4 (2011): 407.

70 Richard White, *The Republic for Which It Stands* (New York: Oxford University Press, 2017), 264–65. Historians contend that one of the catalysts for the Panic of 1873 was the fact that European investors had become hesitant to invest in American securities because of a financial panic in Vienna that began in the spring of 1873. European investors had started to liquidate their investment in American railroad bonds, which drained capital from New York banks at the moment of Jay Cooke & Company's bankruptcy. See Barreyre, "Politics of Economic Crises," 403–23; Hannah Catherine Davies, *Transatlantic Speculations: Globalization and the Panics of 1873* (New York: Columbia University Press, 2018); Scott Reynolds Nelson, "A Storm of Cheap Goods: New American Commodities and the Panic of 1873," *Journal of the Gilded Age and Progressive Era* 10, no. 4 (2011): 447–53; Scott Reynolds Nelson, *Oceans of Grain: How American Wheat Remade the World* (New York: Basic Books, 2022).

71 "Another Panic," *New York Times*, September 19, 1873.

72 *Evening Star*, September 18, 1873.

73 *Beaufort Republican* (Beaufort, SC), September 25, 1873, Chronicling America.

74 *Christian Recorder*, October 2, 1873.

75 Douglas Report, 75.

76 Bruce Report, 181; *Donaldsonville Chief* (Donaldsonville, LA), October 18, 1873, Chronicling America; *Helena Weekly Herald* (Helena, MT), October 2, 1873, Chronicling America.

77 Journal of the Board of Trustees, 139.

78 Douglas Report, 108.

79 Fleming, *Freedmen's Savings Bank*, 84.

80 Commissioners' Report, 1874, 59.

81 Examiner's Report, St. Louis, Missouri, RG 101: Records of the Office of the Comptroller of the Currency, Division of Insolvent National Banks, Freedman's Savings and Trust Company, General Records Received by the Commissioners of the F.S.&T. and by the Comptroller, 1870–1914, Examiners Reports, National Archives, College Park, MD.

82 Examiner's Report, St. Louis.

83 Examiner's Report, St. Louis.

84 Gilbert, "Comptroller of the Currency," 129.

85 For example, the $33,000 loan to the YMCA was secured by a piece of DC property, on Ninth Street and D Street. The joint stock company had no authority to mortgage the property. Douglas Report, 122.

86 Gilbert, "Comptroller of the Currency," 129.

87 Journal of the Board of Trustees, 142–43.

CHAPTER SEVEN: THE BANK'S LAST PRESIDENT, 1874

1 Douglass, *Life and Times*, 487.

2 "Notes from Louisville," *Christian Recorder*, June 19, 1873.

3 "Notes from Louisville."

4 "Notes from Louisville."

5 Frederick Douglass, "Self-Made Men" (undated), Walter O. Evans Collection of Frederick Douglass and Douglass Family Papers, James Weldon Johnson Collection in the Yale Collection of American Literature, Beinecke Rare Book and Manuscript Library, accessed April 1, 2024, https://collections.library.yale.edu/catalog/17374018.

6   Blight, *Frederick Douglass*, 562–64.

7   Douglass, "Self-Made Men."

8   In this speech, Douglass also drew from Cotton Mather, Benjamin Franklin, and Ralph Waldo Emerson, connecting their ideas about self-reliance to the American concept of the economic benefits of capitalism. He also invoked Toussaint Louverture as an example of Black self-making. Waldo E. Martin Jr. argues, "More specifically, it reflected his deep-rooted commitment to both capitalism and the Protestant work ethic." For a discussion of Douglass and the "self-made man," see Waldo E. Martin Jr., *The Mind of Frederick Douglass* (Chapel Hill: University of North Carolina Press, 1984), 253–56.

9   For a discussion of the Colfax Massacre, see LeeAnna Keith, *The Colfax Massacre: The Untold Story of Black Power, White Terror, and the Death of Reconstruction* (New York: Oxford University Press, 2009); Charles Lane, *The Day Freedom Died: The Colfax Massacre, the Supreme Court, and the Betrayal of Reconstruction* (New York: Henry Holt, 2008).

10   For a discussion of Douglass's embrace of photography as a means of communicating Black people's humanity to white viewers, see John Stauffer, Zoe Trodd, and Celeste-Marie Bernier, *Picturing Frederick Douglass: An Illustrated Biography of the Nineteenth Century's Most Photographed American* (New York: Liveright, 2015).

11   *New Era*, January 13, 1870.

12   Célérier and Tak, "Finance, Advertising and Fraud"; Blight, *Frederick Douglass*, 525.

13   *New Era*, January 20, 1870.

14   Douglass, *Life and Times*, 488–89. Douglass's sons, Frederick Douglass Jr., Charles R. Douglass, and Lewis Douglass, were depositors as well.

15   Journal of the Board of Trustees, 92.

16   Douglass, *Life and Times*, 488–89.

17   Purvis was elected as the bank's first vice president in March 1873. Journal of the Board of Trustees, 131.

18   Journal of the Board of Trustees, 114; John Mercer Langston, *From the Virginia Plantation to the National Capitol; or, The First and Only Negro Representative in Congress from the Old Dominion* (Hartford, CT: American Publishing Company, 1894), 340.

19   Langston, *From the Virginia Plantation*, 124–25.

20   William F. Cheek and Aimee Lee Cheek, *John Mercer Langston and the Fight for Black Freedom, 1829–65* (Urbana: University of Illinois Press, 1996).

21   *New National Era*, October 30, 1873.

22   Douglas Report, 76.

23   Douglas Report, 76.

24   Douglass, *Life and Times*, 489.

25   Douglass, *Life and Times*, 489. It is possible that in his autobiography, Douglass was trying to distance himself from his affiliation with the bank, which explains his arm's-length perspective on his own involvement, especially as the bank was veering into bankruptcy.

26   Douglass, *Life and Times*, 484–85.

27   Bruce Inquiry, Report of the Select Committee to Investigate the Freedman's Savings and Trust Company, United States Senate, 1880, 236.

28   Douglass, *Life and Times*, 489.

29   Douglass, 493.

30   Douglass, 489.

31   Douglass, 489.

32   Bruce Inquiry, 238.

33   Bruce Inquiry, 238.

34   Blight, *Frederick Douglass*, 529–31.

35   Bruce Inquiry, 283.

36   Douglass, *Life and Times*, 490.

37   Commissioners' Report, 1874, 119.

38   Examiner's Report, Jacksonville, Florida.

39   *Yorkville Enquirer* (Yorkville, SC), February 19, 1874, Chronicling America.

40   As quoted in Fleming, *Freedmen's Savings Bank*, 151.

41   2 Cong. Rec. 287 (1874), appendix.

42   Fleming, *Freedmen's Savings Bank*, 151–55.

43   As quoted in Fleming, 153.

44   As quoted in Fleming, 153.

45   *Nashville Union and American* (Nashville, TN), April 29, 1874, Chronicling America.

46   Journal of the Board of Trustees, 145.

47   Bruce Inquiry, 238.

48   Bruce Inquiry, 238.

49   *New National Era*, May 7, 1874.

50   *New National Era*, May 7, 1874.

51   2 Cong. Rec. 272 (1874), appendix.

52   *Chicago Daily Tribune* (Chicago, IL), April 28, 1874, Chronicling America.

53   *Chicago Daily Tribune*, April 28, 1874.

54   *Chicago Daily Tribune*, April 28, 1874.

55   *Nashville Union and American*, April 29, 1874.

56   "United States, Freedman's Bank Records, 1865–1874," database with images, FamilySearch .org, F G Bromberg; Mobile, Alabama.

57   2 Cong. Rec. 272 (1874), appendix.

58   2 Cong. Rec. 272 (1874), appendix.

59   2 Cong. Rec. 273 (1874), appendix.

60   2 Cong. Rec. 287 (1874), appendix.

61   2 Cong. Rec. 273 (1874), appendix.

62   2 Cong. Rec. 284 (1874), appendix.

63   2 Cong. Rec. 4490 (1874).

64   Fleming, *Freedmen's Savings Bank*, 136–39.

65   Journal of the Board of Trustees, 146.

66   *New National Era*, June 25, 1874.

67   *New National Era*, June 25, 1874.

68   *New National Era*, June 25, 1874.

69   Journal of the Board of Trustees, 147.

70   Journal of the Board of Trustees, 148; Fleming, *Freedmen's Savings Bank*, 101. It is worth noting that Robert Purvis was "among some of the Wealthy citizens of Philadelphia" during the 1840s, with an estimated net worth of $50,000 ($38 million today in terms of relative wealth). *Memoirs and Auto-biography of Some of the Wealthy Citizens of Philadelphia, with a Fair Estimate of Their Estates—Founded upon a Knowledge of Facts. With an Appendix: Containing Particular Accounts of the Lives of Stephen Girard, Jacob Ridgway, and Obed Coleman, Obtained from Authentic Sources* (Philadelphia, 1846), 50.

71 *Daily Dispatch*, July 3, 1874.
72 Journal of the Board of Trustees, 148.
73 *Christian Recorder*, August 12, 1875.

CHAPTER EIGHT: FALLOUT, 1874–1911

1   *The Weekly Clarion* (Jackson, MS) July 16, 1874, Chronicling America.
2   Frederick Douglass, *The Frederick Douglass Papers*, ed. John R. Kaufman-McKivigan, series 3: *Correspondence*, vol. 3: *1866–1880* (New Haven: Yale University Press, 2023), 279.
3   Commissioners' Report, 1874, 52. See also Giedeman, "Fannie Mae, Freddie Mac," 215.
4   Commissioners' Report, 1874, 1–2.
5   Commissioners' Report, 1874, 2.
6   See *New Orleans Republican* (New Orleans, LA), August 20, 1874, Chronicling America.
7   Bruce Report, 140, 157.
8   Bruce Report, ix–x.
9   Commissioners' Report, 1874, 35. Howard had been questioned by Democrats in Congress about his involvement with the Freedmen's Bureau, which Democrats forced to cease operations in 1872. For a discussion of the Freedmen's Bureau and its aftermath, see Dale Kretz, *Administering Freedom: The State of Emancipation after the Freedmen's Bureau* (Chapel Hill: University of North Carolina Press, 2022).
10 *Christian Recorder*, July 9, 1874.
11 Douglass, *Life and Times*, 492.
12 *Christian Recorder*, November 5, 1874.
13 Commissioners' Report, 1874, 8.
14 Commissioners' Report, 1874, 8.
15 Meigs Report, 1873, 8.
16 Célérier and Tak, "Finance, Advertising and Fraud," 16. They argue that the difference between this amount and the amount due depositors was a result of the miscalculation of money owed to the depositors.
17 Célérier and Tak, "Finance, Advertising and Fraud," 17.
18 Commissioners' Report, 1874, 9.
19 *Christian Recorder*, November 11, 1875.
20 *Montgomery County Sentinel* (Rockville, MD), December 11, 1874, Chronicling America.
21 *Memphis Daily Appeal* (Memphis, TN), December 22, 1874, Chronicling America.
22 Known as the "Douglas Report."
23 *Congressional Record Containing the Proceeding and Debates of the Forty-Third Congress, First Session* (Washington, DC: U.S. Government Printing Office, 1874), 477.
24 Douglas Report, 1.
25 Douglas Report, 42.
26 Douglas Report, iii.
27 Douglass Report, 66.
28 Douglas Report, 68.
29 Douglas Report, 69.
30 Douglas Report, 66.
31 Douglas Report, 76.
32 Douglas Report, 76.

33 Howell did not designate whether he was enslaved or free in 1865 in his Freedman's Bank account ledger.

34 Registers of Signatures of Depositors.

35 Douglas Report, 117.

36 Douglas Report, 118.

37 Douglas Report, 117.

38 Douglas Report, 118.

39 Samuel Shapiro, "A Black Senator from Mississippi: Blanche K. Bruce (1841–1898)," *Review of Politics* 44, no. 1 (January 1982): 83.

40 Bruce was the second Black senator, after Hiram Revels, and the last Black senator until Edward Brooke was elected in 1967, as a Republican from Massachusetts.

41 Bruce Report, iii.

42 Foner, *Reconstruction*, 412–59.

43 Bruce Report, appendix, 27.

44 Bruce Report, 23.

45 By 1880, Huntington and Eaton had passed away.

46 Bruce Report, 57.

47 Bruce Report, 236.

48 White, *Republic For Which It Stands*, 331–33. For information on Gordon, see W. Todd Groce, "John B. Gordon," New Georgia Encyclopedia, last modified June 8, 2017.

49 Bruce Inquiry, 236.

50 Bruce Inquiry, 237.

51 Bruce Report, appendix, 47–49. For a discussion of the Cookes' coded communications, see Oberholtzer, *Jay Cooke*, 410.

52 Fleming, *Freedmen's Savings Bank*, 87.

53 Bruce Report, 244.

54 Bruce Report, 244.

55 Bruce Report, 244.

56 Bruce Report, 244–45.

57 Douglass, *Life and Times*, 493.

58 Bruce Report, 180.

59 Bruce Report, 180.

60 Douglas Report, 179.

61 *Christian Recorder*, October 4, 1883.

62 *Annual Report of the Commissioner of the Freedman's Savings and Trust Company* (Washington, DC: U.S. Government Printing Office, 1893), 11.

63 Giedeman, "Fannie Mae, Freddie Mac," 215.

64 Osthaus, *Freedmen, Philanthropy, and Fraud*, 218.

65 50 Cong. Rec. 2684 (1888).

66 *Christian Recorder*, August 9, 1888.

67 AM Sperry—Freedmen, September 29, 1907, Anson Sperry Collection, RG 101: Records of the Office of the Comptroller of the Currency, National Archives at College Park.

68 AM Sperry—Freedmen.

69 AM Sperry—Freedmen.

70 AM Sperry—Freedmen.

71 AM Sperry—Freedmen.

72 62 Cong. Rec. 243 (1911).

73   General Records Received by the Commissioners of the Freedman's Savings and Trust Company and by the Comptroller of the Currency as Ex Officio Commissioner, 1864–1914, RG 101: Records of the Office of the Comptroller of the Currency, National Archives at College Park.

74   General Records Received by the Commissioners.

CONCLUSION: THE PROBLEM OF FINANCE IN THE AGE OF EMANCIPATION

1   William Wells Brown, *My Southern Hope: or, The South and Its People* (Boston: A. G. Brown & Co., 1880), 199.

2   Mary Susan Harris is listed in the dividend payment record as "Margaret Susan Harris." I've concluded that this record is, in fact, Mary Susan Harris because there was a depositor named "Susan Harris," but this depositor is listed as such in the dividend payment record. There was also a Margaret H. Harris listed in the dividend payment record. Since there was no original depositor record listed as "Margaret Susan Harris," I believe that the record keeper made a spelling mistake, labeling "Mary" as "Margaret." Dividend Payment Record: Richmond, vol. 10, RG 101: Records of the Office of the Comptroller of the Currency, National Archives. For a discussion of the experiences of Black washerwomen in the postwar South, see Tera Hunter, *To 'Joy My Freedom: Southern Black Women's Lives and Labors after the Civil War* (Cambridge: Harvard University Press, 1997), 74–97.

3   *Virginia Deaths and Burials, 1853–1912*, Library of Virginia, Richmond, Virginia.

4   Célérier and Tak, "Finance, Advertising and Fraud," 21, 61.

5   Célérier and Tak, 21.

6   Aaron Carico, *Black Market: The Slave's Value in National Culture after 1865* (Chapel Hill: University of North Carolina Press, 2020), 17–45.

7   Journalist Emily Flitter offers an incisive critique of the predatory relationship Wall Street has had with Black communities. See Emily Flitter, *The White Wall: How Big Finance Bankrupts Black America* (New York: Atria, 2022).

8   Douglass, *Life and Times*, 611.

9   Aditya Aladangady, Andrew C. Chang, and Jacob Krimmel, "Greater Wealth, Greater Uncertainty: Changes in Racial Inequality in the Survey of Consumer Finances," FEDS Notes, Washington: Board of Governors of the Federal Reserve System, October 18, 2023.

10   "2021 FDIC National Survey of Unbanked and Underbanked Households," FDIC, last updated July 24, 2023.

11   Osthaus, *Freedmen, Philanthropy, and Fraud*, 105.

12   W. E. B. Du Bois, "The Negro Landholder of Georgia," *Bulletin of the United States Bureau of Labor* (July 1901), FRASER, accessed April 1, 2024.

13   W. E. B. DuBois, "The Freedmen's Bureau," *Atlantic Monthly*, March 1901.

14   W. E. B. Du Bois, *The World and Africa: An Inquiry into the Part Which Africa Has Played in World History* (New York: Viking, 1947), 257.

Credits

241 "'Waiting' March 29, 1879 Thomas Nast." *Harpweek: Cartoon of the Day.* Accessed 19 Dec. 2023.

248 "Blood Money," Thomas Nast, January 1, 1900.

263 (both charts) Commissioners Report, 1874, 91.

264 (both charts) Commissioners Report, 1874, 91.

265 Freedman's Bank Branch Locations.

Index

Page numbers in *italics* refer to illustrations.
Page numbers after 266 refer to notes.